Bridging the Rift

The New South Africa in Africa

EDITED BY

Larry A. Swatuk and
David R. Black

WestviewPress

A Division of HarperCollins*Publishers*

Copyright © 1997 by Westview Press, A Division of HarperCollins Publishers, Inc.

Published in 1997 in the United States of America by Westview Press, 5500 Central Avenue, Boulder, Colorado 80301-2877, and in the United Kingdom by Westview Press, 12 Hid's Copse Road, Cumnor Hill, Oxford OX2 9JJ

Library of Congress Cataloging-in-Publication Data
Bridging the rift : the new South Africa in Africa / [edited by] Larry
   A. Swatuk and David R. Black
      p. cm.
   Includes bibliographical references and index.
   ISBN 0-8133-2752-0
      1. South Africa—Foreign economic relations—Africa. 2. Africa—Foreign
   economic relations—South Africa. 3. Africa—Economic integration.
   I. Swatuk, Larry A. (Larry Anthony), 1957– .
   II. Black, David R. (David Ross), 1960– .
HF1613.4.Z4A3513   1997
337.68—dc21   96-49701
                                                                                   CIP

10   9   8   7   6   5   4   3   2

Contents

Tables

Acknowledgments

This books marks the apex of a project long in development. It began in 1991 as a research proposal written by David Black under the direction of Tim Shaw and submitted to an organization that shall remain nameless; just what happened to that submission we shall never know. It was resurrected and significantly revised in 1993 by Larry Swatuk and David Black and submitted to the Cooperative Security Competition Program of the Department of Foreign Affairs and International Trade Canada. Fortunately for us, in a time of funding cutbacks the CSCP saw fit to provide us with generous support, for which we shall remain most grateful.

Several papers originally presented at our initial international symposium hosted by York University's Centre for International and Security Studies in late 1994 form the foundation for this book. We wish to acknowledge with thanks the support and participation of, among others, YCISS's Conference Coordinator, Steve Mataija, its director, David Dewitt, and several workshop participants: Fadzai Gwaradzimba, John Saul and Steve Stedman. We also wish to acknowledge the ongoing support of YCISS and the work of Rose Edgecombe; and the support of Dalhousie's Centre for Foreign Policy Studies, its director, Tim Shaw, and Marilyn Langille.

In addition, there have been other workshops, conferences and connections which have collectively made a major contribution to the content and quality of this collection. Specifically, we would like to acknowledge the support of people and institutions throughout Southern Africa: the Centre for Southern African Studies, University of the Western Cape; the Political Studies Departments of Rhodes University and the University of Durban-Westville; the Group for Environmental Monitoring and the Institute for African Alternatives, both in Johannesburg; the Centre for Foreign Relations, Dar es Salaam, Tanzania; World University Service Canada and the Southern African Research and Documentation Centre, both in Harare, Zimbabwe; and the Department of Political and Administrative Studies, University of Botswana.

Larry Swatuk would specifically like to thank the Social Sciences and Humanities Research Council of Canada for financial support of this and related research. David Black would like to thank the Research Development Fund of Dalhousie University and the Centre for Southern African Studies at the UWC for financial support, and Heather Scott for moral support. With regard to production of the book itself, we would like to thank Susan Rolston, Ann Griffiths and our editors at Westview, in particular Barbara Ellington for her constant support from start to (near) finish.

Finally, we owe a significant debt to an anonymous reviewer for her/his trenchant comments and encouragement. Heartfelt thanks to one and all.

David Black and Larry Swatuk
Ottawa and Toronto

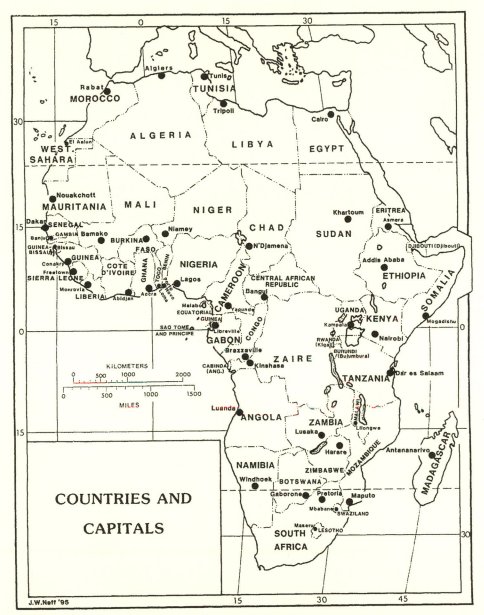

Africa

From *Understanding Contemporary Africa, 2nd edition*, edited by April A. Gordon and Donald L. Gordon. Copyright © 1996 by Lynne Rienner Publishers, Inc. Used with permission of the publisher.

1

The "New" South Africa in Africa

Larry A. Swatuk and David R. Black

Introduction

Despite more than a decade of piecemeal sanctions and economic stagnation and "crisis" (Gelb 1991; Swatuk and Shaw 1991), South Africa retains the most powerful, industrialized and diversified economy in Sub-Saharan Africa. In the post-decolonization phase of African history, most African states and international organizations attempted, with varying but often high degrees of resolve, to isolate South Africa and minimize their economic interaction with the apartheid state. Nevertheless, historical linkages and the continuing strength of South African political and capital interests ensured the persistence of significant economic interchange, regardless of political obstacles.

Today, as South Africans work out their post-apartheid future and as the old political and economic barriers with the rest of the continent crumble, there are increasing social, political and economic interactions between the hobbled leviathan of the South and its continental neighbours, near and far. What repercussions will follow from this process? To what extent will it enhance prospects for political and economic development in the rest of the continent, and to what extent may it further constrain them? Who will be the main agents and beneficiaries of this expansion of South African-African interchange, and who will be its casualties? And what security consequences, broadly conceived, will result?

This chapter serves to introduce these and related issues, principally by highlighting ideas presented in the chapters which follow. We begin, however, with a contextual discussion of "alternative scenarios and working hypotheses," in which we briefly consider the implications of change in South Africa for its region and continent, and lay out the approach and organization of this collection. We then turn to a summary of the chapters, organized around four major themes: (i) South Africa's political economy and its place in the international division of labour; (ii) prospects for Southern African regional security cooperation; (iii) prospects for Southern African regional cooperation on economic and environmental issues; and (iv) prospects for South African-African continental cooperation, focusing on East African and West African cases.

Post-Apartheid Soothsaying: Alternative Scenarios and Working Hypotheses

The implications of a "new," post-apartheid South Africa for the political economies of the Southern African region and of African countries beyond it are attracting increasing analytical attention. Simplifying considerably, one can identify two main alternative approaches within this literature. On the one hand, there are *optimistic* (usually more orthodox) analysts who envision the new South Africa as a regional "engine of growth," generating trade and investment which will spill over (or "trickle down") into African political economies and create new hope for much of the continent (e.g., African Development Bank 1994). On the other hand, there are *sceptical* (usually more critical) analysts who view the prospect of a post-apartheid regional and capitalist superpower with trepidation or even alarm. They anticipate prospects for the region to be "more of the same" at best, increasing domination and exploitation at the hands of a South Africa unchecked by international opprobrium at worst (e.g., Anglin 1991). A number of analysts have advanced and explored both of these alternative scenarios for the future, and various gradations in between.[1]

A third alternative, which has received less attention in writing but is an important subtext in thinking about post-apartheid futures, is the strongly *pessimistic* scenario of spreading civil disorder and economic chaos—the "Lebanonization" of South Africa. Although extremely pessimistic, some would claim that this scenario is still all too realistic, and must not be buried analytically by wishful thinking.

The approach taken by the authors in this collection seeks to transcend stylized and over-generalized scenarios. More particularly, the collection seeks to get beneath a focus on the "high politics" of state-makers and inter-state relations, and to situate these in the context of underlying economic, social, and political forces. While it does not neglect the role of states and international organizations, it argues that these need to be problematized as historically "imagined" (Anderson 1991), and increasingly constrained and (in many cases) dysfunctional entities. Thus, they can only be properly understood in the context of Africa's (and South Africa's) increasingly marginal place within the global economy; the strictures of structural adjustment; historically-resilient and resurgent patterns of production, trade and investment; enduring patterns of migration and trans-boundary movement and exchange; fragile shared ecosystems; and widening and deepening poverty—in short, the enduring bases for sustainable (mal)development and human (in)security.

Adopting this realistic, though not "realist," approach, both optimistic and sceptical alternatives appear over-simplified and -generalized. For starters, much will hinge on the success and character (democratic or authoritarian? internationalist or parochial?) of South Africa's own extremely difficult passage from apartheid and struggle with its socio-economic legacies. Assuming a reasonably orderly transition to a relatively stable post-apartheid regime with a mixed-capitalist economy, the most probable consequence for those African political economies closely entangled with South Africa's will be an acceleration of tendencies toward differentiation and fragmentation not only *between* countries, but *within* them. In other words, in those states where increasing interaction with post-apartheid South Africa has a significant impact—particularly those in its regional periphery—both costs and benefits are likely to be concentrated and uneven. Some groups, sectors and localities will be well positioned to take advantage of new economic opportunities and political alliances, while others will face increasing marginalization.

The emergence of "winners" and "losers" within and between states will produce new inter- and intra-national tensions, as well as new alignments and alliances. These, in turn, will create new pressures and challenges for state and inter-governmental structures, which (particularly given the bureaucratic "build-down" entailed in structural adjustment) they will be hard-pressed to meet. In this context, private sector and civil society institutions, along with decentralized systems of governance, are likely to increase in salience. Over the longer term, strengthened transborder alignments based on ethnic and economic commonalities may ultimately lead towards the reconsideration and realignment of national boundaries—an extremely delicate but quite possibly inevitable process (see Herbst 1992).

But beyond South Africa's periphery, the analyses in this collection suggest that other parts of the continent are likely to be only marginally affected, in the medium term at least. Certainly, South Africa's "demonstration effect" (i.e., its degree of success in sustaining and deepening democracy), its approach to the advocacy of human rights, and its emerging role in regional and continental mechanisms for peacekeeping/building will cause continental ripples (see Chapter 12 below). However, the capacity and willingness of South Africans—in both the state and the private sector—to alter the underlying structural conditions on which sustained development and security will depend is at best limited; while the impact of their activities will be uneven.

There are, of course, potential benefits embedded in the new circumstances of regional and continental fluidity. These may be realized through inter-state and non-state cooperative efforts. While some may yet be realized in the ongoing and painstaking effort to redesign and strengthen institutional structures for regional economic cooperation (see Davies, Chapter 6 and Swatuk, Chapter 7), some of the most promising bases for cooperation lie in a variety of less highly politicized areas. For example, Swatuk highlights the potential to build cooperation through and around regional water issues (Chapter 7), Mugyenyi and Swatuk note the potential for South Africans to learn from Uganda's process of post-conflict societal reconciliation (Chapter 8), and Inegbedion flags the potential for Nigeria-South Africa cooperation on toxic-waste dumping (Chapter 11). There are prospects, in other words, for building cooperation in accordance with the precepts of neo-functionalism (i.e., indirectly, through the creation of patterns, structures and constituencies *away from* areas of high political sensitivity) though in Africa, unlike Europe, this may be most successful in areas other than traditional economic integration. But any such efforts are likely to be difficult and uneven, and most will need to be underpinned by political will born of a sense of urgency. Whether this sense of urgency will emerge quickly enough is doubtful.

As suggested above, the chapters in this collection are organized in a series of expanding concentric circles. Chapters 2 and 3 consider South Africa's place in the global political economy, and prospects for an economic transition which successfully balances the imperatives of growth and redistribution. Given the country's marked relative decline since the 1960s, its serious structural weaknesses, and the vast inequalities fostered by apartheid, the new South Africa faces severe challenges both domestically and internationally. How it chooses to respond to these challenges will certainly affect its region and continent. More to the point, failure to successfully manage and consolidate this difficult transition will render any positive effects associated with the end of apartheid for (Southern) Africa moot.

Chapters 4 and 5 consider Southern African security challenges and prospects—Chapter 4 from the vantage of South Africa, and 5 from that of its neighbours. Chapters 6 and 7 deal with the bases and prospects for regional cooperation/integration in the areas of economics and the environment. The subjects of these four chapters are, in fact, intimately related. Obviously, Southern Africa stands to be most immediately and extensively affected by change in South Africa; as Nelson Mandela has put it, "Southern Africa comands a special priority in our foreign policy. We are inextricably part of Southern Africa and our destiny is linked to that of a region, which is much more than a mere geographical concept" (Mandela 1993). In this spirit, and in keeping with the analytical approach outlined above, these chapters focus on the region *as a whole*. While the state-makers of Southern Africa jealously guard their sovereign prerogatives, their fates are bound together by the integrated historical, socio-cultural, environmental and economic structures of the region they collectively "govern." It makes sense, then, to treat their security and development prospects in like fashion.

While the prospects for the Southern African region have received a good deal of attention, both before and after apartheid, the implications of change in South Africa for the rest of the continent have been relatively neglected. A major priority of this collection, therefore, is to give serious consideration to these implications. In focusing on both East and West Africa, specific biliateral axes have been highlighted. However each one should also be seen, and has been selected, as a proxy for a broader set of issues and relationships. Thus, as Nyang'oro notes, the South Africa-Kenya relationship not only links two continental "growth poles," forming one of the axes to which some (optimistic) observers have argued a continental renaissance may be anchored. It is also at the core of inter-regional relations between Eastern and Southern Africa. By contrast, the Uganda-South Africa relationship is representative of the implications of change south of the Limpopo for the continent's many economic "backwaters"—that is, its weaker political economies. Like many other African countries, Uganda has been struggling to recover from debilitating civil conflict under conditions of structural adjustment, and is dangerously dependent on a single primary commodity export. This relationship also puts into sharp relief the issue of how post-apartheid relations will be influenced (if at all) by alliances during the liberation struggle, since Museveni's Uganda was among the African National Congress's (ANC's) more reliable allies.

In this latter sense, South Africa's relationship with Côte d'Ivoire is the converse of its relationship with Uganda: Houphouët-Boigny's government was one of the few in Africa that regularly "supped with the (Pretoria) devil." Moreover, as Chapter 10 demonstrates, South Africa's links with Côte d'Ivoire have always been the most important element in its wider relationship(s) with francophone West Africa as a whole. Finally, even more than Kenya-South Africa, the Nigerian-South African axis, linking the continent's two most "powerful" political economies, is often treated as vital to Africa's prospects. Moreover, it is central to the prospects for expanding inter-regional ties between Southern and West Africa; and it is indicative of the challenges created by the thriving patterns of informal exchange which characterize Africa's contemporary political economy. This, then, is the logic behind the chapters which follow; let us expand on each sub-set in turn.

South Africa's Political Economy

South Africa's political economy is the central focus of chapters by Timothy M. Shaw and Stephen Gelb. Interestingly, Gelb and Shaw approach their subject—the new South Africa in the international division of labour and prospects for sustained reform and growth—with similar tools of analysis, but reach quite different conclusions. Both focus on the crisis of the economy, in its short-term and more deeply-embedded structural manifestations; Gelb provides a cogent analysis of post-transition efforts to reverse this crisis.

According to Shaw, in the 20 year period after 1965, South Africa's share of world trade declined precipitously, while its share of the world gold market fell from 80% in the 1970s to roughly 35% today. The mini-booms of 1981, 1984 and 1988 were not enough to turn its crisis ridden economy around. Protected and antiquated South African manufacturing entered the post-apartheid era unable to compete with Pacific Rim industrialists.

In terms of debt and capital flows, South Africa's 1993 debt stood at roughly $15 billion, or some ten percent of Gross National Product (GNP); this despite repayments of some $6 billion over 1985-88. Two percent of GDP over the next five years must be paid to the banks. According to Gelb, these constraints are real, and cannot be ignored when determining future policy directions. Shaw concurs: "there is very little room to maneuver between the black community's great expectations and the de facto conditionalities of international capital and exchange."

The government thus faces contradictory needs and forces: on the one hand it must pursue economic policies which will facilitate growth; on the other hand it must take bold steps to redress the inequalities fostered in the past. In other words, it must meet the needs of development.

Many more progressive organizations within South African society have lamented the emerging character of the debate, seeing it as being dominated by the language of neo-liberalism: fiscal responsibility; bringing inflation under control; stabilizing the Rand; cutting public expenditure; ending expensive subsidies for industry and agriculture; opening up the economy to international trade; and aggressively pursuing overseas markets. According to Shaw, senior economic ministers in the Government of National Unity (GNU) seem determined to advance elements of a neo-liberal agenda no matter the price. This is most clearly seen in the addition of neo-liberal tenets to the GNU's white paper on the Reconstruction and Development Program (RDP) (Adelzadeh and Padayachee 1994).

Thus Shaw, surveying the historical decline of South Africa's political economy as well as contemporary trends and compromises, leads us to a rather pessimistic view of its prospects. His analysis points toward the prospect of a more authoritarian variant of corporatism emerging, based on a relatively high level of coercion (see also Shaw 1994). In contrast, Gelb is cautiously optimistic. He argues that the domestic debate between those who advocated "Growth with Redistribution" (in keeping with neo-liberal precepts) and those aligned with the ANC who favoured "Growth Through Redistribution" (i.e., putting redistribution first, and giving a prominent role to state intervention in economic policy) has *not* been decisively resolved in favour of the former. Rather, given the roughly equivalent strength of the major social forces on either side of the socio-economic divide, what has emerged is a combination of the two strategies. In Gelb's view, this is generally to the good, since "too narrow a focus on one or the other of ... (growth or redistribution) may well have undesirable consequences, in terms of severe economic and social dislocation leading to the unsustainability of economic growth."

In both macro-economic and sectoral policies, this compromise has resulted in objectives which are "usually identified, if somewhat simplistically, with 'neo-liberalism' and are intended to restore private sector confidence and profitability and so encourage investment in the short term. But the mechanisms and steps introduced to achieve these intermediate objectives ... have been integrally connected with the need to improve the provision of basic needs and the creation of jobs." These policy objectives and outcomes have been buttressed institutionally by the emergence of a series of national forums in key policy areas, "institutionalizing and regularizing interaction between state officials and private sector actors (including labour)." Of these, the most prominent has been the National Economic, Development and Labour Council (NEDLAC), emerging in 1995 out of the National Economic Forum. NEDLAC's most conspicuous success to date has been the negotiation of a new Labour Relations Act in mid-1995—a highly contentious and politicized piece of legislation which posed a major test for the forum approach. In Gelb's view, "The institutionalization of the negotiating forums represents a major innovation, not just in terms of South Africa's own transition to a post-apartheid democratic order, but in terms of the global response to neo-liberal orthodoxy." It has enabled the government to restore short-term investor confidence while maintaining social stability and political support. Thus, while Gelb, like Shaw, emphasizes the importance of emerging corporatist-style structures in the new South Africa, he sees these structures as taking a more democratic, "social corporatist" form.

Gelb's optimism is not unalloyed, however. In particular, he flags a number of potential pitfalls. These include the question of whether investor confidence and investment levels can be sustained and translated into medium-term growth; the problem of co-ordination across the multiplicity of negotiating forums which have emerged; and the question of how the forums should relate to the national parliament and the principle of parliamentary sovereignty in South Africa's new democracy. Similar sources of conflict may emerge between the national and provincial governments over issues of economic policy. Above all, vital questions remain concerning the ability of the new regime to meet the needs of, and demands for, redistribution. So far, employment creation has fallen considerably short of requirements in this respect, and other redistributive mechanisms associated with the RDP have performed disappointingly. In this respect, the logic of the "growth through redistribution" strategy remains relevant:

"without redistribution, social stability is threatened in the long-run, and without social stability, the sustainability of growth cannot be assured."

A key question confronting economic policy-makers in South Africa seeking to engineer a sustainable recovery is: what markets do South African producers target? For Shaw, South Africa would be wise to pursue as many off-shore markets as possible and feasible. Its best prospects, however, may lie in the pursuit of a renewed regionalism with its vulnerable neighbours—a logic which he argues is reinforced by the dictates of globalization and the concomitant emergence of "new regionalisms."

Certainly, many of the Southern African region's present problems can be traced to an historical process which led to South Africa's present position as the regional political, economic and military hegemon. These problems have been exacerbated by decades of liberation struggle, South African state-directed interventions and, more recently, over a decade of structural adjustment programs. Given the interconnectedness of the region's problems, it may be strongly argued that if it is to move toward a sustainable and prosperous future, it must move as one. This means harnessing and directing newly released energies so that sustainable economic growth and participatory forms of democracy take hold in the region as a whole.

Yet in light of the mammoth tasks of reconstruction and development within South Africa, it will be exceedingly difficult to convince South African policy makers to maintain a regional development focus. It is perhaps telling that, in his insightful analysis of the prospects for economic renaissance in South Africa, Gelb is silent on the issue of foreign economic relations and policies. Still, the government must make choices concerning how to target external markets: to focus on the region and the continent; to focus on markets beyond the continent; or some mix of the two? This leads us to a discussion of the prospects for enhanced regional cooperation, first in the area of "security," and second, in economic and environmental spheres.

Security in Southern Africa

Perhaps one of the most hopeful and immediately tangible outcomes of the demise of apartheid is the regional "peace dividend" that has resulted. Not only has South Africa's destabilization of its neighbours come to an end, but its emerging role as a regional (and perhaps continental) peacekeeper has been the subject of much discussion throughout the sub-continent. Yet the decline of military and paramilitary "threats" has not produced a new era of regional "security." Indeed, from the perspective of broader notions of "common" or "human security," involving a recognition of a range of acute unconventional threats and a focus on people, justice and change, the region's situation remains fragile (Booth and Vale

1995; Solomon and Cilliers 1996). How (if at all) have the region's foreign and defense policy establishments adapted to this new understanding of security? How are they likely to? These issues and dilemmas are the focus of chapters by Peter Vale, and Larry Swatuk and Abillah Omari respectively.

In a region where myriad, growing and seemingly intractable threats derive from region-wide conditions of chronic economic underdevelopment and domestic political instability, a continuing emphasis on traditional notions of "national" security based on "secure borders" patrolled by strong militaries is clearly misplaced. Nevertheless, historically developed forms of political organization and resulting state-centred struggles for majority-rule helped entrench and give weight to traditional approaches to security. South Africa's decade-long policy of total strategy, with its emphasis on securing its international borders from total onslaught and strengthening its domestic security via WHAM (Winning of Hearts and Minds), facilitated inside/outside conceptions of inter-state relations. Security, therefore, continued to be pursued via military strategies of deterrence and compellence for national ends.

The costs of this approach to security are manifold and well-known. In addition to the "residuals" of apartheid, new threats have emerged in all Southern African Development Community (SADC) states.[2] The feelings of alienation from and abandonment by the state on the part of the majority of the region's peoples, exacerbated in some cases by the negative impacts of structural adjustment, have given rise to sub- and supra-national redefinitions of "security" and "community": from Islam and ethnicity to crime networks and cooperatives. Everywhere economic disparities are increasing and serve to exacerbate intra- and inter-state tensions. What is the likelihood that the region's policy makers will overcome this legacy?

Neither Vale nor Swatuk and Omari are particularly optimistic in this regard. To both, in the absence of apartheid, Southern Africa faces no traditionally-defined external security threat. Rather, insecurity and instability throughout the region stem, for the most part, from historical processes of uneven development and the resultant inequalities of resource access and allocation. Problems such as drugs, arms, illegal migrant labour flows, and now AIDS, are merely symptoms of a more widespread disease. "Security," therefore, will not be assured through arms acquisitions and inter-state military cooperation. Instead, according to Swatuk and Omari, security can best be promoted by a concerted attempt to address the region's and continent's economic marginalization from and non-competitiveness within the global economy.

So, whereas the "new" state-centric Association of Southern African States/Inter-State Defence and Security Committee (ASAS/ISDSC) framework presents a positive approach to securing short-term stability, institutionalizing such a framework is hardly a panacea. To be sure, recent movement toward establishing "common security" mechanisms—conflict resolution, peacekeeping, peacebuilding—based on what Swatuk and Omari term "new thinking," are welcome particularly in a region long-marred by inter- and intra-state conflict. However, in the absence of economic development, such mechanisms may well end up serving inter-*regime* defense and security, often at the expense of the region's peoples.

In the specific case of South Africa, Vale is even more pessimistic. He emphasizes the artificiality of the state boundaries and inter-state security problematique imposed on a "single and indivisible" region; and the comforting continuity which has characterized post-apartheid foreign and defense policy thinking thus far. What he has to say resonates through present policy decisions: from the GNU decision to continue exporting arms, to Defence Minister Modise's stern words to the OAU and SADC[3]; from South African support for inter-state cooperation against "drug smugglers" to the swelling ranks of the new South African National Defence Force (SANDF).

In the search for both security and legitimacy, the government is undertaking the integration and reconciliation of previously sworn enemies—notably the ANC's Umkhonto we Sizwe (MK) and the Pan Africanist Congress's (PAC's) African Peoples' Liberation Army (APLA) with members of the former-South African Defense Force (SADF)—into a reformed South African *National* Defence Force. This process, though clearly necessary and unavoidable, throws up its own contradictions. For instance, it enlarges the "civil service" considerably, thereby diverting scarce resources perhaps better used elsewhere.[4]

Moreover, by privileging armed forces, integration rather than integration of former fighters/military personnel/etc. into society at large, it maintains a narrow definition of "security" in the Southern African milieu. In other words, for much of the defense establishment the "nation's security" will be enhanced by a strong, integrated military and police force, as opposed to general disarmament, demobilization, retraining of forces for civilian life, and the freeing up of massive capital and human resources for use in reconstructing society (see, Cock and Nathan 1989; Hough 1990).[5]

This growth in numbers has been accompanied by a parallel defense of the military and policing budget, with like-minded military men protecting their turf at considerable long-term opportunity cost to reconstruction and development. Moreover, their "threat perception" and rationale reproduces old patterns and policies: in Vale's words, "the essence of the regional security perspective remains: the region is a "threat" to South Africa's sovereignty." In the meantime, people in South Africa and in the region turn to other sources for their own protection: from enhanced "security" systems in the white suburbs, to the emergence of gangs and "big men" in the townships.

The continuing dominance of neo-realist thinking in the Department of Foreign Affairs and of neo-liberal thinking in economic ministries and corporate boardrooms—each of which fosters "us/them," "inside/outside" conceptions of global affairs—contributes significantly to South Africa's continuing "laager" mentality. This kind of thinking has ominous implications for regional security. For example, one area where South African industry has developed a global niche is in arms sales. The logic behind continued arms sales seems compelling: (i) "everyone does it, so why should South Africa take the moral high ground at the expense of a proven foreign exchange earner?"; (ii) Armscor is competitive and some of the money earned can go to national reconstruction and development; (iii) the region is full of willing buyers on which to off-load South African arms, so Armscor should sell to the region. Yet, as Vale notes, in so doing South Africa is buying regional insecurity in exchange for hard cash; and long-term regional relations carry a high probability of conflict. This fact leads back to the laager mentality: it reinforces the perception in the defense and security community that "good *electric* fences make good neighbours."

To alter this thinking and the insecurity it produces will not be easy; as Vale notes, political systems are geared for continuity, and bureaucracies are by their nature resistant to innovation, let alone re-invention. Yet, a secure regional future is impossible without such a fundamental re-orientation. Moreover, the current post-apartheid moment offers "strategic footholds" in which it may be advanced. Vale discusses, for example, the potential of the new provincial governments to provide leadership in this regard, citing as an example Mpumalanga Premier Matthews Phosa's May 1995 initiative to seek an "economic bloc" with Swaziland and the southern provinces of Mozambique. "By offering solutions to people on the ground," argues Vale, "Phosa is eroding the myths which created the region's current maps and probing new forms of sub-regionalism."

Given the numerous region-wide threats to security identified above, it is imperative that South African policy makers "discover Pan-Southern Africanism." Until that time, "security" in Southern Africa will accrue to the powerful few at the expense of the powerless many. Moreover, it is a fleeting sort of security, unsustainable in the absence of fundamental regional transformation.

Regional Economic and Environmental Cooperation

Regional cooperation is also the concern of chapters by Rob Davies and Larry Swatuk. Both Davies and Swatuk examine prospects for regional economic cooperation, with Swatuk also assessing prospects for cooperation on environmental issues.

All SADC countries' economies, save for Botswana, Lesotho and Swaziland (BLS), contracted significantly over the course of the 1980s. Causes of poor economic performance are legion and well known. Resulting debts have led to *de facto* and *de jure* adoption of economic structural adjustment programs throughout the region. Trends in world production have moved toward a new international division of labour, involving in part the globalization of production, an exponential increase in the speed and magnitude of finance capital flows, and a general decline in demand for the resources which drove heavy industries in the past.

Southern Africa's states and peoples increasingly find themselves on the periphery of this process. Their products are poorly developed and little in demand save for those covered by limited special preferences *vis-à-vis* the European Union (EU) and those of a few regionally-based multinationals like Lonrho, Anglo American, and De Beers in the areas of sugar, timber, textiles, and minerals. Moreover, regional "development" has been hampered by capital flight and limited foreign investment: the legacy of apartheid-driven sanctions and regional instability (Swatuk 1994).

Everywhere, the capacity of the state to take remedial actions is declining. As a result, unemployment is increasing and a majority of Southern Africans find themselves engaged in some form of informal sector activity, sometimes including such unsavoury pursuits as drug, wildlife, and weapons trading, in order to make ends meet.

Given this deep uncertainty, there is some pressure for South Africa to "go it alone"—that is, to pursue its own development through overseas markets and connections, and turn its back on the region and the continent. This perspective appeals to a variety of South Africans for different reasons. Some South Africans from all racial groups have been inclined to display a "metropolitan arrogance" toward their continental neighbours (Young 1991: 238). Others are understandably concerned that pressing national needs be met. Still others, notably within the business community, see this conclusion as a reflection of hard-nosed economic judgements concerning the location of opportunities in an increasingly competitive world economy.

In light of these facts, a central question addressed by both Davies and Swatuk is how policy makers intend to approach issues of economic and ecological security and development in Southern Africa in the future. Davies, writing from the informed vantage point of a member of South Africa's Parliament, situates his discussion of future regional relations in terms of what he characterizes as the unfinished debate on regional cooperation and integration. He compares and contrasts three distinct approaches to regional economic cooperation/integration: the conventional *trade or market integration* paradigm; the *functional cooperation* or *integration through project cooperation* paradigm, which underpinned SADCC practice during the 1980s; and a more ambitious *development integration* paradigm, which proceeds from a critique of the first two. Thus, it stresses "the need for both macro- and micro-coordination in a multi-sectoral program embracing production, infrastructure, and trade," and "an equitable balance of the benefits of integration." Davies notes that relatively recently, the World Bank and IMF have become advocates of regional integration of the first variety, provided it does not contradict the overall outward-oriented and liberalizing thrust of their structural adjustment programs. He himself clearly favours the development integration paradigm, critiquing the market integration approach reflected in the IMF, World Bank, African Development Bank and EU-sponsored "Cross Border Initiative" (CBI) launched in 1993. Yet he also stresses some important weaknesses in the development integration approach as it has been formulated to date, and concludes that important conceptual and strategic work remains to be done.

Davies then provides a valuable account of the South African GNU's approach to regional economic integration issues in its first two years. In keeping with the views expressed by Swatuk and a variety of other studies (African Development Bank 1994; Ostergaard 1993), he argues that its approach has been characterized, implicitly at least, by an assumption of "variable geometry," with "different arrangements at different levels of integration applying among different groups of countries within the broader region." He then focuses particularly on two sets of issues: the GNU's approach to the Southern African Development Community following South Africa's accession to the treaty of that organization in August 1994; and the negotiations for a revised Southern African Customs Union (SACU) Agreement, ongoing since November of that year.

Several points of debate have been important in both processes. In the context of the SACU negotiations, a key issue has been its relationship with SADC and, concomitantly, the question of whether it should be enlarged to take in new members—thereby potentially challenging/competing with SADC. Davies argues that a second alternative, in which SACU membership remains unchanged and the organization is treated as an important sub-set within a broader regional program centered on SADC, is more viable. His reasoning for this conclusion includes an interesting analysis of the implications of the Marrakesh GATT Agreement, to which South Africa is now subject, for regional integration schemes.

In relation to SADC, a key question immediately confronted by the GNU was whether to work towards a new regional trading relationship on a bilateral or multilateral basis. Davies argues that South African officials have clearly indicated their preference for a multilateral, regional approach—though the pressures for bilateralism (inside and outside South Africa) persist. Another key question is the basis on which integration efforts should proceed. While some have favoured the creation of a full regional Free Trade Area with all due speed, Davies (in line with the development integration approach) argues that "further South African access to these countries' markets would need to be carefully structured and phased," leading to the emergence of an "assymetrical Preferential

Trade Area" in which South Africa opens its market more rapidly than its partners and the arrangement operates on a "somewhat differentiated basis country by country." An important element in his analysis on this point is the ongoing Free Trade negotiations between South Africa and the European Union, which have significant potential implications for other SACU and SADC states. Nevertheless, important questions remain concerning the bases of political support for such an assymetrical regional arrangement in both South Africa and its neighbours, and on how a "somewhat differentiated" approach would be prevented from slipping into a predominantly bilateral, "hub-and-spoke" type of situation.

A number of key questions and challenges remain. These include the need for "greater clarity about what integration is intended to achieve, how it fits in to a broader program including also sectoral cooperation and coordination, and the significance of post-Uruguay Round pressures of globalisation." However, Davies is strongly of the view that both SADC and South Africa stand to gain through cooperation/integration. In rationalizing the existing economic schemes into "new" forms of regional integration, then, the overriding challenge is to find a modus vivendi for incorporating South Africa into the SADC community without raising the spectre of dominance and economic exploitation which has been a major reason for failed economic schemes.

Both Davies and Swatuk make clear that the barriers to substantially enhanced regional trade arrangements are formidable. However, while SADC has undoubtedly fallen short of its aspirations, it has proven politically resilient and has retained a high level of support from regional governments, including South Africa's. Thus, there is a relatively durable institutional basis on which to attempt to proceed. Moreover, notwithstanding considerable mutual indifference and even suspicion between South Africans and their neighbours, there is also a degree of mutual fascination. It is significant in this regard that the ANC is clearly on record as favouring a cooperative and non-hegemonic future for the region and the continent as a whole (ANC 1993; 1994).

Given the highly sensitive nature of economic issues, Swatuk also suggests that the environment may present a somewhat less controversial and more fruitful area in which to build regional cooperation. After all, the environment is universally shared, recognizing no human-made borders, and its protection is central to sustainable development in the SADC region and beyond. He places particular emphasis on the related issues of water resource use and conservation.

South Africa in Africa

The fourth major sub-theme of this collection is the "new" South Africa's role in the continent. In anticipation of South Africa's transition, continental expectations were heightened for the obvious reason that the end of apartheid removed the one remaining white smudge on an otherwise black majority-ruled continent. In other words, it marked the end to Africa's formal colonial period. But for many, "post-apartheid" implied, and implies, much more: South Africa's economic strength would pull the continent out of its enduring economic crisis, while its political stature and leadership would give the continent new direction and expanded influence in the councils of the international community.

To be sure, this remains a powerful and appealing image, particularly to politicians in search of a simple solution for complex and intractable problems. But for our contributors, it is unfortunately more image than reality. As with the South Africa-specific and Southern Africa regional themes, informed opinions regarding South Africa's future relations with the continent waffle between optimism and pessimism. Nevertheless, notwithstanding some new and enhanced possibilities for South African-African cooperation and exchange, the analyses in Chapters 8 to 11 present a composite picture of limited opportunities and uneven benefits, along with some potentially damaging distortions.

Early Thinking on the East African Case

East Africa is featured in chapters by Joshua Mugyenyi and Larry Swatuk, and Julius Nyang'oro. As with South Africa's political economy and Southern African economic and security cooperation, it seems clear to each author that South Africa-East Africa relations will not be driven by "moral imperatives." Thus, for example, Ugandan and Tanzanian support for the liberation struggle is unlikely to translate into any immediate post-apartheid dividends. According to Mugyenyi and Swatuk, trade and commercial relations seem to be dictating continental foreign policy. Similarly, Kenya, which was "never more than lukewarm toward the ANC," is likely to benefit more significantly from South Africa's reintegration into the continent. For Nyang'oro, while this "moral amnesia" is regrettable, it is a fact.

According to Mugyenyi and Swatuk, there has been an increase in commercial and other relations between South Africa and Uganda: e.g., Stanbic has bought out Grindlay's Bank; South African Airways and Uganda Airlines have established formal links; Eskom has indicated its interest in buying out the Uganda Electrical Board; and the South African private sector—particularly in the energy, minerals and health sectors—is "driving very hard bargains." Moreover, many South African manufactured and agricultural goods are now available in Uganda.

However, Uganda's position is typical of other African "backwaters." That is to say, while South Africans have come to Uganda to carve out a niche, Uganda has nothing of significance to sell to South Africa. Its agricultural products are not competitive, it has no manufactures to offer, and tourism seems to be a non-starter until there are improvements in infrastructure, especially given more proximate tourist destinations in the Southern African region. South Africa's reintegration into the continent therefore means that Uganda will have growing bilateral deficits, since it has no goods with which to balance trade.

While Ugandan producers and policy makers are likely to seek both protection from and agreements with South African producers and investors, the prospects are problematic. Businesses setting up in East Africa will be looking for good infrastructure (to get goods to market) and a skilled labour force. If South African firms are willing to (re)locate, according to Mugyenyi and Swatuk, they will probably do so in Nairobi, which is, in relative terms, already "stealing the show." Moreover, there are longer-term problems with any relocation of South African business to the continental hinterland which *does* occur: it will promote deindustrialization in a number of African "backwaters," and, given SAP strictures, will lead to increasing import strangulation.

Nyang'oro's treatment of emerging Kenya-South Africa relations seems to contradict Mugyenyi's claim that Nairobi is stealing the show. To Nyang'oro, while Kenya is not a backwater, neither is it a growth pole. To be sure, South African policy makers have identified Kenya, Nigeria, Zimbabwe, and Côte d'Ivoire as growth poles in the continent. But, as Nyang'oro points out, together these four "poles" account for less than ten percent of total African trade.

As in Uganda, the South African private and governmental sectors have been busy exploring potential linkages with Kenya. A trade show was organized in 1992, and a number of trade missions and fairs have been mounted since that time; diplomatic links were established in April 1994; and there has been some increase in trade including, regrettably, arms exports. Air links were maintained even at the height of sanctions.

For Nyang'oro, however, South Africa's potential role as a spur to continental development has been examined from the wrong way round. Clearly, bilateral trade relations will be pursued, and some South African businesses will set up in regional centres like Nairobi. Yet, Nyang'oro points out that South African business is a thin reed. The "quality" of South African goods is largely a myth, to be cultivated within the continent as long as these manufactures are unable to compete internationally. Moreover, for most South African manufacturers, Africa north of the Limpopo "is a fog." Interest in extra-SACU/SADC markets will therefore be slow to develop. And it must be remembered that South Africa is a net-importer of capital. Thus, aside from the traditional players in the continent (e.g., Anglo, De Beers) who invest in very narrow, highly-capital intensive sectors such as mining, it is unlikely that South African capital will play a significant role in African development.

So for Nyang'oro, the more interesting question to be asked is: what role can South Africa play as a *conduit* for international capital into the continent? He cites the example of the Johannesburg City Council's "Africa Initiative Club" which seeks to be the "gateway to Africa." South African access to the continent is improving in terms of computer link-ups and growth in services (e.g., commercial banking), to name but two areas. These newer linkages reinforce older, often civil societal linkages: media, missionaries, labour, health. Moreover, South Africa also has much to learn from other African states like Uganda (lessons for the ANC in the transition from guerrilla group to state government) and Kenya (lessons for the state in terms of successful modes of repression: from the bulldozing of squatter settlements to the use of rubber bullets). To focus on South African trade and investment is to limit the creative possibilities for increased continental cooperation; yet whether South Africa's economic and political leaders will see the continent in these terms is uncertain at best.

The View from West Africa

These tentative conclusions are reinforced in the West African case studies by John Inegbedion and Cyril Kofie Daddieh. For Daddieh, if the "sympathy factor" is not relevant in determining future South Africa-Africa relations, then neither is the "traitor factor." It should be remembered that Côte d'Ivoire, under the long tutelage of Houphouët-Boigny, pursued linkages with Pretoria to the chagrin of both the OAU and the ANC. South Africa, in turn, used Côte d'Ivoire as a gateway to other French West African states. These relations were disjointed but incremental, and were mediated by Houphouët. South Africa's interest was purely political: to gain acceptance in parts of Africa beyond the "captive" Southern African region.

Economic linkages were minuscule, totalling no more than $10 million in 1975. Given the highly political nature of contact, then, Daddieh suggests that French Africa will lose some of its salience in future relations with South Africa. Many former ANC friends—e.g., Sâo Tomé, Guinea—will lose out as their markets are small and their products uncompetitive and easily substitutable. As with East Africa, there is little Francophone West African states have to offer that South Africa does not already have.

This trend may not include Côte d'Ivoire, however. As Daddieh notes, "Mandela has demonstrated a remarkable capacity to forgive former adversaries, and continues to pursue a policy of reconciliation at home and abroad"; and Côte d'Ivoire is one of the continent's stronger and more promising markets. Thus, South Africa-Côte d'Ivoire relations are likely to increase in range and intensity "as development imperatives and economic actors exert influence on both sides."

Nevertheless, though Côte d'Ivoire—like Kenya—is a relatively major player in African terms, the levels of bilateral trade are still very small.

There is as yet virtually no South African investment in the Ivoirian economy, and little likely to come. In Daddieh's view, South Africans are interested in conserving the old division of labour in West Africa whereby South Africa exports manufactured goods, food products, and base metals in exchange for agricultural raw material inputs for South African industry.

Two further obstacles to increased South African involvement in Francophone West Africa bear emphasis. First, there is the problem of language. Much of East Africa may be "a fog," but it is at least an English-speaking fog. The French language is a significant hurdle to increased cooperation. Second, it is questionable whether South African business can compete with French business in the context of what Daddieh terms "the second scramble for Africa." Paris has long considered this region as its *chasse gardée*, and is not likely to give way easily.

On the surface, the Nigerian case seems to offer more hope for meaningful forms of inter-state cooperation. According to Inegbedion, "not only is each state the hegemon in its sub-region, but Nigeria and South Africa combine between them human, natural and financial resources that surpass the rest of Africa." This kind of thinking led Nigeria's Foreign Minister to state:

> [C]ooperation and better understanding between Abuja and Pretoria ... would ensure a united, stronger Africa that can solve Africa's legion of problems of underdevelopment, unemployment, food shortages, debt and disinvestment" (quoted in Inegbedion, Chapter 11).

To Inegbedion, such claims are unfounded for a number of reasons. Most importantly, there are numerous domestic constraints which make Nigeria unattractive to South African business. Political instability as presently manifest in Nigeria means high risk and serves as a deterrent to foreign trade and investment.

Few today question that Nigeria's economic crises and arrested development have been mainly a function of internal political and economic distortions, both during and after the Cold War. And, as Inegbedion notes, with the emergence of the "new" South Africa, even Nigeria's status as *primus inter pares* in Africa is now contested. For these and other reasons, Nigeria cannot serve as a core state to "uplift" Africa in the immediate future, and Abuja and Pretoria will find it difficult to engage in productive economic cooperation. Nigeria's internal economic and political conditions are simply too anarchic.

However, this does not stop Nigerians from buying and selling goods to and from South Africa and its neighbours. Moreover, Inegbedion envisions Nigerian-South African cooperation in areas beyond trade and investment. One possible area is continental peacekeeping and peacemaking efforts. Another is coordinated activities to stem the flow of toxic waste to the continent. Yet, given the political isolation and intransigence of the Abacha regime in Nigeria, and pressure from Commonwealth and other countries for a restoration of democracy there, it is doubtful whether South Africa will be willing to cooperate with Nigeria at a high political level so long as the current regime remains in place.

In summary, according to Inegbedion, while Nigeria and South Africa may both be sub-regional hegemons, they are not likely to engage in the kinds of economic cooperation that can directly address Africa's underdevelopment. Mere trade between Nigerians and South Africans—much of it shady and unofficial—is not enough to promote economic development if other regional state and non-state actors are excluded. Nevertheless, considerable longer term potential does exist. South Africa remains the economic powerhouse of SADC and the most industrialized economy on the continent. Nigeria is an oil exporter, has the single largest market in Africa, and is the moving force behind ECOWAS. In short, Inegbedion states, what both Abuja and Pretoria lack are political will, commitment and capacity as opposed to resources.

South Africa in Africa: Summary

Despite the obvious potential and compelling logic of continental economic cooperation—consistently reasserted in OAU and ECA documentation—our contributors remain highly sceptical of its practical possibilities. Rather, the overwhelming view, supported by early empirical evidence, is that Africa will remain largely marginal to South Africa's needs and priorities.

Certainly, the journey toward positive changes in regional and continental relations is a considerably less fearful and absolutely more hopeful journey today, in the absence of apartheid, than it was just a few short years ago. However, the early findings marshalled in this collection are sobering. Notwithstanding several new departures and expanding possibilities, there is little reason to expect a South African state struggling with domestic economic and political challenges to provide more than intermittent leadership and limited resources for regional and continental recovery. Moreover, the more aggressive role played by South African capital and other societal interests will be concentrated and uneven in its impact. The ending of apartheid is, perhaps, a "small miracle" in its own right (see Gelb, Chapter 3); but it is neither a continental nor even a regional panacea.

Notes

1. See, for example, Young 1991, who outlines both potential virtuous and vicious cycles of post-apartheid regional relations. Also, Oden 1993; Shaw and Nhema 1995; Stoneman and Thompson 1991; and the articles on the "new" South Africa in *Third World Quarterly*, 15:2, 1994.

2. SADC, formed out of the Southern African Development Coordination Conference (SADCC) established in 1980 with the principal goal of reducing economic

dependence on South Africa, now consists of twelve member states: Angola, Botswana, Lesotho, Malawi, Mauritius, Mozambique, Namibia, South Africa, Swaziland, Tanzania, Zambia, and Zimbabwe.

3. Modise warned the OAU not to expect too much from its newest member, as South Africa was preoccupied with national issues. To the SADC, Modise threatened to take harsh measures if member-states did not control the flow of illegal migrants from their countries to South Africa.

4. See, "Comment: Numbers game," *Business Day*, 14 July 1994.

5. Indeed, the ANC's one progressive plan—i.e. to turns swords to plowshares via the creation of military "brigades" involved in developmental work—was quickly shot down as uneconomic, inefficient, and beneath the esteem of trained fighters.

References

Adelzadeh, Asghar and Vishnu Padayachee. 1994. "The RDP White Paper: Reconstruction of a development vision?" *Transformation* (Durban) 25: 1-18.

African Development Bank. 1994. *Economic Integration in Southern Africa: Executive Summary*. mimeo, Harare.

African National Congress. 1994. *The Reconstruction and Development Programme*. Johannesburg: Umanyano Publications.

———. 1993. *Foreign Policy in a New Democratic South Africa*, a discussion paper. ANC Department of International Affairs, October.

Anderson, Benedict. 1991. *Imagined Communities*. London: Verso.

Anglin, Douglas G. 1991. "South African Relations with Southern Africa: Continuity or Change?," paper presented at the 20th annual meeting of the Canadian Association of African Studies, York University, Toronto, Ontario, May.

AWEPAA. 1992. *Post-Apartheid Regional Cooperation. International Support for Transforming Southern Africa*, conference report. Gaborone, 27-29 April.

Booth, Ken, and Peter Vale. 1995. "Security in Southern Africa: after apartheid, beyond realism," *International Affairs* 19: 285-304.

Business Day (Johannesburg), various.

Cock, Jacklyn and Laurie Nathan, eds. 1989. *War and Society. The militarization of South Africa*. New York: St. Martin's.

Daily Dispatch (East London), various.

Gelb, Stephen, ed. 1991. *South Africa's Economic Crisis*. Cape Town: David Philip.

Gereffi, Gary and Donald L. Wyman, eds. 1990. *Manufacturing Miracles: Paths of Industrialization in Latin America and East Asia*. Princeton: Princeton University Press.

Herbst, Jeffrey. 1992. "Challenges to Africa's Boundaries in the New World Order," *Journal of International Affairs* 46 (Summer): 1.

Hough, M. 1990. "Security, war and the environment," *Strategic Review for Southern Africa* 12(2) (November): 1-13.

Mandela, Nelson. 1993. "South Africa's Future Foreign Policy," *Foreign Affairs* 72(5): 86-97.

Munck, Ronaldo. 1994. "South Africa: the great economic debate," *Third World Quarterly* 15(2): 205-18.

Oden, Bertil, ed. 1993. *Southern Africa After Apartheid. Regional Integration and External Resources.* Seminar Proceedings No. 28. Uppsala: Nordiska Afrikainstitutet.

Ohlson, Thomas and Stephen John Stedman. 1994. *The New is Not Yet Born. Conflict and Conflict Resolution in Southern Africa.* Washington: The Brookings Institute.

Ohlson, Thomas and Stephen John Stedman. 1993. "Towards Enhanced Regional Security in Southern Africa?", in Oden, ed., *Southern Africa After Apartheid.* Pp. 87-107.

Stoneman, Colin and Carol B. Thompson. 1991. *Southern Africa after Apartheid: economic repercussions of a free South Africa.* Africa Recovery Briefing Paper No. 4 (December). New York: UNDP.

Shaw, Timothy M. 1994. "South Africa: the corporatist/regionalist conjuncture," *Third World Quarterly* 15(1) (March): 243-55.

—— and Alfred Nhema. 1995. "Directions and Debates in South Africa's First Post-Apartheid Decade," *Mershon International Studies Review* 39: 97-110.

Solomon, Hussein, and Jakkie Cilliers. 1996. *People, Poverty and Peace: Human Security in Southern Africa.* IDP Monograph Series No. 4 (May). Midrand: Institute for Defence Policy.

Sunday Times (Cape Town), various.

Swatuk, Larry A. 1994. "Prospects for Southern African Regional Integration after Apartheid," *Journal of the Third World Spectrum* 1(2): 17-38.

—— and Timothy M. Shaw, eds. 1991. *Prospects for Peace and Development in Southern Africa in the 1990s: Canadian and Comparative Perspectives.* Lanham: University Press of America.

The Economist (London), various.

Weekly Mail and Guardian (Johannesburg), various.

Young, Tom. 1991. "South Africa's Foreign Relations in a Post-Apartheid World," *South Africa International* 21(4): 236-43.

2

Post-Apartheid South(ern) Africa in the New International Divisions of Labour and Power: How Marginal?

Timothy M. Shaw

A strong America, an advancing China, a struggling Russia and an uncertain Europe make up the new quartet of big powers ... Nobody else seems to qualify. It is unlikely that Africa or the Antipodes is going to produce a member of this dominant group.
—*Economist* (8 January 1994: 21)

Southern Africa's critical choices have less to do with the propensity of individual states to crumble into ethnic fiefdoms than with the commitments made by member states to the region's future. A political truism applies to Southern Africa in the mid-1990s: weak commitments by weak states create weak regional communities.
—Peter Vale (1994: xxii)

Profound changes in the global political economy impact on both the analysis and praxis of development in South(ern) Africa as they do else-where in the world. The combination of on-going structural change and adjustments and post-Cold War strategic/diplomatic transformations makes a reconsideration of past assumptions and anticipations imperative. To be sure, the political economies of South and Southern Africa in the remaining years of the twentieth century are largely a function of historical patterns of political and socio-economic relations. Given significant shifts in the "New" International Divisions of Labour (NIDL) and Power (NIDP), it is important, however, to situate national and regional tensions and directions in the context of such global trends (on the NIDL see, for example, Mittelman 1994a and 1994b; on the NIDP, see, for example, Boardman 1994).

This chapter attempts to juxtapose "internal" and "international" political economies of South and Southern Africa at the middle of the last decade of the twentieth century. It is not intended to be at all conclusive or definitive. Rather, it seeks to stimulate discussion and speculation, building on analytic and policy discourses in the burgeoning literature (ANC 1994; Baker 1993; Lipton and Simkins 1993; Nattrass 1994a and 1994b; Shaw and Nhema 1995). It therefore seeks to address one key question: Given the trends toward economic globalization and differentiation, and the numerous opportunities as well as difficulties these phenomena create in the developing world, what are the prospects for the emergence of new forms of sustainable, cooperative, regional relations in post-apartheid Southern Africa? In order to do this, we must first establish the key historical trends in the South and Southern African political economy, and the sources and extent of their marginalization.

Causes and Characteristics of South African Decline in the Global Political Economy

Along with the rest of an increasingly marginalized continent (Shaw 1993), while South Africa remained an important element in world trade, it was less so by the beginning of the 1990s than at the end of the 1970s (Holden 1992). According to Strydom (1987: 205), "South Africa ... shed some of its share in world trade over the period 1965 to 1985. Most probably the Newly Industrializing Countries have conquered part of South Africa's foreign markets." Economic, strategic and political pressures on the National Party (NP) state intensified at the end of the 1980s because of a combination of costs of apartheid structures and security, and changes in global structures and economy. The regime was forced to "liberalize" somewhat not only because of diplomatic, demographic and strategic pressures; it also had to begin to "privatize" because of intense economic pressures from external creditors and contexts, notably declining exchange, profit, and investment (EIU Quarterly *Country Reports* and Annual *Country Profile*; Baker 1993; Lipton and Simkins 1993).

The "state capitalist" system created largely by the NP after 1948 was slowly being undermined by privatization reforms and liberalization pressures, even ahead of the contemporary period of political transition. Such privatization of the heights of the Afrikaner economy did not, by itself, lead to the demise of apartheid, despite the long-standing corporate thesis about industrialization and modernization leading to political, if not economic, liberalization. It did, however, serve to erode the patrimonial resources of Afrikanerdom and to change or reduce the inheritance awaiting the post-apartheid regime.

The current stage in South Africa's continuing crisis can be dated from 1985, when political rebellions induced both reform and repression, and economic pressures produced default and redirection (Commonwealth 1989: 108-19). South Africa has long been experiencing relative deindustri-alization, however. In the 20-year period after 1965 its share of world trade except gold declined from 1.5% exchange to 0.9% exports and 0.6% imports (Strydom 1987: 204). When combined with its falling share of the world gold market—from 80% in the 1970s to just 35% today—its post-war economy was clearly in crisis. The mini-booms of 1981, 1984 and 1988, during which secular declining terms-of-trade momentarily improved, were not enough to stop decline and devaluation. Indeed, GDP per capita has been falling along with share of manufacturing since 1975, which eventually trickled-down to worsen already unacceptable Human Development Index (HDI) performances (see Tables 2.1 and 2.2). Protected and antiquated South African manufacturing was increasingly unable to compete with Pacific Rim industrialists, even if some of the latter have begun to invest selectively in the region's own periphery (Stein 1995).

The Newly Industrialized Country (NIC) and near-NIC structure and status of Pacific Rim states are quite distinct from rather orthodox forms of corporatism in the old (and perhaps new) South Africa (Baskin 1993a and b; Friedman 1991; Nattrass 1994a and b; Shaw 1994). Increasingly, South Africa's extra-African exports have relied excessively and chronically on raw materials for any post-recession growth. While gold and diamond sales were always something of an official or corporate secret, the importance of these mining activities to South Africa's economy cannot be denied. Gold, for example, accounts for 50% of total mineral production and more than

TABLE 2.1 Southern Africa Human Development Indicators

	Human Development Index	GNP rank minus HDI rank	HDI rank[a]
Angola	0.271	-35	155
Botswana	0.670	-29	87
Lesotho	0.476	4	120
Malawi	0.260	-1	157
Mozambique	0.252	14	159
Namibia	0.425	-43	127
Swaziland	0.513	-21	117
Tanzania	0.306	22	148
Zambia	0.352	-4	138
Zimbabwe	0.474	-3	121
South Africa	0.650	-33	93

[a] A positive figure shows that HDI rank is higher than that for GNP; a negative figure the opposite.

Source: UNDP, *Human Development Report 1994* (New York: Oxford University Press, 1994), pp. 130-1.

TABLE 2.2 South Africa: Economic Indicators

	1980	1987	1988	1989	1990	1991	1992	1993[a]
GDP at current prices (R bn)	60.3	154.5	198.1	233.4	264.2	297.9	327.1	365.2
Real GDP growth (%)	6.6	2.1	4.2	2.3	-0.5	-0.4	-2.1	1.1
Merchandise exports ($mn)	25,698	21,088	22,632	22,399	23,383	23,715	23,645	23,925
Merchandise imports ($mn)	18,268	13,925	17,210	16,810	17,045	17,449	18,216	17,980
Current account balance ($mn)	3,508	2,936	1,218	1,579	2,253	2,664	1,388	1,814
Gross budget deficit/GDP (%)	-2.29	-6.99	-5.27	-0.23	-5.14	-6.11	-9.03	-6.90
Gross investment/GDP (%)	30.4	19.3	21.5	20.8	19.3	n.a.	n.a.	n.a.
Total external debt ($mn)	26.1	22.6	21.2	20.6	18.6	17.1	16.4	16.4
Debt service ratio (to exports) (%)	7.9	16.9	16.5	14.0	16.0	13.5	14.7	14.7
Gold ore production (tonnes)	572.4	601.8	619.0	605.5	600.6	601.0	608.5	619.5
Coal production (mn tonnes)	116.0	176.5	178.0	173.9	174.8	175.2	174.0	n.a.
Food production per capita (1979-81 = 100)	97	85	87	90	?81	80	82	72
Exchange rate (average rand per dollar)[b]	0.78	2.03	2.25	2.62	2.59	2.76	2.85	3.26
Reserves (months of import cover)	0.5	0.5	0.5	0.7	0.7	0.6	0.6	0.7
Inflation rate (%)	13.8	6.1	12.8	14.7	14.4	15.3	13.9	9.7

[a] Estimates

[b] June 1994 R 3.53 x 51

Source: World Bank, IMF, FAO, Government of South Africa.

30% of total export earnings (ODI 1994: 3). However, changing technological and policy environments have led to the proliferation of gold mines and
coins elsewhere in the world, particularly in Latin America. At the same
time, the production costs of gold in South Africa continue to rise.

The Pacific Rim, especially Japan and Taiwan, is now crucial for South
Africa's gold and diamond sales. Indeed, both formal and informal sector
diamonds pass from South Africa, Namibia and other parts of Africa
(including both Angola and Zaire) to Holland, Hong Kong and Israel with
minimal paperwork. De Beers' Central Selling Organization (CSO) has had
to be very nimble to maintain its global cartel given Angolan, Russian, and
Sierra Leonean informal production and distribution.[1]

According to a recent ODI Briefing Paper (1994:5), "[p]rospects for
chrome, nickel, zinc, copper and uranium prices remain depressed, while
South Africa has continued to lose market shares in most of these minerals
in the 1990s." Hence the imperative of Southern African Development
Community (SADC) markets for value-added products, leading to renewed regional apprehensions, especially in its nearest competitor, Zimbabwe, about the economic power of post-sanctions South Africa.

The economic as well as political crisis became glaringly apparent in the
debt default of 1985 on $12 billion of private bank loans (Ovenden and Cole
1989: 75-107; Sampson 1987: 38-59; and EIU *Country Profile, South Africa
1988-89*: 48). The reasons for this default resided primarily in structural
causes, especially declining foreign investment and exports, despite drastic
devaluations of the rand as well as rising rates of interest and inflation.[2]

Like many other oil- and energy-deficient regimes in the South, South
Africa's debt grew rapidly in the first half of the 1980s as it attempted to
buy its way out of an economic-cum-political crisis (Ovenden and Cole
1989: 76). Because of continuing outflows rather than inflows of capital as
well as a regular deficit on its invisible account, South Africa can now only
afford such levels of debt-servicing by running a substantial trade surplus,
which the end of sanctions may facilitate but will not guarantee (EIU
Country Profile, South Africa 1988-89: 42). Net capital outflow reached $6
billion in 1988, having started in the 1985 crisis. Reflective of this crisis
period, GDP growth over the next five years was negative: -7% in 1985; -3%
in 1988; and -1% in 1990 (Lachman and Bercuson 1992: 33). Debt-servicing
via trade surplus makes South Africa peculiarly vulnerable to terms-of-
trade fluctuations, particularly of gold, diamonds and oil—none of which
have performed well—as well as the imposition, escalation and now elimination of sanctions. While South Africa has regained access to long-term
foreign loans, by the mid-1990s, most "new" foreign capital consisted of
transitory portfolio/mutual fund flows, returning trademark and franchise
owners and joint ventures, i.e., unpackaged direct foreign investment.
When combined with high rates of inflation, minimal growth at the end of

the 1980s and into the 1990s, and continued government deficits, it is clear that South Africa has little room to maneuver.

State-Response to Crisis: Corporatism

Debt in South Africa, as in the rest of the continent, is a symptom rather than the cause of crisis, however. In the case of South(ern) Africa, adjustments have generated political as well as economic consequences. These were particularly problematic for the Afrikaner regime as its post-war "state-capitalism" was restructured into a unique, racist form of "corporatism." Subsequently, the President's Economic Advisory Council was superceded in the early-1990s by a proliferation of national, regional and sectoral forums.

The political economy of South Africa has long been distinctive, not only because of institutionalized racism but also because of tendencies towards corporatism which became quite overt in the last decade of "reform" and the first months and years of negotiation and transition. The economic dominance of the randlords and political hegemony of the Broederbond were subsequently reflected in the inter-relationship between highly oligopolistic companies and the ubiquitous Afrikaner state. After 1948 this national capital and state capital coalition worked to contain the third partner in any such "triple alliance," i.e., international capital. The post-World War II Afrikaner state was highly "nationalist" in both political and economic spheres. At the same time, Afrikanerdom was ambivalent about "anglophone" capital, especially as the former became more militarized. Yet, despite all the strains, a distinctive form of racially-exclusive corporatism functioned in South Africa throughout the post-war period and remained largely unthreatened until the mid-1980s.

One central dimension of current Government of National Unity (GNU) policy is the refashioning of South African corporatism to include the black labour "aristocracy" and black capital. For example, this labour "aristocracy" is being advanced through a $4 million International Finance Corporation (IFC) investment in the South African Franchise Capital Fund and $9 million in the African Life Assurance Company. Black capital is being fostered, in part, through affirmative action and the deconcentration of white oligopolies (see Gelb, Chapter 3). These sorts of activities are both compatible with neo-liberal philosophy and central planks in the Reconstruction and Development Program (RDP).

Doubts about the sustainability of such state capitalism had arisen before the mid-1980s crisis, however. This was so in part because of an inefficient and outdated manufacturing sector as well as an increasingly moribund and expensive gold industry which even the uncertainties of the Gulf War and continuing attempts to rationalize failed to revive (Blumenfeld 1991a: 5-6). Ironically, liberalization—official and informal, under National Party and ANC—may exacerbate rather than resolve these problems. Clearly, commercialization and privatization serve to undermine some of the inherited features of Afrikaner state capitalism. Unfortunately, they may also lead to further un- and under-employment among both Afrikaner and Black employees. Significant sections of the bureaucracy, petty-bourgeoisie and labour aristocracy stand to be hardest hit. Windfall, one-time "profits" related to the lifting of sanctions could be reinvested in post-apartheid "development regions" (and therefore delay or offset the effects of restructuring), but macro-strategy for the new South Africa remains problematic, notwithstanding an increasingly threadbare consensus over the ANC's RDP (see below; also, Munck 1994; Nattrass 1994a and b).

Popular Responses To Crisis: A Burgeoning Informal Sector

Adjustment throughout Africa has served to shrink both state and formal sectors; informal sectors have expanded to fill some of these spaces (Shaw 1991). South Africa has always had such ubiquitous sectors—from shebeens to migration—and these have expanded as un(der)employment and deindustrialization have proceeded. Such sectors thrive in the sprawling high-density slums and squatter cities of South Africa and may have criminal as well as illegal characteristics, especially when related to drugs, guns and gangs, the latter at times being connected to some marginalized political groups.

Even before privatization, South Africa had at least one million (officially) to five million (unofficially) unemployed, mainly Blacks, or some 30-50% of the Black labour force. This was one result of a "20% effective boycott of South African exports" which helped generate the momentum towards a non-racial transition (Hermele and Oden 1988: 22). Anglo American has long been calling not only for urban renewal but also for the encouragement of the informal or small business sectors, noting the rapid rise and effective institutionalization of Black taxi owners: the R3 billion capital of 100,000 taxis with their 300,000 workers and a turnover of some R3 billion means that "the taxi industry directly employs twice as many people as such industrial giants as Iscor and Eskom." In addition, the 500,000 hawkers and street traders have an estimated turnover of at least R1 billion annually (Anglo American 1988: 16).

The Private Sector Responds

At the formal level, the twin pressures of economic crisis and sanctions led, by the end of the 1980s, not only to political "reform" but also to economic diversification in terms of sectors, locales and partners. Thus, large South African companies like Anglo American and Rembrandt have diversified out of both South Africa and mining. At the same time, multinational corporations (MNCs) withdrew or disinvested, typically by exchanging direct capital investment for non-equity, some of which is now returning. These tendencies have been reinforced by the GNU's RDP which advocates, among other things, deconcentration, competition, beneficiation, and affirmative action. Such trends represent South Africa's belated attempts to respond to "globalization" or "Japanization" and are characteristic of the NIDL—e.g., licenses, franchises, supply and service contracts—i.e., control via technology rather than equity. Yet it is precisely in such areas of "flexibilization" and "just-in-time" production that South African capital is weak, despite its new extra-continental ambitions. As Strydom (1987: 206) cautions: "It would appear that South Africa is unlikely to play an important role in the trade in invisibles."

Moreover, despite such attempts at diversification, most of South Africa's trade is still with four Organization for Economic Cooperation and Development (OECD) partners[3]—so rendering it vulnerable to disruption—and a few of its major companies still dominate exports. In short, as revealed by the recent disinvestment and the slow reinvestment processes, the South African economy, despite myths to the contrary, is peculiarly vulnerable in terms of sectors, partners, debt, foreign capital, and technology, as well as demand.[4]

The Search For Foreign Investment

Of the 1,000 or so MNCs in South Africa in the mid-1980s (35% each from the US and UK), over 200 had partially "withdrawn" by 1988, 150 from the US and 60 from the UK (Hermele and Oden 1988: 34). Most of their shares were bought by large-scale national capital: Anglo American, Rembrandt, Sanlam, SA Mutual, among others. These four alone now control over 80% of the shares on the Johannesburg stock exchange, up from 70% in the early 1980s; by itself, Anglo increased its share from over 50% to some 60%. Only a few of these cut-priced spoils were picked up by Black capital, Ford and Pepsi being the exceptions. The list of MNCs which had partially withdrawn if not completely disinvested came to include hitherto household names in South Africa as well as across the North Atlantic: Barclays, Coke, Ford, GM, Mobil, Pepsi, Proctor and Gamble, to name several (Commonwealth 1989). By the mid-1990s, their focus was on the Pacific Rim, especially China and the near-NICs, rather than South Africa. Indeed, ironically, the GNU may feel compelled to turn to Armscor and its exports in the post-apartheid and post-Cold War era to help "kick-start" its flagging economy (see Vale, Chapter 4).

Such disinvestment reinforced by privatization advanced the expansion of the national bourgeoisie as MNCs sold off shares if not control to reduce exposure. Both state and international or comprador fractions declined under these policies and processes while national and military fractions increased their power and importance. Might these forces constitute the social bases for future national fascism, particularly if they are reinforced or legitimated by economic and strategic insecurities? Such tendencies have periodically emerged, as in the rise of the Conservative Party, vigilante groups and assassination squads.

In contrast to these seemingly "lower class" reactions, the more bourgeois forms of liberal responses are represented by the new hegemonic coalition centred initially on the Democratic Party but soon superceded by the NP-ANC alliance. The combination of high-cost apartheid, structural adjustment and incremental sanctions undermined the social bases of the previously dominant NP, leading to revisionist debates about the nature of the state (Helliker 1988). The demise of Bantustan ruling groups may be contrasted with the palpable embourgeoisement of the new, primarily Black, "ruling" class in "transitional" central and regional governments and in the rapidly multi-racializing private sector.

The Legacy of Apartheid Security and Foreign Policies

The military is one state institution which has rarely been adjusted or reduced anywhere in Africa, until very recently including South Africa, despite new de facto official aid and private investment conditionalities. Despite economic and related difficulties, South African military expenditures quadrupled yet again in the 1980s, reaching R8 billion or 15% of the budget. If related costs of apartheid are included—e.g., Homelands and Black ghettos—then the "apartheid share" of state spending might rise to 30% (Blumenfeld 1991a; Hermele and Oden 1988: 24; Moss and Obery 1992). However, one of the few bright spots in the otherwise depressed South African economy is the "peace dividend" from declining military expenditures in recent years, along with prospects of some savings from dismantling duplicative and inefficient separate development institutions (Lachman and Bercuson 1992: 21-2; also, Swatuk and Omari, Chapter 5).

Over the apartheid period, the distinctive foreign policy of a "pariah state" became all too apparent as South Africa was publicly excluded from UN, Commonwealth and other international fora from the 1960s onward. To be sure, it always remained a member of the IMF and International Bank for Reconstruction and Development (IBRD) and its transnational tentacles were ubiquitous. But both formal and informal diplomacy was limited by exclusions and sanctions. South Africa found formal diplomatic recognition beyond the OECD only in some Latin American regimes. Informal economic and strategic connections were nurtured with other pariahs or "neutrals" such as Israel, Panama, Switzerland and Taiwan (Aluko and Shaw 1985; Shaw 1974).

Because of gold and diamonds, let alone Anglo American's myriad subsidiaries, South Africa could always engage in clandestine economic and strategic operations (see, for example, Naylor 1987; and Pallister et al 1988). At the same time, Armscor seemed to operate its own secret foreign policy at the global level in an endless quest for military technology and hardware. Elements in the South African Defence Force's (SADF's) intelligence and covert organizations behaved similarly in the region.

However, with the rapid dismantling of a variety of diplomatic and social sanctions, the "new" South Africa has rapidly (re)established links with the old Africa and the new Eastern Europe and Pacific Rim, enabling it to anticipate a continental as well as regional role (Maasdorp and Whiteside 1992; Oden 1993; Thede and Beaudet 1993; Vale et al 1991). This has led to some speculation regarding an emerging "concert" of African powers (with, perhaps, Nigeria and Egypt) to secure order, if not peace and development, after the end of Cold War interventions.

The novel aspects of renewed civil society within South Africa and revisionist economic and strategic policies around it, some of which have been highlighted above, are yet to be fully incorporated into the analysis and practise of national and regional foreign relations (Martin 1991; cf. Southall 1994). Nevertheless, given profound changes in the global political economy, as well as South(ern) Africa's transition away from apartheid, the new South Africa has begun to redefine its own foreign and security policies (see Vale, Chapter 4; and Swatuk and Omari, Chapter 5).

Dialectics of Dependence and Destabilization in the Region

Contemporary contradictions in Southern Africa have a long history (see Chapter 5 below). This history of conflict and cooperation in the region has endowed it with a distinctive political culture as well as political economy, largely determined by settler colonialism and capitalism but reinforced initially by formal infrastructures and institutions (Maasdorp 1992; Shaw 1974) and now increasingly by informal exchange.

Dual Destabilization

The pre-1980s struggles for political independence and strains over economic (inter)dependence were intensified in the 1980s by two interrelated forms of destabilization: politico-strategic and socio-economic.[5] The former was largely a function of South Africa's "total strategy," while the latter is largely a function of World Bank/IMF structural adjustment conditionalities. Initially economic in focus, these reforms now also embrace political and social liberalizations, and operate in cross-conditional ways.

Together, this pair of destabilizations have continued to divert and retard prospects for regional cooperation and development as neither physical security nor political stability can be assured. The combination of apartheid and adjustment undermined established regional patterns and plans and led to a preoccupation with short-term crisis management in both diplomacy and economy (Black et al 1988; EIU 1988). The devastating impact of South Africa's regional destabilization on both population and production are well-documented, and continue to haunt and retard post-apartheid development, particularly in Angola and Mozambique (see, for example, Hanlon 1986 and 1991; UNICEF 1989).

Patterns and programs of structural adjustment in the region serve as revealing indicators of national resilience and resourcefulness in response to international economic changes and policy conditionalities. In both empirical and theoretical terms, structural adjustment has transformed development and foreign policies and practices in Southern and Sub-Saharan Africa.[6]

If short-term adjustment has had negative consequences for economic growth in South Africa, it has had a devastating impact on "sustainable" human development in Southern Africa (Stoneman and Thompson 1991; Swatuk 1993; UNDP 1994; also Table 2.1 above). The classic, national negotiations insisted upon by the Bank and Fund have served to divert and divide SADC states and exacerbate inequalities, notably between the "self-reformers" (Botswana, Namibia, Swaziland), "weak- or late-reformers" (Angola, Lesotho, Zimbabwe), "strong-reformers" (Malawi, Mozambique, Tanzania), and "ex-reformer" (Zambia, at least until its intense readjustments after mid-1989) (see, World Bank 1989: 32).[7]

The Need for Home-Grown Adjustments

Reform conditionalities are now being stretched to include formal political pluralism and capped military expenditures. Yet, as Fantu Cheru has cautioned, "The problem of dependence cannot be solved by the more intense application of conventional development strategies that created the problem in the first place" (Bryant 1988: 260). Instead, he calls for a more radical, comprehensive, alternative development for SADC which includes a combination of basic human needs (BHN), self-reliance, and ecologically-sound structural transformation.

In Southern as well as South Africa, the imperative of structural change—but not the standard Bank/Fund package—is a function not only of the high costs of debt but also of the obsolescence of colonial commodity economies in the NIDL. Even those African exports for which some demand continues to exist are now in competition with similar commodities from Asia or Latin America (Harris 1993). Such "fallacy of composition" is, of course, one reason why standard Bank/Fund packages are flawed.

The NIDP, with its possible "peace dividend," may yet assist some sectors in the North once the lingering global recession finally lifts. But "strategic" metals in the South will be even less in demand as the superpowers' military-industrial complexes downsize.

The short-term pressures to adopt adjustment "reforms" are intense. Only relatively well-integrated economies such as those of Botswana, Zimbabwe, and post-apartheid South Africa can really resist adopting the standard structural adjustment formula for any length of time. But everywhere—including these three countries—devaluation, deregulation, desubsidization, and privatization have led to disruption, inflation and contraction. Diminished regimes are increasingly reduced to two preoccupations: on the one hand, endlessly negotiating with the Bank, Fund and donor consortia; and, on the other hand, maintaining minimal social order in hard times through rarely- or minimally-adjusted security structures.

The rise and fall of such policies in Zambia is symptomatic both of the imperatives of economic redirection and the implausibility and unsustainability of orthodox conditionalities. The cases of Angola and Mozambique indicate that even peace-keeping, let alone peace-building and economic reform, is problematic given the legacy of destabilization. I turn, in the final section, to speculation on the longer-term implications for South(ern) Africa's political economy of such contemporary forms of destabilization. In other words, I will seek to tentatively answer the question posed at the outset: what are the prospects for the emergence of new forms of sustainable, cooperative, regional relations in post-apartheid Southern Africa?

Prospects for South(ern) Africa at the Start of the Twenty-First Century

The dialectics of conflict and cooperation, destabilization and (inter)dependence in the sub-continent are likely to continue beyond the 1990s and into the post-apartheid state and region (see, for example, Moss and Obery 1992; Thede and Beaudet 1993). Indeed, the intensity of regional inequalities may increase rather than diminish after the mid-1990s' transition as the costly inefficiencies of apartheid are progressively eliminated. Nevertheless, there is a case to be made that South Africa needs SADC, in addition to SACU, and perhaps the Common Market of Eastern and Southern Africa (COMESA), more than ever (see Davies, Chapter 6). Despite remaining the regional centre, the "new" South Africa is unlikely to become either a NIC or near-NIC, notwithstanding dreams about being the "Japan of Africa."[8]

In the present period of profound and problematic structural and technological changes, South Africa's extra-continental trade in the crucial industrial and service sectors continues to decline. In the mid-1980s, it probably had a regional surplus in visible and invisible trade of $1.5 billion to set against extra-continental deficits (Bryant 1988: 56). Until apartheid's legacies of inefficiency and antiquity are transcended, South African industry has few prospects of sustained expansion in either national or continental markets (see Chapters 8 through 11 below).

Despite intense efforts to diversify products and markets, and some success in the Pacific Rim and Latin America, South Africa is still dependent on trade with the European Union (EU), especially Germany and Britain. Exchange with the former will likely revive as the costs of reunification are digested. Trade with the old Second World, especially with the "new" Central Europe if not with the "new" Central Asia, may also contribute to diversification in the second half of the 1990s.

It is only in the historically dependent and currently vulnerable regional economy that prospects for growth are good, however. At the same time, Southern Africa is to be the new South Africa's foreign policy centrepiece (see Vale, Chapter 4; and Swatuk and Omari, Chapter 5). Such renewed regionalism is now reinforced by the broader dictates of globalization and related new regionalisms: If Southern Africa is to be recognized as part of the NIDL, it must be able to negotiate with the EU, North American Free Trade Area (NAFTA), and Asia-Pacific Economic Community (APEC), among others. It is also reinforced by on-going and developing patterns of regional intercourse—at the level of civil society, and in terms of both formal and informal transaction flows (see, for example, MWENGO and AACC 1994; and Venter 1994).

Moreover, South Africa could yet play a catalytic role in redirecting liberalization away from a global openness towards a regional orientation, by both example and activity. This would, of course, also serve its own national and sectoral interests. But it would also enable it to indicate its usefulness in negotiations on behalf of the region given the global trend towards regional blocs and the World Bank's apparent new pragmatism over such regionalisms.

There will continue to be intense pressures on any post-apartheid regime to redistribute internally rather than externally, but these patterns of redistribution are not necessarily incompatible; meanwhile, regional leaders expect some recognition and compensation for their commitment to ending apartheid over the last quarter-century. Further, in the absence of the anti-apartheid glue to hold the continent together, some alternative focus is imperative if (Southern) Africa's marginalization is to be avoided or minimized in the so-called New World (Dis)Order. Should such new regionalism include and encourage informal sectors and civil societies then any regional renaissance might show the way for similar arrangements elsewhere in the South. The counter-developmental impacts of those dual destabilizations highlighted above are presently generating popular "counter-hegemonic" responses.[9] These responses will most likely find form in informal sector developments and activities in the shorter term and, perhaps, formal sector self-reliance in the longer term (see ECA 1989).

In such developments lie opportunities to transform the threat of heightened global, neo-liberal competition via economic regionalization into a foundation for globally sustainable development (see, for example, Mittelman 1994b and 1995). At the same time, there remain formidable obstacles to such eventualities. For example, both conditionalities and the legacies of apartheid will serve to dichotomize social forces so that the diminished post-apartheid state will be reduced to reliance on force to maintain order and power, i.e., (re)militarization, whilst the people will become empowered to create their own popular organizations for production and distribution, i.e., democratization (Shaw 1991 and 1993). Such struggles will now occur in a post-Cold War global environment in which civil society has been recognized to be a crucial ingredient in both democracy and development. But how much accumulation, by whom, and for what will remain problematic elements in any forseeable scenario in regions like Eastern Europe and Southern Africa. This, then, is the paradox: South Africa needs its region more than ever, and could be an important and creative source of leadership in the NIDL(P). Yet the legacies of the past have left both South and Southern Africa ill-equipped to exploit this potential. Overcoming this paradox will be a formidable task indeed.

Notes

1. According to R.T. Naylor's exposé of *Hot Money* (1987: 394), such diamond transactions financed the "Israeli-South African military alliance," including its nuclear elements. And now De Beers Centenary has a public sales agreement with the new Russian Federation and the Republic of Sakhia, reflecting post-apartheid and post-bipolar structures (De Beers 1991).

2. This is not to under-estimate the importance of South Africa's growing economic isolation, particularly over the course of the 1980s. It does, however, regard international economic sanctions and responses to heightened political repression as a secondary factor in the crisis.

3. These are the US, the UK, Japan and Germany. Trade with the latter pair is particularly important given their privileged places in the NIDL.

4. In the NIDP, South African producers suffer from not only a decline in demand for formerly-crucial "strategic minerals," but also from an increase in base metal competitors in Russia and Eastern Europe.

5. For an elaboration of this notion of "dual destabilizations" see Larry A. Swatuk, *Dealing With Dual Destabilization in Southern Africa: Foreign Policy Making in Botswana, Lesotho and Swaziland 1975-1989*, unpublished Ph.D. dissertation, Dalhousie University 1993.

6. These realities have led to a new subset of comparative development studies (see, for example, Black et al 1988; Campbell and Loxley 1989; Matthew Martin 1991; Shaw, Davies and Sanders 1993; Skalnes 1995). It has also accelerated a re-ordering of state and non-state actors in the region as changing conditionalities lead to new economic, political and social adjustments (see, for example, Shaw and Korany 1994; Swatuk and Shaw 1994).

7. In this typology, South Africa might be regarded as an emerging strong, self-reformer (see Gelb, Chapter 3).

8. Such notions are reminiscent of similar claims made by Nigerians in the early 1980s, only then the comparison was with Brazil, not Japan. Similarly, Zimbabwe's senior economics minister has been quite fanciful in making claims about that country's NIC potential (see Shaw and Davies 1993).

9. See, for example, the editorial introduction and articles by Eddie Webster, Leo Panitch, Judith Marshall and Gretchen Bauer in the issue of *Southern Africa REPORT* sub-titled "Globalization: The Trade Union Response" (Vol. 11, No. 3, April 1996: 1-16).

References

African National Congress. 1994. *Reconstruction and Development Program*. Sixth Draft. Johannesburg, January.

———. 1993. *A New Foreign Policy for South Africa: a discussion document*. Johannesburg.

Aluko, Olajide, and Timothy M. Shaw, eds. 1985. *Southern Africa in the 1980s*. London: George Allen and Unwin.

Anglo American Corporation of South Africa (various). *Annual Report*. Johannesburg.

Baker, Pauline H., et al., eds. 1993. *South Africa and the World Economy in the 1990s*. Cape Town: David Philip for IDASA and Aspen Institute.

Baskin, Jeremy. 1993a. *Corporatism: some obstacles facing the South African labour movement*. Research Report No. 30. Johannesburg: Centre for Policy Studies, April.

———. 1993b. "The Trend Towards Bargained Corporatism," *South African Labour Bulletin* 17(3) (May/June): 64-9.

Black, David R., et al. 1988. *Foreign Policy in Small States: Botswana, Lesotho, Swaziland and Southern Africa*. Halifax: Centre for Foreign Policy Studies, Dalhousie University.

Blumenfeld, Jesmond, ed. 1991a. "South Africa's Post-Apartheid Dividend," *World Today* 47(1) (January): 3-7.

———. 1991b. *Economic Interdependence in Southern Africa: from conflict to cooperation?* London: Pinter.

Boardman, Robert. 1994. "Triangles, Wrecked Angles and Beyond: The Post-Cold War Division of Power," in Larry A. Swatuk and Timothy M. Shaw, eds. *The South at the End of the Twentieth Century*. Pp. 28-40.

Bryant, Coralie, ed. 1988. *Poverty, Policy and Food Security in Southern Africa*. Boulder: Lynne Rienner.

Campbell, Bonnie K. and John Loxley, eds. 1989. *Structural Adjustment in Africa*. London: Macmillan.

Carlsson, Jerker and Timothy M. Shaw, eds. 1988. *Newly Industrializing Countries and the Political Economy of South-South Relations*. London: Macmillan.

Canadian International Development Agency (CIDA). 1992. *Southern Africa Regional Policy Framework*. Hull: CIDA, February.

Commonwealth. 1989. *South Africa: the sanctions report*. London: Penguin.

Davies, Rob and William G. Martin. 1992. "Regional Prospects and Projects: what futures for Southern Africa?" in Sergio Vieira, William G. Martin and Immanuel Wallerstein, eds. *How Fast the Wind? Southern Africa 1975-2000*. Pp. 331-64. Trenton: Africa World Press.

Davies, Robert, David Sanders and Timothy M. Shaw. 1993. "Liberalization for Development: Zimbabwe's adjustment without the Fund," in Giovanni Andrea Cornia, Rolph van der Hoeven and Thandika Mkandawire, eds. *Africa's Recovery in the 1990s*. Pp. 135-55. London: Macmillan.

———, et al. 1991. *Zimbabwe's Adjustment without the Fund*. Innocenti Occasional Paper No. 16. Florence: UNICEF.

De Beers Consolidated Mines and Centenary. 1991. *Annual Reports 1991*. Kimberley and Lucerne, April.

Development Bank of South Africa. 1990. *Annual Report 1989-90*. Johannesburg: Halfway House.

Economic Commission for Africa (ECA). 1989. *African Alternative Framework to Structural Adjustment Programs for Socio-Economic Recovery and Transformation*. Addis Ababa: ECA, July.

Economist (London), various.

Economist Intelligence Unit (EIU). 1992-93. Quarterly *Country Reports* and Annual *Country Profiles* on South Africa, Tanzania and Mozambique, Zambia, Zimbabwe and Malawi. London: EIU.

————. 1988. *Southern Africa: the price of apartheid*. London, EIU.

Fine, Robert. 1992. "Civil Society Theory and the Politics of Transition in South Africa," *Review of African Political Economy* 55 (November): 71-83.

Fowler, Alan B. 1991. "The Role of NGOs in Changing State-Society Relations: perspectives from Eastern and Southern Africa," *Development Policy Review* 9(1) (March): 53-84.

Friedman, Steven. 1991. "An Unlikely Utopia: state and civil society in South Africa," *Politikon* 19(1) (December): 5-19.

Hanlon, Joseph. 1991. *Mozambique: who calls the shots?* Bloomington: Indiana University Press.

————. 1986. *Beggar Your Neighbours: apartheid power in Southern Africa*. London: James Currey.

Harris, Betty J. 1993. *The Political Economy of the Southern African Periphery*. London: Macmillan.

Helliker, Kirk. 1988. "South African Marxist State Theory: a critical overview," *Politikon* 15(1) (June): 3-15.

Hermele, Kenneth, and Bertil Oden. 1988. *Sanctions Dilemmas: some implications of economic sanctions against South Africa*. Uppsala: Swedish Institute for African Studies (SIAS).

Holden, Merle. 1992. "Trade Reforms: finding the right road," *South African Journal of Economics* 60(3) (September): 249-62.

International Development and Research Centre (IDRC). 1991. *Economic Analysis and Policy Formulation for Post-Apartheid South Africa: Mission Report*. Ottawa: IDRC.

Lachman, Desmond and Kenneth Bercuson, eds. 1992. *Economic Policies for a New South Africa*. International Monetary Fund Occasional Paper No. 91. Washington, DC: IMF, January.

Lipton, Merle, and Charles Simkins, eds. 1993. *State and Market in Post-Apartheid South Africa*. Johannesburg: Witwatersrand University Press.

Maasdorp, Gavin. 1992. "Economic Prospects for South Africa in Southern Africa," *South Africa International* 22(3) (January): 121-27.

Maasdorp, Gavin and Alan Whiteside, eds. 1992. *Towards a Post-Apartheid Future: political and economic relations in Southern Africa*. London: Macmillan.

Martin, Matthew. 1991. *The Crumbling Facade of African Debt Negotiations: no winners*. London: Macmillan.

Martin, William G. 1991. "The Future of Southern Africa: what prospects after majority rule?," *Review of African Political Economy* 50 (March): 115-34.

Mittelman, James H., ed. 1995. *Globalization: opportunities and challenges*. Boulder: Lynne Rienner.

——. 1994a. "The End of a Millennium: Changing Structures of World Order and the Post-Cold War Division of Labour," in Larry A. Swatuk and Timothy M. Shaw, eds. *The South at the End of the Twentieth Century*. Pp. 15-27.

——. 1994b. "The Globalization Challenge: surviving at the margins," *Third World Quarterly* 15(3) (September): 427-43.

Moss, Glen and Ingrid Obery, eds. 1989. *South African Review 5*. Johannesburg: Ravan for SARS.

Munck, Ronaldo. 1994. "South Africa: the great economic debate," *Third World Quarterly* 15(2) (June): 205-17.

MWENGO and AACC. 1994. *Civil Society, the State and African Development in the 1990s*. Harare: MWENGO, and Nairobi: AACC.

Nathan, Laurie and Joao Honwana. 1995. *After the Storm: Common Security and Conflict Resolution in Southern Africa*. The Arusha Papers: A Working Series on Southern African Security No. 3. Bellville: CSAS, February.

Nattrass, Nicoli. 1994a. "South Africa: the economic restructuring agenda, a critique of the MERG report," *Third World Quarterly* 15(2) (June): 219-25.

——. 1994b. "Politics and Economics in ANC Economic Policy," *African Affairs* 93(372) (July): 343-59.

Naylor, R.T. 1987. *Hot Money and the Politics of Debt*. London: Unwin and Hyman.

Oden, Bertil, ed. 1993. *Southern Africa after Apartheid: regional integration and external resources*. Swedish Institute for African Studies Seminar Proceedings No. 28. Uppsala: SIAS.

Ovenden, Keith and Tony Cole. 1990. *Apartheid and International Finance: a program for change*. Ringwood, Victoria: Penguin.

Overseas Development Institute (ODI). 1994. *Economic Policies in the New South Africa*. Briefing Paper 1994 (2) April. London: ODI.

Pallister, David, Sarah Stewart and Ian Lepper. 1988. *South Africa Inc.: the Oppenheimer Empire*. London: Corgi.

Rugumamu, Severine M. 1994. *New Security Threats in Africa: an overview at the end of the millennium*. Centre for Foreign Policy Studies Working Paper Series. Halifax: Centre for Foreign Policy Studies, Dalhousie University.

Sampson, Anthony. 1987. *Black and Gold: tycoons, revolutionaries and apartheid*. London: Coronet.

Shaw, Timothy M. 1994. "South Africa: the corporatist/regionalist conjuncture," *Third World Quarterly* 15(1) (March): 243-55.

——. 1993. "Africa in the New World Order: marginal and/or central?" in Adebayo Adedeji, ed. *Africa Within the World*. Pp. 78-93. London: Zed for ACDESS.

——. 1991. "Reformism, Revisionism and Radicalism in African Political Economy in the 1990s," *Journal of Modern African Studies* 29(2) (June): 191-212.

——. 1974. "Southern Africa: cooperation and conflict in an international subsystem," *Journal of Modern African Studies* 12(4) (December): 633-55.

—— and Rob Davies. 1993. *The Political Economy of Adjustment in Zimbabwe: convergence and reform*. Ottawa: North-South Institute.

—— and Bahgat Korany, eds. 1994. "Special Issue: The South in the New World (Dis)Order," *Third World Quarterly* 15(1) (March): 7-146.

—— and Alfred Nhema. 1995. "Directions and Debates about National and Regional Development in South(ern)Africa's First Post-Apartheid Decade," *Mershon International Studies Review* Supplement, 39(1).

Skalnes, Tor. 1995. *The Politics of Economic Reform in Zimbabwe*. London: Macmillan.

Southall, Roger. 1994. "The New South Africa in the New World Order: beyond the double whammy," *Third World Quarterly* 15(1) (March): 121-37.

Southern Africa REPORT. 1996. "Globalization: The Trade Union Response," 11(3) (April).

Stein, Howard, ed. 1995. *Asian Industrialization and Africa: studies in policy alternatives to structural adjustment*. London: Macmillan.

Stoneman, Colin and Carol B. Thompson. 1991. "Southern Africa after Apartheid: economic repercussions of a free South Africa," *Africa Recovery Briefing Paper No. 4* (December).

Strydom, P.D.F. 1987. "South Africa in World Trade," *South African Journal of Economics* 55(3) (September): 203-18.

Stubbs, Richard and Geoffrey R.D. Underhill, eds. 1994. *Political Economy and the Changing Global Order*. London: Macmillan.

Swatuk, Larry A. 1993. *Dealing With Dual Destabilization: Foreign Policy Making in Botswana, Lesotho and Swaziland. 1975-1989*, unpublished Ph.D. dissertation, Dalhousie University, Canada.

―― and Timothy M. Shaw, eds. 1994. *The South at the End of the Twentieth Century: rethinking the political economy of foreign policy in Africa, Asia, the Caribbean and Latin America*. London: Macmillan.

――, eds. 1991. *Prospects for Peace and Development in Southern Africa in the 1990s: Canadian and Comparative Perspectives*. Lanham: University Press of America.

Thede, Nancy and Pierre Beaudet, eds. 1993. *A Post-Apartheid Southern Africa*. London: Macmillan.

United Nations Childrens Fund (UNICEF). 1989. *Children on the Front Line*. Third edition. New York: UNICEF.

United Nations Development Program (UNDP). 1994. *Human Development Report*. New York: Oxford University Press.

Vale, Peter. 1994. "Fashioning choice in southern Africa," in Minnie Venter, ed. *Prospects for Progress*, Pp. xvi-xxiv. Cape Town: Maskew Miller Longman.

――, Graham Evans, James Barber and David Walsh. 1991. "The Outlook for Southern Africa," *International Affairs* 67(4) (October): 697-753.

Venter, Minnie, ed. 1994. *Prospects for Progress: critical choices for Southern Africa*. Cape Town: Maskew Miller Longman.

Whiteside, Alan W., ed. 1989. *Industrialization and Investment Incentives in Southern Africa*. London: James Currey.

World Bank. 1989. *An Economic Perspective on South Africa*. Washington: Southern Africa Department, May.

3

South Africa's Post-Apartheid Political Economy

Stephen Gelb

The popular view is that South Africa's transition to democracy was a "small miracle."[1] It was miraculous that a racially-divided society was able to avert civil war in the democratization process. But, some academic analyses of the transition suggest, the small miracle is also likely to be a brief one, because the new government will be overcome by economic difficulties (Friedman 1994). As it entered the democratic post-apartheid era, South Africa faced the challenge, indeed the necessity, of rejuvenating a stagnant economy and raising the growth rate, while at the same time redistributing income and wealth to create greater equity. Achieving these goals simultaneously was likely to prove impossible, it is argued, and the fledgling democracy might well be destroyed in the attempt, to be followed by a reversion to authoritarianism, this time practised by a black government.

This pessimistic and paradoxical perspective—success in following a "democratic," or negotiated, path to democracy, followed by failure to consolidate the democratic structures—is found widely in the literature not only on South Africa, but also on other societies' transitions. The essence of the argument is that in the course of negotiations, the democratizing forces are forced to make significant concessions to economic, political and military powerholders under the old regime, in order to persuade the latter to participate in the democratic process. These concessions, expressed in institutional arrangements and in policy orientation, ensure the new government follows a conservative approach towards the economy, ignoring their own support base, despite the louder voice of popular demands in the democratic system. One possible result, according to the argument, is that the newly-elected government retreats to the use of executive power to force through economic reforms in the face of popular opposition; in other words, "authoritarianism with a democratic face" or what Guillermo O'Donnell has labelled "delegative democracy."[2] Alternatively, the government reneges on policy reform agreements with major economic powerholders, leading the latter to engage in capital flight and investment strikes, producing economic decline and perhaps an attempt from "the right" (pre-transition forces) to install a new, authoritarian government.

Is this the appropriate lens through which to view South Africa's transition? Elsewhere, I question the applicability of the "miracle" metaphor to South Africa (Gelb 1996). In this chapter, I evaluate the economic policies of South Africa's Government of National Unity to assess whether continued economic difficulties are likely to lead to the short-circuiting of the democratic process. The next section spells out the key dimensions of the problems of restoring growth and equalizing distribution. I then discuss the policy strategies put forward during the transitional process by powerholders under the old regime and by the democratizing forces, labelled respectively "growth with redistribution" and "growth through redistribution." Sections 3 and 4 argue that the policies adopted by the Government of National Unity (GNU) in office since May 1994 represent a positive-sum compromise between these two approaches. In Section 5, I look at some of the positive consequences of this compromise especially in terms of the improvement in investor confidence, and then Section 6 identifies some of the possible obstacles and difficulties to be faced. The conclusion returns to the possibility that the "miracle" will be a brief one, particularly given the slow pace of redistribution.

The Challenge: Growth and Redistribution

Growth

The economy has experienced a two-decade long economic crisis, or long-run stagnation, reflected in a decline in the Gross Domestic Product (GDP) growth rate from about 5.5 percent in the 1960s, to 3.3 percent in the 1970s, to 1.2 percent in the 1980s (see Table 3.1). Although this long period of stagnation includes cyclical upswings in the growth rate, these have been short-lived and limited, with downward cycles tending to be deep and more durable. The economy was in the longest and deepest recession of the post-1945 era from the 2nd quarter of 1989 until the second quarter of 1993, with a negative growth rate of -0.2 percent from 1990 (Gelb 1991).

Associated with, and contributing to, low growth rates have been a range of macro-economic problems, including declining levels of fixed investment, which dropped from over 25 percent of GDP in the 1970s to around 16 percent at present, with net investment being approximately

TABLE 3.1 Average Annual Growth Rates in Real GDP and other Real Indicators

	1961-65	1966-70	1971-75	1976-80	1981-85	1986-92
GDP	5.94	5.15	3.49	3.13	1.36	1.03
GDI	4.62	5.81	6.39	4.02	0.03	0.27
Private Consumption	4.62	6.00	5.08	2.64	2.65	1.97
Employment	3.18	2.53	2.41	1.42	0.07	0.23

Notes: Gross Domestic Income (GDI) - real GDP adjusted for movements in the external terms of trade.
Employment - wage and salaried employment including domestic servants.

Source: South African Reserve Bank (SARE) National Accounts Data Base. *Quarterly Bulletin*, September 1992, SARB South African Labour Statistics 1992. CSS.

zero. The rate of inflation hovered persistently around 15 percent during the past 20 years, until the current recession forced it down to single figures. There have also been severe fiscal difficulties: the budget deficit rose to 8.5 percent of GDP in 1992 in the context of the recession, while total government debt surpassed 60 percent.

A major reason for the low investment rates has been the vulnerability of investor confidence to political uncertainties during the slow disintegration of apartheid in the 1980s, and the long transitional period from apartheid to democracy between 1990 and 1994. These uncertainties also affected the foreign exchange reserves, most notably during 1984-85, when widespread political resistance followed by repression in the form of a State of Emergency declaration led local and foreign investors to withdraw funds. The central feature of this process was the refusal of foreign banks to renew their South African loans, which resulted in the almost total exclusion of the country from international capital markets. This was important in persuading the local business community to press more strongly for a transition to democracy. But the difficulties experienced during negotiations, including the breakdown of CODESA, exacerbated the uncertainties and increased the outflow of funds. Capital flight (officially acknowledged) was positive throughout the decade from 1985, and in the year to June 1993 amounted to over three percent of 1992 GDP.

Fluctuations in the terms of trade of primary exports (especially gold) contributed to macro-economic instability and so to long-term economic decline. The gold price in US dollars declined in 1976, 1982, 1987 and 1992, while it rose steeply in 1979-80 and more slowly between 1985 and 1987. Given the importance of gold to South Africa's foreign exchange earnings, the price declines helped to force the economy into recession, and also encouraged the central bank to allow the exchange rate to depreciate during the 1980s to stabilize the profitability of the mining sector, thereby making imports (including investment and intermediate inputs for manufacturing) more costly.

Macro-economic instability exacerbated underlying problems in the economy. The lack of international competitiveness of the tradable manufactured goods sector, both exports and import-competing industries, has required most capital goods and a wide range of intermediates to be imported, while exports of manufactured goods have been very low, leaving this sector with a massive and chronic trade deficit. This has in turn been linked to an overly protective trade regime, and to the decline in the productivity growth rates of both capital and labour resulting from rising wages and the rising cost of capital goods. Manufacturing total factor productivity growth dropped from 2.3 percent per annum in the 1960s, to 0.5 percent in the 1970s and then to a disastrous -2.9 percent during the first half of the 1980s, before a small improvement in the decade since (see Table 3.2).

Redistribution

During the 1970s, South Africa was one of the most unequal societies in the world, in terms of the distribution of income (McGrath and Whiteford 1994). Table 3.3 shows the extreme racial maldistribution of income: in 1970 the share of total personal income going to whites was more than three times that of Africans. In per capita terms, the disparity was even greater: 12.8 to 1. During the intervening period of growth decline, the racial income gap has narrowed quite considerably, but remains substantial. In 1987, the white share of personal income was less than twice that of Africans, while South Africans of asian and "coloured" descent had also improved their share. The income gap expressed in per capita terms had decreased by about 25 percent.

Racial inequality in income distribution is also reflected in differential access to basic public sector goods and services. In 1986, whites received nearly 2.5 times the national average level of government spending on education, health and pensions, while Africans received only two-thirds of this average (van der Berg 1992). Table 3.4 shows some indicators of racial differences in health and education outcomes.

TABLE 3.2 Growth in Total Factor Productivity (annual average percentage rates)

	1961-70	*1971-80*	*1981-85*	*1986-91*	*1961-91*
GDP	1.6	-0.4	-0.5	0.7	0.4
GDP (non-government)	1.8	-0.4	-1.3	0.7	0.3
Agriculture	-0.4	2.4	-0.3	5.3	1.6
Mining	2.5	-5.8	-3.7	-3.2	-2.3
Manufacturing	2.3	0.5	-2.9	0.6	0.5

Source: World Bank Staff estimates.

TABLE 3.3 Percentage Share of Personal Income and Employee Remuneration
by Race and Ratios of Per Capita Income

	Africans	Asians	Coloreds	Whites
Personal income				
1960	22.4	2.0	5.5	70.1
1970	22.3	2.4	6.3	69.0
1975	25.6	2.8	7.2	64.4
1980	28.3	3.2	7.5	61.0
1987	31.5	3.6	7.9	57.0
Employee remuneration				
1975	31.6	2.7	8.8	56.9
1980	35.6	3.0	8.4	53.0
1987	38.0	2.7	7.6	51.7
1992	38.5	3.4	8.4	49.7
Ratios of per-capita income				
1960	1.0	2.1	1.9	12.3
1970	1.0	2.6	2.1	12.8
1975	1.0	2.8	2.1	10.9
1980	1.0	2.9	2.1	10.0
1987	1.0	3.2	2.1	9.5

Sources: Bureau of Market Research (1989) and World Bank staff estimates
based upon data taken from South African Labour Statistics (1993).

TABLE 3.4 Health (1988) and Education (1990) Indicators by Race

	Whites	Asians	Coloureds	Africans
Pass rate for school-leaving exam (%)	95.8	95.0	79.4	36.7
Pupil-classroom ratio	15	27	23	45
Infant mortality rate per 1000 live births	11.9	19.0	46.3	80.0
Life expectancy	71	67	61	62

Source: MERG, *Making Democracy Work: A Framework for Macroeconomic Policy in South Africa* (Cape Town: Oxford University Press, 1994), Tables 4.11, 4.14, 4.19 (Row 2 assumes a pupil-teacher ratio of 35-1).

These data do not reveal the change in inequality within racial groups which, it appears, has deteriorated substantially since the mid-1970s. According to McGrath and Whiteford, the bottom 40 percent of income earners in the African population received 12.3 percent of total African income in 1975, and the top ten percent received 32.5 percent. In 1991, these proportions had changed to 6.4 percent at the bottom, and 46.6 percent at the top, that is, a much greater concentration of income within the African population. Amongst whites, a similar pattern occurred, the top ten percent increasing their share of white income from 25.9 percent to 32.7 percent, and the lowest 40 percent of earners dropping from 18 percent to 13.7 percent (McGrath and Whiteford 1994).

Absolute poverty levels are also inordinately high. A 1989 study concluded that 45 percent of all households received incomes below the minimum living level, while for Africans the proportion was 53 percent (Fallon and Pereira da Silva 1994: 41). The level of absolute poverty is linked to the problem of unemployment. As Table 3.5 suggests, employment growth was just fast enough to absorb new labour during the 1960s when economic growth was more satisfactory. Since the 1970s, unemployment has been exacerbated by economic decline (also reflected in the employment growth rate in Table 3.1). After years of maintaining the fiction of single digit black unemployment, the government acknowledged in 1993 that the actual figure is 46 percent for the total population (and higher for Africans) if the informal sector is included, having risen from 39 percent during the last recession. Of significance here is that the labour force growth rate is of the order of 2.6 percent.

Adding to the problem is the low level of labour absorption of the economy—the proportion of new labour force entrants who actually find jobs—which has dropped from 74 percent in the late 1960s, already quite poor though the economy was performing at its peak, to around 12.5 percent in the late 1980s. Similarly the production elasticity of employment, the percentage increase in the employed labour force associated with a one percent increase in the level of output, dropped from 0.64 in the 1970s to 0.46 in the late 1980s.

TABLE 3.5 Estimated Proportions of Labour Force not in Wage Employment

	1960	1970	1980	1985	1992
Africans	0.28	0.27	0.37	0.43	0.55
Asians/Coloureds	0.29	0.21	0.18	0.29	0.34
Whites	0.15	0.15	0.16	0.18	0.21

Source: Sadie (1991) and World Bank staff estimates.

Meeting The Challenge: Two Alternatives

During the transitional period between 1990 and 1994, the formal constitutional negotiations were paralleled by more disparate and less formal discussions about economic policy, in which important roles were played not only by the government and the ANC and other black political organizations, but also by business associations, trade unions and other economic interest organizations.[3] A consensus quickly emerged that the two overarching challenges facing a new government were reviving economic growth and improving distributional equity, as outlined above. But wide differences remained over the relationship between these two objectives, and in particular over the obstacles to sustaining an improvement in economic growth over time. Nonetheless, two broad approaches to the issue can be discerned (Gelb 1990).

Growth with Redistribution

The 'establishment' position, supported by the (then) National Party government and the white business and middle classes, focused upon the obstacles to growth posed by macro-economic constraints. The emphasis here was firstly on the balance of payments, where the difficulties of maintaining a large enough surplus on the current account to finance the capital outflows limited foreign exchange reserves, so that there was for example only six weeks import coverage in September 1993. A second major concern was the fiscal imbalance. The Public Sector Borrowing Requirement rose from two percent of GDP in 1990 to 9.7 percent in 1993 before dropping slightly in 1994, while the share of total public debt went from just under 40 percent to 55 percent between 1990 and 1994. Associated with these increases was a drop in both government and personal savings, though these were offset by a rise in corporate savings. The unstable macro-economic environment was seen as a major contributor to the persistence of double digit inflation (until 1993), together with wage increases in excess of productivity improvements. It was argued very strongly that attempts to redistribute, whether by directly expanding incomes or by increasing public sector provision of goods and services to the poor, would quickly be self-defeating. Their negative impact on the macro-economic constraints would lead to higher inflation and/or balance of payments crises, and in either case contractionary policies would have to be implemented.

The policy stance which emerged from this diagnosis of the problems prioritized restoring macro-economic stability and raising industrial profitability. This, it was implied, would boost investor confidence and lead to more rapid growth. In turn, an improvement in growth performance would lead to job creation and improve popular welfare.[4] Thus, the issue of redistribution was seen to be logically consequent upon the recovery of growth in the short term and its sustainability in the long run.

The specific policies recommended began with the need for financial discipline, that is, a lower government deficit and positive government savings, and high interest rates to discourage credit creation and lower money supply growth. Lower fiscal deficits would have to be achieved primarily through expenditure cuts (rather than higher revenues), so that the positive impact of lower government borrowing on private sector investment (less "crowding out") could be complemented by tax cuts for both corporations and individuals. The former would boost investment, and the latter provide incentives for individuals to work harder and save more. Industry would be further encouraged to become more competitive internationally by a range of measures to reduce protection from imports, especially for intermediate goods used as inputs in export industries, and to assist in establishing export markets, as well as tougher measures against anti-competitive practices in domestic markets. Support for small businesses and informal sector activities was identified as crucial to the job creation process.

A critical aspect of the policy package was the need for strict limits on wage increases. Offsetting this, a number of policies with redistributive goals were specifically identified, though the extent to which these dimensions of the policy package could be implemented was strictly subject to the growth achieved. Development for previously disadvantaged groups would occur through improving the educational and health systems, and transforming the urban environment to eliminate the apartheid legacies of inadequate housing and transport. This development was important for sustaining growth, both by eliminating wasteful resource allocations by both private and public sectors, and perhaps more important, by improving the commitment and skill level of the labour force over the medium to long term, and thus enhancing productivity.

Growth Through Redistribution

In contrast to the above approach, the ANC and its allies in the trade unions, civic associations, and other popular organizations, argued that economic growth would be most rapidly accelerated by a more direct focus on meeting basic needs, involving redistributive processes which would expand the consumer market as well as aggregate investment through the public sector and provide the required growth stimulus.[5] The emphasis, not surprisingly, was on obstacles to long-run growth arising out of poverty and the socio-political instability caused by it. The argument was that by re-focusing production on the provision of basic goods and services for the domestic market, and specifically targeted at the poor who had been largely excluded from access to these markets by apartheid, economic growth and employment would simultaneously be increased. As economic activity picked up and socio-political violence abated, investor confidence would be restored leading to an improvement in macro-economic stability, with rising foreign capital inflows as well as enhanced tax revenues due to higher incomes.

The public sector was seen to have a critical role in managing, and if necessary undertaking, major programmes to deliver housing and physical infrastructure—running water and sewerage, roads, electricity, telephones—to urban and rural communities lacking these basic amenities. Investment programmes in these sectors would use labour-intensive technologies and production methods, so as to create as many jobs as possible. In addition to infrastructural investment projects, heavy emphasis was placed on the provision of services and the development of human resources. A massive expansion of education and training was envisaged, to reach all sectors of the population. Health and social welfare delivery was to be totally overhauled, with a National Health Service focusing on primary health care, and increased social security support to the unemployed, indigent, and aged.

Other economic policies flowed from the expansion of basic needs provision as the starting point. The creation of new productive capacity and, as important, new structures of ownership and management in industry would re-orient flows of both products and income towards blacks and women, especially Africans, previously discriminated against in goods and factor markets. Small, especially black-owned, businesses were a major target for redistribution, since they could play a role in both job creation and production of basic wage goods.

Thus affirmative action policies were an important vehicle, relating to hiring practices, access to credit and procurement of goods and services by entities in both the private and public sectors. In addition to affirmative action policies to widen participation in economic activity, it was argued that participation and control over economic governance should be broadened, by establishing negotiating forums in which economic and social interest groups would be represented, and which would have a role in policy formulation and implementation.[6]

Macro-economic and financial policy was treated as being facilitative and supportive of the primary thrust of the strategy, rather than the central focus as in the first approach. The destabilizing potential of macro-economic imbalance was explicitly identified, implying the need to avoid excessive money creation which might lead to inflation, as well as excessive reliance on capital inflows by relying mainly on domestically-generated savings.[7] But this was far from the main focus of attention within this strategy, and the possibility of macro-economic constraints binding growth from the outset was not addressed.

Implementing a Response

The two strategies outlined above both recognize the need to restore investor confidence as the essential precondition for the recovery of growth, but they differ on the most appropriate route to achieve this intermediate goal, the first being concerned primarily with macro-economic stability and the second focusing upon social stability.

Too narrow a focus on one or the other of these concerns may well have undesirable consequences, in terms of severe economic and social dislocation leading to the unsustainability of economic growth. This is because each of the two approaches outlined above tends in "pure" form to marginalize an important social force which, if amongst the "losers" from economic policy, would be likely to react negatively and disrupt the implementation of policy. On one hand, real wage cuts have in many economies been a critical element of macro-economic stabilization strategies, seen as necessary to support both demand compression policies to reduce inflation and currency devaluation to improve the balance of trade. In South Africa, a likely response to such policies would be a rise in strikes and political opposition from the strong and well-organized trade unions in the industrial and commercial sectors. On the other hand, were too much emphasis to be placed on broad social upliftment, private sector investors would expect "excessive" public sector deficit and debt levels to result, producing further macro-economic instability. Their response therefore would be a reduction of investment and capital flight, that is, a "capital strike." Thus the expectation of macro-economic chaos becomes a self-fulfilling prophecy and reduces growth potential.

Such outcomes, it is evident, are likely only if the "losers" from economic policy are sufficiently well-organized and powerful as interest groups to force, through disruptive action, the rest of the society to share the burden of their loss. In South Africa, both capital and organized labour would appear to have this capacity. But an important reason for the political transition in South Africa being negotiated—and so based on compromise—was the relatively equivalent strength of these major social forces on opposite sides of the socio-economic divide. This made the adoption of an exclusive version of either of the two strategies outlined above unlikely. Instead, a combination of the two strategies has been implemented.[8]

But what is the nature of this compromise? And is it coherent? The inability to reach real compromise could lead to policy lurching back and forth from one strategic approach to the other, as opposing political forces get the upper hand in turn, or at least force the dominant elements to introduce ad hoc policies to meet their needs. Alternatively, incoherence could be reflected in individual ministries of the government adopting elements of opposing strategies. Both patterns have occurred in other countries, the first in several Latin American economies during much of the post-1945 period, and the second in Turkey during the 1980s. The consequences are the unsustainability of growth, and the disappearance of income redistributions in rising inflation.[9]

The Policy Stance

The policy stance of the new Government of National Unity (GNU), since it took office in May 1994, suggests we may have reason to expect a more positive and constructive outcome in South Africa than in the comparative experiences mentioned above. The combination of the two approaches to economic policy has been accomplished in a manner which reflects a significant degree of agreement amongst key economic policy makers, and relatedly, substantial coherence in the overall approach to policy.

The key step in this process has been the recognition, at least implicitly, by the leadership of the ANC that social stability is more relevant to investor confidence in the long-run, and that it is essential to maintain confidence in the short-run as well. In this respect, it is financial investors in particular whose expectations of the future need to be addressed, so that a clear policy commitment to macro-economic stability is essential for a government wishing to avoid either public finance or balance of payments crises.[10] The incoming government was forcibly reminded of the potential for macro-economic disruption during its first months in office. First, there was continuing (if dropping) capital flight from the private sector during the last three quarters of 1994.[11] In addition, there was a rise in government bond yields—the cost to the government of financing its deficit—in September 1994, as private sector financial institutions reduced their willingness to supply funds to the public sector in the face of rising inflation (Suzman 1994).

In line with its overall orientation towards the constitutional negotiations—a willingness to compromise with forces potentially disruptive of progress towards democracy—the ANC effectively conceded immediate control over macro-economic policy to the investment community. The management of the Reserve Bank was left intact, and its institutional independence inscribed in the interim constitution. Derek Keys, the businessman who was appointed Minister of Finance in 1992, continued in this role after May 1994, but resigned in October. A banker, Chris Liebenberg, was brought in from outside the political arena to replace him. Within the ANC itself, newly-appointed ministers were at pains to stress their commitment to fiscal discipline. For example, Jay Naidoo, former general secretary of COSATU and minister in charge of the Reconstruction and Development Programme, pointed out that RDP spending would be within the parameters of the need to lower existing deficit and debt levels.[12]

Thus a very cautious, even conservative, fiscal stance was adopted—the deficit was lowered from seven percent to 6.6 percent in the 1994/95

Budget, and then to 5.7 percent in the 1995/96 Budget. Within this overall limit, the government is making significant moves to shift the priorities of spending towards basic needs provision. The 1995/96 Budget raised overall social spending by five percent of total government spending, and more than doubled housing spending in Rand terms. Secondly, there have also been renewed moves toward the privatization of state assets as a means of raising public funds and transforming the asset portfolio of the public sector to reflect the priorities of the new government, especially in terms of its objective to develop infrastructure for black communities (Mathews 1995). Thirdly, the continuity in management at the South African Reserve Bank has also meant continuity in policy, with anti-inflation policy the overarching priority pursued, as since 1989, through the use of high nominal interest rates and a stable nominal value for the exchange rate. Interest rates have not been lowered in line with the dropping inflation rate, so that real, inflation-adjusted rates have reached double digits, amongst the world's highest. In an important departure from standard "neo-liberal" prescriptions, the Reserve Bank has resisted intense pressure from the business community for the rapid scrapping of all currency controls and the two-tier exchange rate, and implemented this gradually and piecemeal, maintaining strict regulation of foreign investments by South African corporations.[13] Most important for the long-run perhaps, was the stated intention to use finance as a lever to force government departments to alter the focus and nature of their operations. Thus the RDP Fund was set up not with new funding, but by reducing line departments' budgets. The latter were then permitted to apply for additional funding from the RDP Fund by developing projects approved by the RDP Ministry (subsequently closed with responsibility for the RDP re-allocated to the Ministry of Finance and the Office of Deputy President Thabo Mbeki—see Blumenfeld 1996).[14]

Policy in specific sectors reflects similar concerns with the macro-economic arena: intermediate policy objectives are those usually identified, if somewhat simplistically, with "neo-liberalism"[15] and are intended to restore private sector confidence and profitability and so encourage investment in the short term. But the mechanisms and steps introduced to achieve these intermediate objectives in the South African case have been integrally connected with the need to improve the provision of basic needs and the creation of jobs. In housing, for example, the January 1995 White Paper laid out increased government subsidies to home buyers, as well as tougher regulation of the construction industry to improve competition and thereby cut house prices. Another central element in the new policy was provision for tough regulation of mortgage repayment. Widespread boycotts of mortgage and service repayments had been an important part of the breakdown of authority in black residential areas in the process leading up to constitutional negotiations. These boycotts, which of course provided significant financial relief to hard-pressed poor households, continued through the negotiation period and into the post-election stage, and now pose a major financial and political problem for the GNU. A new approach to repayments was seen as essential to lowering risk and improving incentives for financial institutions to lend to poor households wishing to buy houses. Notwithstanding the centrality of the state in housing policy in these various ways, it was the private sector that was seen very clearly to be the actual supplier of housing, rather than the state.[16]

To take a second important policy issue, that of trade liberalization, announcements in the first half of 1995 by the government lowering tariffs in the textile/clothing and auto industries emphasized the need to phase in policy over an extended time period to enable firms to adjust to new conditions of competition, while also promising retraining initiatives to re-absorb workers made redundant.

All of these instances suggest that while the GNU has been sensitive to the "new imperatives" facing governments in the 1990s—in particular, reducing the public sector's share of the economy, and becoming more open to international trade and financial flows—its response cannot straightforwardly be labelled "neo-liberal," but reflects an approach that is more politically nuanced and concerned with longer-term issues, of both redistribution and efficiency, than the stereotypical neo-liberal perspective.[17]

The development of this distinctive approach to policy reflects in part the success of the disparate informal discussions about economic policy referred to earlier. One dimension of this process involved the parties to the constitutional negotiating process. But as important as the political parties was the involvement in the economic debate of other organizations representing interest groups in "civil society," especially labour and business. Their participation was formalized in the course of the transition process by the establishment of a wide range of negotiating forums.

The initial emergence of the forums reflected the demand by COSATU to be involved in macro-economic policy decisions, in the wake of the government's introduction of a value-added tax in 1991. The trade unions' success in achieving this demand reflected the government's limited political capacity for policy formulation and implementation during the transition period. But as forums proliferated from 1992, it also became evident that they were filling a gap in the government's administrative policy-making capacity, since in many cases the policy research and formulation process was led by the business and labour groups, rather than government.

By mid-1993, there were 15 national forums concerned with different industries or public services such as education and health, seven regional forums, five serving metropolitan areas and possibly hundreds at the local government level. The most important was the National Economic Forum, a tripartite body with a range of organizations representing different groupings of business and labour.[18] A permanent body, the National Economic, Development and Labour Council (NEDLAC), was established in 1995 to succeed the National Economic Forum. In addition to labour, business and government, relevant interest groups such as community organizations are represented in its "Development" chamber. In other sectors, proposed or newly-established statutory bodies such as the national and provincial Housing Boards, and the Commission for Higher Education, build on the forum concept in providing for broad "stakeholder" participation.

The forums institutionalize a bargaining process over policy and impose the need to reach compromises over the sharing of the benefits and costs of policy. This not only enhances democracy by widening participation in policy processes, but also provides an essential political context for the combining of the alternative development strategies. As will be elaborated below, there are some potential problems arising from the prominence of the forums in the policy-making process. But thus far, discussion and debate of policy within the forums appears to have contributed to a consistent and coherent strategy, partly by enabling the government to win support for its cautious macro-economic strategy as the framework for other policy initiatives.

Perhaps the most important advantage offered by the forums is simply in enabling negotiation over policy to take place amongst all interested parties simultaneously (rather than serially between government and individual interest groups, that is, through lobbying), thereby imposing the need to have explicit discussion of the sharing of costs and benefits of policy and reducing the opportunities for special arrangements and concessions for particular groups. This increases the prospects of mutually consistent and politically sustainable policies.[19]

In a more general sense, by institutionalizing and regularizing interaction between state officials and private sector actors (including labour), the forums may well contribute to the emergence in South Africa of an effective "developmental state." Current conventional wisdom suggests that the state's contribution to development is optimized if the relation between state and society is characterized by "embedded autonomy," or, in an alternative formulation, that the state has "infrastructural power" (Evans 1992). By this is meant that there is frequent and close contact between government and private sector in the policy formulation process, enabling policy to be formulated with the full benefit of information about market trends and shifts, but that government officials are sufficiently independent to avoid particularistic appeals from private interests. Thus government is able to act effectively in the broad social interests.

In the East Asian economies which stimulated this conception of the developmental state, state officials were able to impose "reciprocity" on businesses which received assistance, that is, to force them to meet specified performance targets, especially in relation to exports, in return for receiving protection and subsidies. This was in part enabled by bureaucrats' independence or insulation from private interests, which in turn rested on these societies' authoritarianism. But authoritarianism is not a sufficient condition for a "strong" state able to impose conditions on interest groups in society (and may not be a necessary condition, either). Obviously authoritarianism is undesirable for post-apartheid South Africa, and this is not the lesson to be drawn for South Africa from the East Asian NICs.

The lesson rather is that development requires a "strong" state, able to lead society by formulating a strategy and creating a broad base of support for it within society. Alice Amsden has argued, based primarily on the East Asian experience, that there is a correlation between strong states and relatively equitable income distributions, which limit the power of business to subvert reciprocity, while providing incentives to labour to compensate for being subject to discipline (Amsden 1992). While South Africa clearly does not fall into the class of equitable societies, the emerging institutional framework might offset the differential access to resources on the part of interest groups. In other words, the forums may enable an analogous outcome in terms of state power, first by enabling close contact between bureaucrats and relevant interest groups in the formulation of policy, and secondly by equalizing class power and enabling interest groups to assist state officials in monitoring each others' compliance with agreements.

The most significant product to date of the forum process has been the successful negotiation in NEDLAC of a new Labour Relations Act, agreed in NEDLAC in July 1995, and passed by Parliament in August. The process was not without its difficulties. For several months, two key aspects of the new Act remained unresolved: weakened trade unions insisted upon centralized bargaining, while management opposed the innovation of workplace forums, fearing a loss of control at shopfloor level. Following mass action on the streets by COSATU and other union federations, agreement was reached on these and other deadlocked issues, with the general consensus being that there had been something of a tilt towards labour (von Holdt 1995).

The fact that agreement over the LRA ultimately involved open conflict cannot be regarded as a negation of NEDLAC or of the forum process more generally. The forums do not eliminate conflicts of interest or guarantee that compromise can be reached. But it can be argued that without the negotiating possibilities provided by NEDLAC, agreement on the LRA would have been reached only with a much greater level of conflict, if at all. Thus the passing of the LRA should be seen as both a successful test of NEDLAC and also as a significant extension of the emphasis on consultation amongst stakeholders into the workplace and sectoral level bargaining.

Consequences

The institutionalization of the negotiating forums represents a major innovation, not just in terms of South Africa's own transition to a post-apartheid democratic order, but in terms of the global response to neo-liberal orthodoxy. The most important consequence has been that the government has been able to restore short-term investor confidence while maintaining relative social stability and its political support in its traditional constituencies. In other words, it has been able, at least thus far, to achieve the objectives of neo-liberal orthodoxy, and of the "growth with redistribution" approach, while not paying the political price which has generally been exacted of governments pursuing this path.

There are several positive signs of improved confidence. The most important is the recovery of fixed investment, which rose by seven percent in 1994, contributing to overall growth of the GNP of 3.5 percent in 1994, equivalent to one percent per capita growth. This improved performance continued into 1995, at least for the manufacturing sector. There is no doubt that the Government of National Unity, and especially its leading element, the ANC, was fortunate to take office at a time when the economy was in any event moving into a cyclical upswing after four years of very deep recession. At the same time, it is important to emphasize that the revival of economic growth has been led by investment, rather than by personal or government consumption expenditure as had been the case in previous economic recoveries during the 1980s.

An important aspect of the investment recovery has been the announcement of many large projects in minerals processing, transport and electronic communications, science and technology educational and research infrastructure and electrification of black communities, as well as the ubiquitous shopping centre and hotel and convention centre developments (*Weekly Mail and Guardian*, 21 October 1994). On one hand, the number of such multi-billion rand projects suggests that the long-term expectations of big business in South Africa are positive, since these are projects with a payback period of many years. In other words, the improvement in confidence should not be understood simply as a short-term phenomenon. On the other hand, the spread of these projects across a wide span of sectors, including exports and commercial and community infrastructure, is itself significant: since the latter element—community infrastructure—is one focus of the "growth through redistribution" strategy, the implication is that all significant actors, most especially big business, have accepted that development policy should not reflect an exclusive emphasis on either one of the two strategic approaches. Indeed, policy debate and discussion during 1995 began to shift increasingly to an emphasis on mechanisms to enable "infrastructure," particularly in urban communities, to become the lead sector in aggregate investment.

The reversal in business confidence was underlined by a June 1995 poll of business and union leaders which put support for Mandela and the ANC, in a straight choice against de Klerk and the National Party, at 70 percent for both economic interest groups. This represented a major shift for business leaders in response to ANC cabinet ministers' more investor-friendly stance, but also reflecting the view that the ANC was more capable of maintaining political stability, indicated by the continuing support of the trade union constituency. At the same time, the poll was yet another sign of the increasing irrelevance and marginalization of the National Party (as well as other historically white, centrist groupings), whose most important claim during the transitional period had been to represent a business-oriented position.

Internationally, investor confidence has also improved significantly. Most important from the perspective of short-term confidence and macro-economic stability is that South Africa is back in international credit markets. By the end of 1994, both of the major credit rating agencies, Moody's and Standard and Poor's, had begun to include South Africa in their ratings, an essential criterion for credibility in the international money markets. In December 1994, the government floated its biggest bond issue for many years, and was successful in raising US$750 million, selling everything on offer. With the Johannesburg Stock Exchange also climbing, and attracting foreign investors, overall capital inflows became positive from the second quarter of 1994, and were expected to reach as much as 3.5 - 4 percent of GDP during 1995. Indeed, by mid-1995, the Reserve Bank was beginning to express concern about the inflows, worrying about the large proportion of short-term flows in the total which could make South Africa similarly vulnerable to a reversal of flows as Mexico was at the end of 1994. Nonetheless, this was a significant shift from the pattern of persistent outflows over the previous decade, and the inflows made it possible to finance a trade deficit, that is, enabled substantial increases in imports of investment goods.

Large numbers of new direct investments have also taken place, as well as the return of many corporations, especially from the US, which had "warehoused" their local operations during the era of disinvestment, by selling their equity to local management while retaining an option—now exercised—to repurchase. Thirty US companies came into South Africa in the year to September 1994, a rise of over 20 percent in the total (*Globe and Mail*, 11 October 1994). Much of the new investment has gone into high profile industries, such as food, especially fast food, and services, especially upmarket and international tourism. In addition, high tech industries, with smaller volumes but high value-added ratios, such as computer hardware and software and airlines, have been targeted. Two other features of foreign direct investment are worth mentioning. One is that foreign investment is now coming in from developing countries, as well as industrialized countries. Amongst the more important sources of new capital are Malaysia and India. The second point is that almost all new foreign investment is occurring in partnership with local black entrepreneurs, or, in the case of fast foods and other consumer industries, through the extension of franchises to black entrepreneurs.

"Black empowerment," or the opening of access to ownership and wealth to black entrepreneurs, has in fact been perhaps the most visible development in the South African economy since the 1994 election. It has occurred not only through the vehicles of foreign investment partnerships and franchises, but also via sales of stock in major domestic corporations, usually assisted by credit extended on relatively easy terms. For several of South Africa's conglomerates, establishing partnerships with now politically influential black businesspeople has been the central aspect of a more complex process of "unbundling," or corporate restructuring and rationalization, with the additional objectives of avoiding the impact of competition policy and re-focusing assets for international expansion following the relaxation of exchange controls. The new class of black "big" business created by this process remains very tiny, probably of the order of 50-100 people, running what are essentially leveraged investment funds, rather than productive enterprises or even financial intermediaries in the usual sense of the term. Control of the levers of private sector economic power remains substantially white—a recent magazine profile of four of the most prominent of the "new" black businessmen suggested that their holdings amounted to approximately US$640 million—a minute share (less than 0.5 percent) of the overall capitalization of the Johannesburg Stock Exchange, but a huge shift from only two years previously (*Finance Week* 1995).

Problems

There are many positive signs which provide hope that South Africa will succeed in introducing the intended re-orientation of economic policy while avoiding the economic collapse and high social costs experienced by many African and Latin American countries which pursued similar economic reform strategies in the 1980s under IMF/World Bank guidance. But the problems are not all resolved—the road ahead remains filled with potential pitfalls. This section identifies and discusses some of them, leaving consideration of progress on redistribution and its implications to the next, concluding, section.

Most obviously, it remains to be seen whether the improvement in investor confidence and in fixed investment levels will be sustained and translated into growth over the medium-run.[20] This is likely to depend upon the degree to which the current growth upswing establishes new markets, both for exports and for domestic (black) consumption, which can then provide an engine for subsequent growth. Thus the success of current policy initiatives, such as trade liberalization or support for small and medium-sized enterprises, and of current investment projects, whether in minerals-processing or in infrastructure, cannot yet be evaluated.

Turning to the political economy aspects, it is evident that the existence of forums does not guarantee that satisfactory compromises will be reached, only that the prospects for the latter are enhanced. Two important issues which need to be addressed in relation to the forums are, firstly, the need for co-ordination across forums, and secondly, related to this, the role of the forums in relation to the national parliament.

With forums established at a national level, as well as for individual sectors and provinces (though coverage at these levels is unlikely to be complete), it is perhaps inevitable that cross-cutting and contradictory agreements will be reached in different forums. It cannot be assumed that having the same interest groups represented in different forums will ensure that coherent policies emerge, since co-ordination within national trade union federations or business associations, and even within government, is usually far from perfect. It is a well-known problem of corporatist-type negotiating institutions that the "peak associations" whose officials actually participate in the negotiations are not able to guarantee compliance of member organizations with the agreements forged. With a multiplicity of forums, a strong possibility exists of localized alliances emerging amongst parties in sectoral or provincial forums to oppose national-level agreements. An obvious example of this possibility is in relation to the budgetary process, where attempts to cut spending in a sector or province may well be frustrated by joint action by the negotiating parties in the relevant forum, including government representatives from the line department.

A second problem that could come to plague the constructive role of the forums is their relationship with the national parliament. There remains substantial ambiguity concerning the sovereignty of parliament *vis-à-vis* the forums, individually and collectively. *De jure*, of course, parliament is supreme, but *de facto* this may not be the case. In the case of the Labour Relations Act, there was concern amongst parliamentarians that they were discouraged from full consideration of the bill before them, both because of cabinet concern to enact the law as quickly as possible, and on the grounds that any proposals to change the bill would upset the delicate agreement forged in NEDLAC. If this process were to become generalized, it would not merely vitiate democracy, but also generate conflict between the legislative and executive arms of government, and introduce substantial inflexibilities and deadlocks into the policy-making process.

Aside from possible obstacles arising from the forums, two other potential political difficulties for the sustainability of medium-term growth can be mentioned. The first is the limited administrative capacity of the state to formulate and implement policy, that is, the ability of civil servants to design effective and efficient state actions and regulations. This is to be distinguished from the other dimension of state capacity, the political capacity to manage the demands and reactions to policy of interest groups, which is likely to be enhanced by the emergence of the forums and the associated "culture" of negotiation discussed above. Administrative capacity had declined quite precipitously during the waning of apartheid from the mid-1980s, as reflected in the inability of the previous government to develop strategies of adaptation for its own survival.[21] Though it can decline quite rapidly, administrative capacity is built up extremely slowly, and it is unlikely that this dimension of state capacity will improve markedly for some years, given both the influx of new and inexperienced civil servants into government structures, and more importantly the possibility of internal opposition to GNU policies from elements within the "old" bureaucracy still unhappy with the transition. These factors have clearly contributed to the limited improvement since May 1994 in the supply of basic goods and services. The delay in delivery has been perhaps the central criticism thus far of the GNU's performance, notwithstanding the fact that the public sector is not solely responsible for delivery.[22]

A second issue which may threaten the stability of the growth process is potential conflict between the national government and provincial governments over economic policy. One factor here is of course the political division between the ANC, on the one hand, and the Inkatha Freedom Party and the National Party on the other, each of the latter in control of a major province. But there are also differences between the central government and ANC-controlled provincial governments, as exemplified by the tensions which surfaced during 1994 between the (then) Minister of Housing, Joe Slovo, and the Premier of Gauteng, Tokyo Sexwale. What was evident from Sexwale's extravagant promises around the number of new houses to be built in the province, accompanied by his attempt to enlist a private sector corporation to implement directly the delivery of housing on behalf of his government, in direct contradiction to Slovo's painstaking efforts to shape a broadly inclusive agreement amongst all relevant actors, was that the former saw the prospect of building a political support base for his own government (and by implication for himself) which was independent of support for the ANC more generally.

Further examples of this sort of tension are the entirely predictable outcome of the decentralized nature of South Africa's new constitution, which defines areas of provincial legislative competence very broadly, overlapping substantially with those of the central government,[23] and defines the distribution of fiscal resources between national and provincial governments somewhat loosely, creating a new institution, the Financial and Fiscal Commission, to help specify in detail the size of national government grants to the provinces. Provinces are not allowed to levy income or expenditure (sales) taxes, and their borrowing activities are very tightly circumscribed. But the criteria for determining their revenue allocation from the fiscus include, for example, fiscal performance, needs of provinces and economic disparities between them, and developmental needs, as well as the recommendations of the Financial and Fiscal Commission. This leaves open considerable room for political conflict and negotiation, focused upon the latter body.

The lack of precision about the powers and responsibilities of the provinces to receive revenues and spend them makes it inconceivable that the provincial governments would become merely administrative and spending agents of the central government, as some senior politicians in the latter appeared to expect and hope. This outcome is partly a consequence of the federalist pressures brought to bear within the constitutional negotiating process by both the National and Inkatha Freedom Parties. But it is also a result of the ANC's concern to reach the point of holding democratic elections, which meant a willingness to shelve firm resolution of contentious issues in favour of general formulations open to varying interpretation.[24] The resulting institutional arrangements provide incentives to provincial politicians, of whatever political stripe, to develop the political and policy-making capacities of their governments, so as to enhance the effectiveness of their lobbying of the central government and pressuring of it in negotiations over fiscal allocations and relative policy authority. This situation reflects significant potential for loss of fiscal control, with the consequent danger of excessive public debt or inflationary rates of money supply growth, either of which can undermine overall economic growth.[25]

Redistribution: The Achilles Heel?

While there are grounds for cautious optimism that growth can be sustained, the record thus far on equity improvements under the new government must be seen as less encouraging. Visible progress on redistribution is inevitably slower to appear than evidence of improvement in the growth rate. Yet the "growth through redistribution" position was premised in part on the need for social stability through improvements in living standards to underpin long-term growth prospects. Does the slow pace of redistribution therefore threaten the latter, and give support to the "brief miracle" understanding of South Africa's transition discussed at the outset of the chapter?

Looking first at what has happened, the most important mechanism for reducing absolute poverty levels is employment creation, and here performance has been inadequate. As noted above, the employment elasticity of the South African economy—the relation between output growth and employment creation—dropped to extremely low levels during the 1980s, as reflected in a rising capital-output ratio. Not surprisingly, the improvement in growth since late 1993 has not been accompanied by a sufficient rise in this ratio: the upswing in economic activity has commonly been characterized as a 'jobless recovery', though in fact, there has been some increase in job creation. Total employment has risen at only 1.3 percent per annum, as compared with the labour force growth rate of twice that figure (Stals 1995).

There is no agreement on appropriate policy interventions to improve the situation. For many economists, the blockage lies in the labour market itself, with strong union organizations for workers with low productivity levels preventing the decline in wage levels necessary for (especially smaller) firms to hire more workers (Fallon 1992). For others, the more significant problem is the composition of investment, and in particular the heavy emphasis on high tech production and capital-intensive projects in the minerals processing sector and amongst foreign investors.[26] The allocation of investment resources in these directions, and the extensive use of financial mechanisms to promote black ownership stakes in existing large corporations, is sometimes also identified as an obstacle. All of these factors may undermine potential investment by small and medium-sized enterprises, with negative implications for employment creation, since this category of firms is more labour-intensive.[27]

But even with increased investment by labour-intensive firms, employment growth may not be sufficient to lower the unemployment level in the medium term. What is necessary to raise the rate of increase in jobs above that of the labour force is continuous improvements in the productivity of both capital and labour, and these improvements simply may not be achieved.[28]

Turning to other aspects of redistribution, the increased share of basic needs items in overall government spending has been noted above. While the African share of current public spending on basic goods and services has naturally increased significantly as per capita spending has been equalized, or in some areas biased in favour of previously disadvantaged groups, this naturally does not mean that access to such goods and services is now equitable. Non-Africans still have greater access to these public services, since the capital stock invested in their provision is located overwhelmingly in what are still primarily non-African residential areas, and since much of the provision of these goods and services is now undertaken by the private sector for higher income groups.

As noted above, the GNU established a ministry within the president's office to oversee the implementation of the Reconstruction and Development Programme. There has been considerable ambiguity as to whether its primary task was to formulate and implement projects to enhance delivery of basic goods and services, or to transform the overall public sector through re-directing the spending of all government departments in line with new priorities. While the lack of success in the latter task was not a surprise, the slow pace of delivery in respect to the former made the RDP ministry the most frequent target of government critics from all quarters. While there were good reasons for the RDP ministry's difficulties, including the need to establish administrative and accountability structures and processes *ab initio*, and the desire to use consultative mechanisms when developing projects with communities, the strategic error on the part of the ANC was possibly to rely upon a newly-established ministry, given the importance of the political objective of improvements in living standards for its working-class black constituents. This may explain, in part, the March 1996 shift of the RDP Fund and its associated project planning, monitoring and evaluation functions to the Department of Finance (Blumenfeld 1996).

It is important to recognize that the government remains committed to redistribution as a policy priority, though its approach now locates redistribution within a framework of short-term macro-economic discipline. This commitment will not easily be abandoned, given the vigorous support for it within the ANC, including its powerful parliamentary caucus and provincial governments. Thus a direct confrontation with popular demands appears unlikely, though unhappiness with the pace of delivery will continue. A second critical factor is that no effective political challenge is on the horizon: with the effective collapse of the PAC, and the refusal of the South African Communist party to take a position independent of the ANC, there is certainly no political organization which appears capable of rallying popular voices from below to threaten the ANC's rule and force it towards a form of "delegative democracy." Nor are the trade unions likely to lead any such challenge, since policy compromises forged through the forums take account of their concerns: indeed, this is a crucial aspect of those redistributive processes which are occurring, and underlines the importance of forums for economic growth and democracy. Without either political or trade union leadership, it is hard to see popular resentment, however intense, as a real threat to governmental power.

On the other end of the spectrum, the right, the serious threat to democracy is political, not economic, coming, as is well-known, from the unresolved violent conflict between the Inkatha Freedom Party and the ANC in the province of KwaZulu-Natal. This may yet force the GNU into a more authoritarian stance. Analysis of this issue is clearly beyond the scope of this paper, having little to do with economic policy issues. But in a sense there is an overlap with the endemic political violence: the limited scope of redistribution thus far and the lack of formal economic opportunities is certainly a contributing factor in the rise in criminality, organized and individual, as one means of livelihood for the huge mass of unemployed. Organized crime should be seen in strictly economic terms as providing incomes for otherwise unemployed people, and in this way as unaccounted growth. While crime may retard growth in the formal economy by lowering investment and influencing its sectoral and geographical patterns , at this stage it does not threaten to lead to economic collapse, and thus invite an authoritarian response. But like the political violence, crime could possibly spiral out of state control.

Contrary to the "brief miracle" hypothesis, this would be a result of the lack of redistribution, not its excessive pace. In other words, the implicit logic of the "growth through redistribution" strategy remains relevant: without redistribution, social stability is threatened in the long-run, and without social stability, the sustainability of growth cannot be assured. The democratic government has not yet resolved the major conundrum of its legacy. But it is in its early days—it has not yet had sufficient opportunity to do so, and the path down which it has started provides a fair prospect that it can succeed in restoring growth and improving equity over the longer term.

Notes

1.   This phrase was coined by Nelson Mandela and was adopted as the title of a generally useful collection of essays on the constitutional negotiations and 1994 election (see Friedman and Atkinson 1994).

2.   This describes the situation found in some new democracies in Latin America, where democratically-elected governments have reversed direction in economic strategy from their electoral platforms, and centralized power in the executive in order to force through conservative economic policy reforms. Multi-party elections in these societies amount to little more than plebiscites, a means to delegate power to the president or prime minister and his close advisors (see O'Donnell 1994).

3.   This process was more disparate in that it took place via a host of conferences and workshops, as well as bilateral meetings between political organizations and sectoral and national business interest groups, and between political organizations and officials of the previous government. It was less formal in that discussions in these various contexts did not always represent officially mandated positions of the participating organizations. From 1993, a more formal dimension was introduced, in that the constitutional negotiations took up some issues relating to economic policy, while at the same time, the National Economic Forum and a range of more specific sectoral forums were established. The ANC itself did not participate in the National Economic Forum, however.

4.   The most complete statement of this view is found in Central Economic Advisory Services, *The Restructuring of the South African Economy: A Normative Economic Model*. A summary statement is Ministry of Finance, *The Key Issues in the Normative Economic Model*.

5.   The most elaborated version of the programme is *The Reconstruction and Development Programme* (ANC 1994), but the broad framework is essentially similar to ANC economic policy statements developed in September 1990 and July 1991. An important difference between earlier and later versions is the diminishing importance of the role envisaged for the state in the production and delivery of goods and services, as nationalization slipped lower on the ANC's agenda. A

second important shift was the increasing prominence within the proposed industrial strategy of policies specifically intended to boost exports of manufactured products. Movement by the ANC on both issues reflects the growing recognition of the need for compromise with business, as the most powerful economic interest group.

6. Although the broadening of democratic participation in economic governance was part of ANC economic policy goals from 1990, the mechanisms for achieving this objective expressed in the RDP naturally built upon the widespread emergence of negotiating forums from 1991, to deal with macro-economic issues, sectoral change in industry and social services, and local and regional government.

7. In this respect, tax reform was identified as an important mechanism, with a wide range of proposals being made to shift the incidence of tax away from poor and middle-income individuals, towards the wealthy and corporations, while at the same time improving the efficiency of tax collection.

8. This is true notwithstanding the use of the RDP "label" by an extremely wide range of private and public organizations to legitimate their activities in terms of the political direction of the new government, or at least its dominant partner.

9. In the Latin American cases, governments since the 1950s have cycled between "populist" parties' efforts to create a national industrial base by using policy to secure the interests of urban manufacturers and workers, and authoritarian reactions to the runaway inflation induced by these policies, imposing austerity so as to restore price stability. The inevitable adverse political reaction to austerity then re-starts the cycle (see Diaz-Alejandro 1981; Foxley 1983).

In Turkey, orthodox fiscal and financial and trade liberalization policies imposed during the early 1980s seemed to be successful in the middle of the decade, but by 1990 had been totally undermined by the proliferation of "extra-budgetary funds" which were used as expenditure vehicles for a wide range of goods and services provided by the public sector, so as to keep the official fiscal deficit artificially low (see Onis 1992; Onis and Riedel 1993).

10. The self-fulfilling dimension of the relation between investor confidence and macro-economic stability should be noted. In addition, it should be remembered that the Transitional Executive Council, the temporary all-party body which governed South Africa between December 1993 and April 1994, signed an agreement with the IMF for a standby facility of US$750 million, ostensibly to offset the balance of payments consequences of drought (which had in fact broken by the time the agreement was signed). The terms of this facility specified a reduction in the fiscal deficit as well as trade liberalization.

11. See South African Reserve Bank, *Quarterly Bulletin*, June 1995, Table 6, p. 12. Note that there was a positive inflow of long-term private capital during the first quarter of 1994.

12. See Patti Waldmeir et al, 1994. See also speeches in October 1994 by Naidoo and by Alec Erwin (former trade unionist and Deputy Minister of Finance; now Minister of Trade and Industry) in *Human Resource Development in the RDP* (Johannesburg: Ravan Press, 1995). Naidoo and Erwin are amongst those accused by leftwing critics inside and outside of the ANC of "selling out" to neo-liberalism. See for example Padayachee and Adelzadeh 1994. This is a facile view, which identifies as "neo-liberal" any strategy which responds to the concerns identified by neo-liberals. These authors fail to take account of both the actual macro-economic constraints existing in relation to the fiscal and foreign balances, and the political

constraints reflected in the structure of the Government of National Unity. Furthermore, their understanding of short-term macro-economic issues and of investor confidence is impoverished.

13. The hazards of too rapid an opening of the financial system to the international economy are recognized clearly in South Africa after the previous attempt to do so in the early 1980s contributed significantly to the foreign debt crisis of 1985, which in turn was an important factor pushing the National Party government into negotiations by 1990. It is also recognized more widely to be inappropriate, even by proponents of the "Washington consensus."

14. The power of the RDP Ministry to pressure other departments to transform was limited, given its marginal budget. The Finance Ministry was in a much stronger position *vis-à-vis* other departments, so that the initial situation seemed to institutionalize tensions between the RDP and Finance Ministries. Thus, the March 1996 shift of primary responsibility for the RDP Fund to Finance should remove this source of tensions.

15. The neo-liberal policy strategy, or "Washington consensus," is usefully summarized by John Williamson in Chapter 2 of Williamson 1994. There is a great deal of overlap with the "growth with redistribution" approach discussed above, as was explicitly but informally acknowledged by some of the contributors to the previous South African government's Normative Economic Model.

16. This shifted subsequently. The death of Joe Slovo, Minister of Housing and architect of the White Paper, shortly after the latter's adoption, was one factor in what developed into an impasse in housing delivery. But there were clearly other problems of a financial and institutional nature, as by mid-1995 the private construction industry was urging the state to re-assume its historic role as builder in the lowest income segments of the housing market, arguing that the risks were too great for private business. Interestingly, Housing Ministry officials stood firm on limiting their role.

17. It is only quite recently that proponents of neo-liberalism have come to see that simply cutting back the state's economic activities and regulatory role does not restore growth, but that the state has a range of essential economic roles. So what is needed, it is now argued, is a re-orientation of state institutions, and an improvement in their efficiency. See for example the contributions by Naim, Nelson and Haggard and Kaufman to *Journal of Democracy* 5(4) (October 1994): Special Issue on Economic Reform and Democracy.

18. Importantly, the ANC refused to participate in the National Economic Forum, though it was involved in most other forums. This reflected, it seems, ambivalence on the part of some ANC leaders about the possible effect of forums in vitiating government control over policy. Though the ANC does participate in NEDLAC, the NEF's successor body established in 1995, misgivings over its role continue to be expressed by some ministers.

19. Consistency and political sustainability are both particularly desirable when policy is concerned with macro-economic stabilization, especially fiscal reform, and with trade liberalization, as implied by the experience of IMF and World Bank programmes in both Africa and Latin America during the 1980s.

20. It is to be expected, of course, that the growth process will undergo a cyclical downswing in due course. This in and of itself does not imply that the growth process is unsustainable—the question is how long and deep the downswing is,

and whether a cyclical upswing follows without major policy changes, that is, without a process of structural reform.

21. Evidence for this claim is anecdotal and uneven, as to my knowledge, the issue of state capacity, in the sense used here, has not been the subject of systematic research in South Africa.

22. There is some merit in the response from the cabinet ministers responsible, that adequate systems and capacity need to be established before embarking on major spending initiatives. But the time required to accomplish this is precisely a reflection of the low level of administrative capacity.

23. See Schedule 6 of the 1993 (interim) Constitution.

24. A useful discussion of how the federal issue was dealt with in the constitutional negotiations is R. Humphries et al, "The shape of the country: Negotiating regional government," in Friedman and Atkinson 1994.

25. In the short term there is the problem of very large deficits inherited by some provinces from the former "homelands."

26. This argument was made by other World Bank research. See B. Kahn et al, "South Africa: Macro-economic issues for the transition," World Bank Southern Africa Department, May 1992, and B. Levy, "How can South Africa efficiently create employment? An analysis of the impact of trade and industrial policy," World Bank Southern Africa Department, January 1992. Levy also pointed out that such projects not only do not create employment, but also may hold back overall productivity growth.

27. In addition, these firms frequently are black-owned and produce consumer goods, further reasons to support their investment plans.

28. See S. Gelb et al, "Targeting 3 percent employment growth—alternative scenarios," unpublished mimeo, National Economic Forum, 1993, presenting results using a quantitative macro-economic model of the South African economy. More precisely, total factor productivity—the sum of labour productivity and capital productivity, each weighted by its share in total income—needs to increase by 2-3 percent. Investment in labour-intensive sectors tends to raise capital productivity, but lower labour productivity, and vice versa for capital-intensive investments. Thus, the net impact on total factor productivity, and hence on employment growth, is difficult to predict.

References

African National Congress (ANC). 1994. *The Reconstruction and Development Programme*. Johannesburg: ANC.

Amsden, Alice. 1992. "A theory of government intervention in late industrialization," in L. Putterman and D. Rueschemeyer, eds., *State and Market: Rivalry or Synergy?* Boulder: Lynne Rienner.

Blumenfeld, Jesmond. 1996. "Pragmatists versus Populists in the 'New' South Africa," *The World Today* (July): 185-89.

Bureau of Market Research, cited in P. Fallon and L. Pereira da Silva, *South Africa: Economic Performance and Polices*, Informal Discussion Papers on Aspects of the South African Economy No. 7, Southern Africa Department, World Bank, 1994, p. 41.

Diaz-Alejandro, C.F. 1981. "Southern Cone stabilization plans," in W.R. Cline and S. Weintraub (eds.), *Economic Stabilization in Developing Countries*. Washington, DC: Brookings Institution.

Evans, P. 1992. "The state as problem and solution: predation, embedded autonomy and structural change," in S. Haggard and R.R. Kaufman, eds., *The Politics of Economic Adjustment: International Constraints, Distributive Conflicts and the State*. Princeton: Princeton University Press.

Fallon, P. 1992. "An analysis of employment and wage behaviour in South Africa," World Bank Southern Africa Department, May.

—— and L.A. Pereira da Silva. 1994. *South Africa: Economic Performance and Policies*, World Bank Southern Africa Department, Discussion Paper 7 (April).

Finance Week (Johannesburg), 30 March 1995.

Foxley, A. 1983. *Latin American Experiments in Neoconservative Economics*. Berkely: University of California Press.

Friedman, S. 1994. "Afterword: The brief miracle?," in S. Friedman and D. Atkinson, eds., *The Small Miracle: South Africa's Negotiated Settlement*. Pp. 335-36. Johannesburg: Ravan Press.

—— and D. Atkinson, eds. 1994. *The Small Miracle: South Africa's Negotiated Settlement*. Johannesburg: Ravan Press.

Gelb, Stephen. 1996. "The political economy of transition—South Africa in comparative perspective" (forthcoming).

—— et al. 1993. "Targeting 3 percent employment growth—alternative scenarios," unpublished mimeo, National Economic Forum.

——. 1991. "South Africa's Economic Crisis: An Overview" in S. Gelb, ed., *South Africa's Economic Crisis*. Cape Town: David Philip, and London: Zed Press.

——. 1990. "Democratizing Economic Growth: Alternative Growth Models for the Future," *Transformation* (Durban) 12.

Globe and Mail (Toronto), 11 October 1994.

Government of South Africa, Central Economic Advisory Services. 1993. *The Restructuring of the South African Economy: A Normative Economic Model*. Pretoria: Government Printer, Pretoria.

Government of South Africa, Ministry of Finance. 1993. *The Key Issues in the Normative Economic Model*. Pretoria: Government Printer, 24 pp.

Journal of Democracy 5(4) (October 1994): Special Issue on Economic Reform and Democracy.

Kahn, B. et al. 1992. "South Africa: Macro-economic issues for the transition," World Bank Southern Africa Department, May.

Levy, B. 1992. "How can South Africa efficiently create employment? An analysis of the impact of trade and industrial policy," World Bank Southern Africa Department, January.

McGrath, M. and A. Whiteford. 1994. *Inequality in the size distribution of income in South Africa*. Occasional Paper No. 10, Stellenbosch Economic Project, p. 1.

Mathews, Rogers. 1995. *Financial Times* (May 26).

O'Donnell, G. 1994. "Delegative democracy," *Journal of Democracy* 5.

Onis, Z. 1992. "Redemocratization and economic liberalization in Turkey: The limits of state autonomy," *Studies in Comparative International Development* 27(2) (Summer).

Onis, Z. 1991. "The logic of the developmental state," *Comparative Politics* 24(1) (October).

—— and J. Riedel. 1993. *Economic Crises and Long-Term Growth in Turkey*. Washington, D.C.: World Bank.

Padayachee, V. and A. Adelzadeh. 1994. "The RDP White Paper: Reconstruction of a development vision," *Transformation* 25.Stals, C.L. 1995. "Governor's Address," South African Reserve Bank, *Annual Economic Report*, (August).

Suzman, Mark. 1994. "Longing for an economic miracle," *Financial Times* (September 8).

Van der Berg, S. 1992. "Social reform and the reallocation of social expenditure," in R. Schrire, ed., *Wealth or Poverty? Critical Choices for South Africa*. Cape Town: Oxford University Press.

von Holdt, K. 1994. "The LRA Agreement," *South African Labour Bulletin* 19(4) (September).

Weekly Mail (Johannesburg), 21 October 1994.

Waldmeir, Patti, et al. 1994. "Pretoria seeks to calm fears on spending," *Financial Times*, May 20.

Williamson, J. ed. 1994. *The Political Economy of Policy Reform*. Washington, D.C.: Institute for International Economics.

4

Backwaters and By-passes: South Africa and "Its" Region

Peter Vale

Too many revolutions have been swallowed by all-powerful states.
—Rob Walker, 1988

We have no eternal allies, and we have no perpetual enemies. Our interests are eternal, and those interests it is our duty to follow.
—Lord Palmerston, 1848

The suffering generated by the ending of the Cold War suggests why sensation is a poor substitute for the hard lessons of experience. This is why the current celebration over the re-emergence of South Africa is misleading. For all its undoubted domestic accomplishments, the country remains an international enigma.

Consider these puzzles in the "new" South Africa's foreign policy: very powerful within its own region, it has sold arms to its neighbours; liberated from an oppressive system, the post-apartheid state has cozied up to suspect regimes in different corners of the globe; purportedly concerned about widening income gaps world-wide, the Government of National Unity uncritically supports market-driven solutions to international economic divides (Southall 1994; Suttner 1995; Vale 1995).

This chapter is preoccupied with tracking some of the foreign policy outcomes which have flowed from South Africa's domestic transition. In particular it is concerned with what these may hold for Southern Africa where the "new" South Africa will be called upon to secure peace and generate prosperity. While these particular regional outcomes are desirable, they are not necessarily achievable. This in turn opens the possibility that intermediate outcomes are more so.

Will these generate a more secure and prosperous Southern Africa? The answer is "no," as this chain of random questions suggests: Can Southern Africa grow fast enough to provide jobs for its people? Can Southern Africa share its dwindling water resources? Can Southern Africa divide its land, meeting the expectations of the majority and feeding them at the same time? Can Southern Africa escape national unravelling which appears to mark the course of international relations in every other corner of the globe? Can the region be at peace if South Africa remains powerful? These questions, rather than the hope of a Southern Africa nirvana, reflect the "realities" faced by the people of the region.[1]

Policy Makers and "Their" Publics

Understanding the dichotomy between rulers and ruled is an essential sub-theme of this chapter. The reinvention of democracy in Southern Africa has opened space for controlled contestation between the governed and their governors. In this process, ideas and understandings are contested and, through this process, citizens often come to hold different understandings of what constitutes political reality for their governments.

All this is not surprising, as South Africa shows. The struggle to end apartheid was a contest for the state (see Swatuk, Chapter 7). Once it was over, South Africa's politics have been drawn towards the timeless contest between politicians and people. In practice, however, the contest between citizens and their governments is regulated by the power of the state and the instruments which it uses to defend what it sees as its interests.

To appreciate this, consider foreign policy-making. Foreign policy flows from the selective interpretations of states and the bureaucracies which serve them and which they both create and re-create. Outcomes follow from a process of selection—the proverbial search for the lowest common denominator. For policy makers, the prism of national interest is said to be central, but inevitably "interpretations" and "understandings" determine their choice. Although themes can become constant, the process of selection invariably differs from case to case, from situation to situation, from "fact" to "fact" (Booth and Vale 1995: 291).

In the "new" South Africa, the making of foreign policy—of which regional policy is an essential component—is an increasingly contested area. The ending of apartheid certainly removed the central prop—race discrimination—which isolated the minority-ruled state for four decades, but very little else has changed.

What Does this Mean for Southern Africa?

The terrible destruction which apartheid visited upon the region in the 1980s has returned to haunt the "new" South Africa.[2] The region, it seems, continuously infers, interrupts and irritates the South African government's efforts to set the "domestic" agenda. But—and this is the policy point—South Africa's image of its own role in the region has lingered beyond the formal ending of apartheid. South African policy makers continue to cling to understandings of regional relations through a prism of "national interest" coloured by "threat" analysis. Why this happened is not difficult to understand. Orthodox analysis of national interest invariably begins with near-neighbours. What kinds of threats do they pose? Will they attack? How can they be repulsed? The same questions lie, of course, at the heart of Clausewitzian thought.

The search for self through the eyes of others is an important, though neglected, foundation moment in international relationships (George 1994; Walker 1993). When these are set by the simple binary discourse of the military, regional relations are reduced to slogans. This, of course, happened in South Africa where, during the apartheid years, the dangerously simplistic strategic doctrine of the "total onslaught" determined the course of regional relations. As it almost invariably does, paradox marks the spot for deepening conflict. All apartheid's brutality and bullying did not make the region more secure. By stressing its negative traits and emphasizing its strategic and economic vulnerabilities, South Africa's military weakened Southern Africa.

The notion of Southern Africa—like the notion of Europe—is a single and indivisible one.[3] For policy makers, this raises the uncomfortable issue of the "water's edge." Where does regional policy begin and where does domestic policy end? But like so many questions in policy-making circles, this one turns on particular understandings. Myth and reality are constant companions in the elaborate processes of international relations where selective memory and the construction of multiple identities combine in intricate patterns. When these blend together, they are drawn into the idea of the state. The idea of "South Africa" was no exception to this primordial impulse.

Underlying the narrative which first envisioned and later created the South African state were a series of associations with, and around, its physical location in the region and the world. Conventional interpretations suggest that the South African state is bordered by the Atlantic Ocean in the west, Botswana and Namibia to the north-west, Zimbabwe in the north, Mozambique and Swaziland in the north-east and to the east, the Indian Ocean. But this construction fails to explain a state called Lesotho which is an independent enclave set entirely within South Africa; it also fails to explain Swaziland which is a near-enclave. In both cases, more ethnic Basotho and Swazis, respectively, live in South Africa than in the nation-states which purport to capture their national consciousness. The conclusion is inescapable. The maps which have shaped the course of South Africa's relations with its neighbours are as arbitrary as the legends which have assembled (and disassembled) ideas of its own and its neighbours' nationhoods.

This "creation" of both nations and states has been a long-standing feature of the regional dynamic. It was, for instance, integral to apartheid's domestic mischief. As part of its grand scheme, minority-ruled South Africa created, nourished and sustained four "international" states.[4] Around these, elaborate institutional structures developed with all the trappings of statehood. Although bogus in a strict constitutional and political sense, these creations were carried forward by policy makers, including—it needs to be stressed—foreign policy makers.

"Statehood," and the political designs which underpinned it, gave the TBVC "states" impressive economic weight. Certainly, in the geographical areas in which they were located, growth was recorded. True, the capital base for this growth was situated in the Johannesburg Stock Exchange and, also true, the types of development which flowed were not readily sustainable. They were, nevertheless, areas of activity and—within the apartheid context—these states developed a sizeable political currency. Although formally buried along with apartheid's debris, their ghosts may well return to haunt the new South Africa for some time.

The tales around geography and politics take on the cast of reality as legends are both refined and reified by state makers and -maintainers. Inscriptions become reality through the power of ideas. This has also happened in South Africa where well-placed institutions and influential individuals helped buttress what Barry Buzan (1991) has called the "idea of the state." So, as an example, the South African Institute of International Affairs (SAIIA) helped underpin the "independence" of South Africa's homelands (SAIIA 1974); thereafter, others, like the Africa Institute and the South African Development Bank, through their various projects and publications, helped maintain them.

Such selective views of South Africa's reality were reinforced by the "tall tales" the minority told themselves during the Cold War. Their country, they argued, was charged with holding Western strategic interests in an area of the world which was crucial for the long-term survival of free-market capitalism. In this way, the holding myths of the Cold War buttressed and sustained the manner in which South Africans engaged and understood their own role in the wider international community. This understanding provided fertile ground for the idea of "total onslaught."

South Africa's minority were not alone in this, of course. The power of the Cold War and its purchase on the tide of human affairs for close on five decades cannot be under-estimated. E.L. Doctorow sees the effects of its "capture" of history in this way:

> [It] was a fifty-year nuclear altercation with two full-fledged non-nuclear clashes, Korea and Vietnam, fought in its shadow, and innumerable surrogate wars, covert subversions of foreign governments, coups, incursions,

skirmishes, forays, international incidents, and nuclear weapons tests performed in its service. What is more, though the enemy to be contained was the Soviet Union, the creative animus of our warring was unleashed, to an astonishing degree, upon ourselves (Doctorow 1994: xi).

Given these understandings of South Africa's international "reality" and the absence of a competing message, there was little room for a more nuanced, people-driven approach to determining South Africa's role in the region. The country's move towards democracy has not changed this. Instead of focusing on destiny and vision, South Africa's "new" regional policy was caught between the national interests of the old South Africa and the unfolding uncertainty generated by the ending of the Cold War. This raises the issue of South Africa's transition.

Politics in the "new" South Africa is, above all, about compromise and re-invention. This is symbolized in the country's Government of National Unity (GNU): a four-year interim arrangement during which representatives of the main political parties jointly govern the country.[5] Given these arrangements, the bureaucracy has been primarily charged with carrying the transition and, secondly, with redefining its role in supporting the state. The dominant theme is continuity, not change. Although recast, the national interests of the state called South Africa have been sustained beyond apartheid, and carried forward in the various Departments of the state.

The existential situation is quite different, however. Shorn of the weight which apartheid placed on the state, both state makers and state-maintainers are now positioned to articulate a new set of objectives. In the absence of a thorough, far-reaching and democratically-driven foreign policy review, the most efficient way of meeting the international future was to re-invent a set of interests for the "new" South Africa. This explains why, for all its change, statements concerning the international relations of the post-apartheid state sound ominously like those of the "old" South Africa. This has found its strongest enunciation in the revised foreign policy document issued, after the country's first democratic election, by the African National Congress. It reads, in part:

> The essence of South Africa's foreign policy is to promote and protect the interests and values of its citizens. We prize our commitment to peace and the promotion of human dignity in the far corners of the globe, but recognize that the security of our people and their yearning for a non-racial, non-sexist democracy also lies close to our foreign policy (ANC 1994).

Given the unsettling conditions generated both by the ending of the Cold War and apartheid, it is easy to understand the appeal of these sentiments for bureaucrats and politicians. The platform for this was established during the formal transitional process. The Sub-Council on Foreign Affairs of the country's Transitional Executive Council recommended that:

the foreign policy of South Africa should primarily be shaped by its domestic policies and objectives, and should be directed at serving the needs and interests of its peoples (Recommendations from the Sub-Council on Foreign Affairs 1994).

The effect of this approach on Southern Africa is, however, potentially devastating. South Africa's regional policy is being shaped by a series of myths which are rooted in the institutional memory of the apartheid state.

In a fragile and poorly developed region, South Africa as the strongest state is reaching towards the twenty-first century armed with several strands of realist thought which, unfortunately, have survived in spite of 100 years of colonialism, racism, apartheid and a Cold War: state-centrism, national interest, foreign policy based on perceived threats from "outside" the state, and defence policy based on military preparedness.

This hostile view of the world and the region has been seized upon by a new generation of state-promoters. The Institute of Defence Policy, for example, is driving South Africa's regional security agenda in South Africa (Booth and Vale 1995). Its efforts aim, essentially, at re-creating the South African defence force by establishing a new role for it on the sub-continent, in particular, and on the continent, in general. However, this "new" role is largely based on old thinking about security (see Swatuk and Omari, Chapter 5).

If this is the security dimension of South Africa's approach to the region, its economic engagement is taking its cues from a confused series of signals around the centrality of market driven solutions to human problems. Because both the ending of the Cold War and apartheid have ruined the compass of international navigation, new bearings have emerged. For many in South Africa and elsewhere, these are provided by a new economic determinism which is rooted in the purported "success" of the market revolution of the 1990s. In this view, market forces and trade relations are set to become the navigational poles for global politics.

This dimension of regional relations has been reinforced by the holding power of South African capital. Their role in the transition has been central because they have managed to carry a debate that links economic progress, transition and democracy (see Gelb, Chapter 3). In part this has been possible only by default. The collapse of the socialist alternative has almost entirely silenced a competing narrative, notwithstanding the relative strength of the South African trade union movement. As a result, many believe that the market option is the only option for South Africa's international relations. Put differently, the country has little or no choice but to fall into line with the dominant international economic system. To ensure its "success" means that it will have to become a compliant state within the emerging global economic order (*Report of Commission Three* 1993).

In following this approach, South Africa's evolving trade relations with its neighbours have become strained and testy: the region is after all the natural hinterland for South African manufactured goods (see Davies, Chapter 6; and Swatuk, Chapter 7). But given international competition, this is a zero-sum game: South Africa's export success will, in all likelihood, destroy the possibility for industrial growth in the rest of the region (see Keet 1994).

There is also a security cost to this economic determinism. South Africa's arms industry is purported to be very competitive; while this is contested ground, it remains an attractive option for South African business interests. In addition, the logic for continuing the sale of arms beyond the apartheid system is compelling when measured against international norms: everyone does it, so why should South Africa take the moral high ground at the expense of a proven foreign exchange earner? There is also a compelling internal argument: money earned from the sale of weapons can be used for national reconstruction and development.

All this has profoundly touched Southern Africa where Armscor, the country's parastatal arms manufacturer, is selling weapons to the region (*Commission of Inquiry into Alleged Arms Transactions between Armscor and one Eli Wazan and Other Related Matters* 1995). South Africa, it seems, is buying regional insecurity in exchange for hard cash. This highlights the region's central paradox: on the one hand, there are the needs of nation-building in South Africa; on the other hand, there is the equally pressing and indissolubly related need to overcome regional underdevelopment. The former seeks to limit South Africa's involvement in the region except where it directly enhances South Africa's nation-building capacity (e.g., through the export of manufactured goods, be they bullets or blankets). The latter seeks to integrate South Africa on more equitable terms, so that all states in the region move forward together (see Davies, Chapter 6).

Change in South Africa has excited great expectations throughout the region. Not only is the pan-Africanist ideal of a single, seamless continent much closer but, more immediately, the region's people believe that they will now be able to enjoy the fruits of the region's single economy.

Faced with serious reversals within their own states, the region's people have, it seems, put their faith in South Africa and its remarkable President, Nelson Mandela. But this has brought them up against another face of South Africa: one which is grounded in the security fears of the apartheid state; one which is fearful of outsiders and hostile towards their intrusion.

This brings us back to policy. During the transitional process, South Africa's regional policy has aimed to harness the dialectic of change in the service of continuity; it has mapped the future out of the fears of the past; it has used the argument about the market ostensibly to entrench its own security but appears, instead, to have deepened feelings of insecurity. Given all this, South Africa's victory over racism has given the people of the region little cause for celebration.

Charting the Future

These are early days, to be sure. Although the word miracle has been regularly associated with its transition, it has not been possible to simply sweep away the past. The charting of a new regional policy has been acutely impaired by the process of transformation within key ministries in South Africa. And, in the public domain, the debate on South Africa's relations with the region is, if not silent, then largely inarticulate.[6]

Important though these immediate influences are in determining policy direction, they will be overshadowed by the simple fact that Southern Africa is serviced by a single economy. Understanding this is the key to the region's future incorporation. Although South Africa's policy is resistant, the centripetal forces of globalization are drawing the region closer together in real ways. Economies of scale are shrinking it. The region's labour force considers itself, and often acts, as a single unit. Electricity supply and water are increasingly managed as a single market. And much of the region's business community sees the region as a single market.

But change in the post-Cold War period shows that every centripetal force is matched by a centrifugal one. Globalization is a two-way process. Important features of the regional landscape are disintegrating. In some places, driven by deepening ethnic consciousness and a disillusionment with the nation-state project, irredentism has emerged as a powerful force; in others, the lure of Southern Africa itself is weakening. This is why Angola, as it thinks about its own future, is looking across the Atlantic and towards its northern neighbours.

As the forces of regional integration and disintegration play out, South Africa's formal management of Southern African issues remains grounded within dated approaches to policy questions. As a result, outcomes remain wholly unpredictable and deeply unsettling. These will generate insecurity among states and societies and touch the course of regional events.

Rekindled by the influence of new state makers, the debate on the region's security, for example, has evoked a sense of *déjà vu*. South Africa's planners continue to argue for military preparedness on the basis of the binary—"we" versus "they"—logic which was a feature of their Cold War/destabilization strategy. A draft of the Defence White Paper, published in June 1995, while admitting that "the prospects for peace and stability are greater than ... at any other time in recent decades," continued to urge the importance of military preparedness in terms of the imagined wars so loved by military planners (Government of South Africa 1995: 18).

True, the arc of security interests has opened. And equally true, there is a recognition that socio-economic complications retard, rather then advance, the cause of security in the region. But the essence of the regional security perspective remains: the region is a "threat" to South Africa's sovereignty. As a result, state makers in post-apartheid South Africa remain geared to fight a war in Southern Africa.

Understanding the impact of this view in the region is only possible through the matrix of Herz's security dilemma. As strong and rich South Africa is itself armed, its neighbours are pushed towards the acquisition of their own arms. This is a familiar quandary in security studies. During the Cold War it was frequently manifest, particularly in Eastern Europe where the domination of the region by the Soviet Union generated structural insecurity amongst its neighbours (Booth and Vale 1995).

Escaping this trap is a challenge for South Africa's policy makers. Can they envisage a region in which the notion of threat is not present? Their immediate answer seems to be no. Although genuflecting to the idea that security can be opened towards the widening agenda of "new security thinking," there is little evidence that South Africa's military and intelligence planners believe that sociological, political and constitutional solutions have anything to offer to long-term security in the region.

As Swatuk and Omari point out in Chapter Five below, this is contrary to evidence on the ground. Southern Africa's borders are crumbling. As elsewhere, the centripetal forces of globalism seem to be eroding many of the vestiges of national sovereignty. Beyond the border-posts, it is increasingly difficult to demarcate where one "state" ends and the next begins. Nothing highlights this more dramatically than the flow of migrants throughout the region.

Migrant labour has been a feature of the Southern African landscape for more than a century; indeed, the growth of the region's single economy turned on the free flow of labour. The mining and industrial base at the core of South Africa's wealth, and of the region's economy, was based on the ready participation of neighbouring peoples. If the free flow of labour fuelled the region's relative economic strength—however asymmetrically—it also created the illusion that its absorptive capacity was endless. Global change, which has shrunk world labour requirements, has shown the region to be finite: for all its natural resources and the talent of its many peoples, Southern Africa cannot create jobs for all.

In the divide between expectations of infiniteness and the reality of finite capacity, lie the seeds of conflict and, almost as important, deep disappointment for Southern Africa's peoples. Squeezed by the crisis of the African state and, from the 1980s, by the structural adjustment crisis, the peoples of the region have turned towards South Africa. Armed with their understandings of the past and anticipating a better future, Southern Africans are marching on South Africa.

Can South Africa Carry this Burden?

As Southern Africans search for nodes on which to build stability, they are having to balance the pathologies of weak states and failing polities against the increasing self-assurance of post-apartheid South Africa. Not only is South Africa the world's darling, it is in the throes of a potent project of nation-building which has seen the country draw together in both celebration and economic reconstruction. In its exuberance, its sheer size and its military and economic power, the "new" South Africa promises, as noted earlier, to distort the equation necessary to ensure regional stability.

Early approaches to and perceptions of the problem of illegal migration provide a trenchant example of this kind of distortion. Estimates suggest that there are anywhere between two million and nine million migrants in the country.[7] This influx has brought to the fore the unappealing face of nationalism in a region which, formally, is intent on forging a unity of purpose. For, media and even official portrayals of migrants in the "new" South Africa have been extremely negative; proposed "solutions" have bordered on the jingoistic. As a result, opposing illegal migration has become a powerful unifying force in South Africa's search for common national values (Solomon 1996). Unfortunately, however, "demonizing" the "other" also reinforces the security dilemma and weakens the region.

Yet, South Africa's new vitality also has opened up new footholds which can, with great imagination, help generate an entirely different regional configuration. This is where the country's foreign and domestic policy increasingly mesh.

The new South Africa's approach to regional relations turns, as I have argued, on the same myths which helped both found and consolidate the state itself. These assumed, to all intents and purposes, that the colonial creations which became nation states were permanent fixtures. The states of the region are not 'textbook cases', however; they are the creations of outside powers. The debate on South Africa's constitutional future demonstrates this in clear and unequivocal terms.

An important and, at the time of writing, highly uncertain feature of this equation is the search for power by South Africa's nine provinces. As they seek to understand themselves in a globalized world and their role in "building" a new state, these new entities are increasingly called upon to play a role in the world beyond South Africa. As they define their own personalities, South Africa's nine provinces are increasingly involved in foreign policy issues.

The immediate evidence for this is obvious. Seven of the nine provinces abut one or more international border(s). Only two, Gauteng and the Western Cape, do not directly touch foreign soil. These, however, interface with intense international traffic: the former through the country's busiest airport; the latter through the harbour in Cape Town. These various international links suggest that the central state is losing the capacity to exclusively determine and control the country's foreign relations. As provinces (and other political actors within them) become more self-assertive, the processes of South Africa's international interactions are programmed to deepen, but also become more varied and complex. Already there are signs that provincial leaders understand that lasting security at a local level means generating accord with the states around them.[8]

These imaginative responses to the new issues of the region can appear as quite natural to the rhythm of its peoples. This is why the announcement, in May 1995, by Matthews Phosa, the Premier of South Africa's Mpumalanga (formerly Eastern Transvaal) province, that he would seek an "economic bloc" with both Swaziland and the southern provinces of Mozambique was greeted with equanimity. For centuries the indigenous people of this fertile triangle of African lowveld have considered themselves united by the bonds of blood, barter and the search for a better life. They speak a common language, the area engages in a rich exchange of goods, labour and contraband, and—as has happened so often in Africa—the border between the states is a powerful growth point.

In essence, Phosa has re-asserted a series of regional truths. Southern Africa's peoples belong together by more than dint of geography; ancient ties of kinship straddle each of the region's contemporary and historical national boundaries. This historical confluence of forces has been reinforced by porous national borders which have helped build a single, albeit highly uneven, economy. By offering solutions to people on the ground, Phosa is eroding the myths which created the region's current maps and probing new forms of sub-regionalism.

Through this formal process of building ties which, in many cases, have continued to exist informally, a surprising number of everyday problems may be overcome. As people [re]unite, localized economies of scale will come into effect, particularly if entrepreneurs are given space to develop in lands beyond their juridical borders. Within free areas of movement, the creative impulse of border economies can be harnessed and extended.

This new route for Southern Africa accepts that national borders dare not be used as water-tight instruments of control; and that the writing of the region's future history needs to be based on a single axiom: what is good for states is not necessarily good for ordinary people. There is no point in pretending that this path will be uncontested, however. Having intensely struggled for the state, South Africa's new leaders are not simply about to surrender it to forces which may lead to its dilution.

More importantly, one of South Africa's provinces, KwaZulu-Natal, shows strong evidence of wanting to break away from the country. There is no guarantee that others will not, in future, share similar feelings. Given its immediate political priorities of nation-building, the country's center will not be inclined to encourage further irredentism. But this open question remains: in a shrinking world, how long can they hold the ring?

Tying Up Loose Ends

Like so many other things in our world, the study of South Africa's regional relations can never be what it once was. The ending of the Cold War and the onward march of a New International Division of Labour have changed conventional understandings of events. One of the central tragedies, however, is that political systems are invariably geared for continuity not change; bureaucracies, and the routines necessary for their survival, resist innovation, let alone re-invention.

Although limited, the space offered by the ending of apartheid and the towering international reputation of South Africa's President, Nelson Mandela, have created strategic footholds in Southern Africa. These will not be permanent, however. The process of learning is always less painful than the infinitely more important process of unlearning old habits. Moreover, the way in which various ministries, particularly Defence and Foreign Affairs, have approached the transition process suggests that caution and rote-learning is thought to be the safest course to follow in times judged to be, not full of opportunity, but rife with peril and uncertainty.

This has important consequences for those who make policy. Until the 1990s, international relationships relied on the parameters set by the Cold War to determine policy. Actions were set within predetermined confines; indeed, it was from the comfort of these confines that the minority conducted its foreign policy. The consequences of actions were predicated on the permanence of this international condition. The Cold War provided both licence and limitation.

But the painful consequences of its ending have changed this: no longer set within predictable parameters, the policy choices have shifted in a new direction. The cost calculation for states no longer rests on taking decisions which will affect policy; the cost now falls on the price of not making policy choices. As argued in this chapter, to not make policy choices means either to fall back on previous, outdated policy routines—as seems to be the case with foreign policy—or to abdicate your right to make policy and lose it to others—as seems to be the case with economic policy.

This has important consequences for an international backwater like Southern Africa. The price for not settling the South African issue was, almost assuredly, another African disaster. But having having apparently dodged this fate, South Africans have to change the way in which they run the affairs of the region. If they fail to do so, the option they most feared— deepening poverty and intensified conflict—can still occur. But it may also be avoided. The challenge to those who have traditionally made South Africa's regional policy is to liberate themselves from a narrow threat-based understanding of the country's regional priorities and to understand that South Africa's real interests in Southern Africa can only be determined by the interests of all those who have helped to create it.

Notes

1. For a more comprehensive discussion of these "realities," see Chapter Five of this volume.

2. For the record we need to note that destabilization is estimated to have cost $62.4 billion and, far more importantly, is said to have left more than one million people dead. The presence of an estimated ten million landmines in Mozambique, and several million in Angola, ensure that the "residual" effects of destabilization will be felt for many years to come.

3. Chapters 5 and 7 of this volume go some way toward redefining the Southern African "region" beyond separate "state" identities.

4. These were the ethnically-designed states called "Transkei," "Bophuthatswana," "Venda" and "Ciskei" (collectively called the TBVC states); they were recognized by no other state but South Africa and conducted diplomatic relations in, and amongst, themselves.

5. The 1996 withdrawal of the National Party from the GNU did not fundamentally alter its approach to governing.

6. This was clearly demonstrated in media reports of the Annual SADC Consultative Conference held in Midrand South Africa in February 1996. The press chose to highlight the divisiveness of the meeting, rather than focus on tangible achievments and opportunities (See, for example, *Weekly Mail and Gaurdian*, 2-8 February 1996; and *The Star*, 2 February 1996).

7. Statistics, it is said, reveal everything: the variance in this particular one may spell disaster. A hard, but certain, lesson of contemporary public policy is that states which cannot collect reliable statistics are unlikely to be able to deliver to their citizens let alone the millions who live deeper in the shadows!

8. The following arguments are based on Peter Vale and Khabela Matlosa 1995.

References

African National Congress (ANC). 1994. *Foreign Policy in a New Democratic South Africa*. Johannesburg.

Booth, Ken and Peter Vale. 1995. "Security in Southern Africa: after apartheid, beyond realism," *International Affairs* 19: 285-304.

Buzan, Barry. 1991. *People, States and Fear*. Second edition. Boulder: Lynne Rienner.

Commission of Inquiry into Alleged Arms Transactions between Armscor and one Eli Wazan and other Related Matters. 1995. Pretoria.

Doctorow, E.L. 1994. *Poets and Presidents. Selected Essays. 1977-1992*. London: Papermac.

Frost, Mervyn. 1993. "South Africa in the World: Political and Diplomatic," in *Report of Commission Three: South Africa and the World: A new vision*.

George, Jim. 1994. *Discourses of International Relations Theory*. Boulder: Lynne Rienner.

Government of South Africa. 1995. *Defence White Paper*.

Keet, Dot. 1994. *The Neo-Liberal Challenge to Prospects for Development Co-operation and Integration in Southern Africa*. Institute for African Alternatives (IFAA) Occasional Paper No. 11. Johannesburg: IFAA.

Report of Commission Three: South Africa and the World: A new vision. 1993. Unpublished report on a conference organized jointly by the South African Institute of International Affairs and the Centre for Southern African Studies, University of the Western Cape, Johannesburg.

Solomon, Hussein. 1996. "From Uncertainty to Confusion: the Illegal Immigrant Question in South Africa," paper presented to the international meeting on *South Africa Within Africa: Emerging Policy Frameworks*, Johannesburg, 24-27 January 1996.

Southall, Roger. 1994. "The New South Africa in the New World Order: beyond the double whammy," *Third World Quarterly* 15(1) (March): 121-37.

Suttner, Raymond. 1995. "Parliament's Role in Foreign Policy," *Indicator South Africa* 12(3) (Winter): 74-8.

Swatuk, Larry A. and David R. Black. 1995. *The "New" South Africa in Africa: Issues and Approaches*. York Centre for International and Strategic Studies Occasional Paper No. 30. March. Toronto: YCISS, York University.

South African Institute of International Affairs(SAIIA). 1974. Unpublished papers from a conference entitled *International Implications of the Independence of Transkei*, Umtata, Transkei, Eastern Cape.

Vale, Peter. 1995. "Continuity Rather Than Change: South Africa's 'New' Foreign Policy," *Indicator South Africa* 12(3) (Winter): 79-84.

———. 1994a. "External Pressure for Change in South and Southern Africa," in Gavin Maasdorp and Alan Whiteside, eds., *Towards a Post-Apartheid Future*. London: Macmillan.

———. 1994b. *Of Laagers, Lepers and Leanness: South Africa and Regional Security in the mid-1990s*. Bergen: Christian Michelson Institute.

——— and Khabela Matlosa. 1995. "Beyond and Below: The Future of the Nation-State in Southern Africa," *Harvard International Review* XVII(4) (Fall): 34-7, 83-4.

Walker, R.B.J. 1993. *Inside/Outside: toward a social theory of international relations*. Cambridge: Cambridge University Press.

———. 1988, *One World, Many Worlds: Struggles for a just world peace*. Boulder: Lynne Rienner.

5

Regional Security: Southern Africa's Mobile "Front Line"

Larry A. Swatuk and Abillah H. Omari

A common security approach will remain necessary in the post-apartheid era despite the fact that there is little prospect of external aggression against individual states or the region as a whole ... [M]any of the domestic threats to states are shared problems and undermine the stability of neighbouring countries. In addition, since the sub-continent is politically volatile and its national and regional institutions are weak, internal conflicts could easily give rise to cross-border tensions.

— Nathan and Honwana (1995: 6)

[T]he continent's security problems must be tackled as an urgent priority to pave the way for stability, democratization and prosperity ... [I]n accepting this challenge, Africans need to adopt a cautious approach, not only towards what is possible and what is not, but also in building from national institutions upwards and not from regional institutions downwards ... Even so, the return to stability, democracy and prosperity in South Africa and Southern Africa is sure to be slow and tortuous.

— Cilliers (1994: 49)

It is hardly a revelation to say that Southern Africa is a region in crisis, for this line of argumentation has an impeccable pedigree. From Halpern's study of "hostages" to apartheid in the 1960s, to Grundy's look at "conflict" and "accommodation" in the 1970s; from Carter and O'Meara's examination of the "continuing crisis" at the start of the 1980s, to Johnson and Martin's discussion of "apartheid destabilization" at that decade's end, there has been no shortage of informed analysis of high-political struggle in the regional "sub-system" (see Bowman 1968; Carter and O'Meara 1982; Grundy 1973; Halpern 1964; Hanlon 1986; Johnson and Martin 1989). Yet, to say that the region is highly troubled today is to be somewhat out of step with presently more optimistic moods and times.

To be sure, there are important reasons for more optimistic perspectives on the region at the end of the millennium. First, the end of the Cold War has removed one layer of complexity in analyses of and approaches to regional security in Southern Africa (Buzan 1991). Second, this has paved the way for several positive developments, among them, Namibia's independence, political settlements in Angola and Mozambique, democratic elections in Zambia, Lesotho, Malawi and Tanzania, and the end of apartheid in South Africa.

Third, at the theoretical level, these global and regional shifts in praxis have allowed hitherto marginalized and/or unconventional approaches to the study of (regional) security to gain legitimacy.[1] Arms races, alliance systems and well-patrolled state borders have been joined by socio-economic disparities, environmental change, and the spread of populations, cultures, pollutants, and infectious diseases as primary "threats" to "security" in the late-20th century world. In addition, notions of "human security" and "common security," as complicated and nebulous as these concepts are (see below),[2] now challenge traditionally emphasized "state security" as the ultimate policy goal for the next millennium.

Taken together, numerous scholars and policy makers regard these changes in analysis and praxis as hopeful markers for regional renewal. According to Southall (1995a: 3),

> An era of regeneration and inter-state cooperation throughout the Southern African region seems possible with the fall of apartheid, the democratization process that has taken place throughout the region, and the winding down of the externally fuelled civil conflicts in Angola and Mozambique ... Central to the new optimism that now defines the region has been the conviction that relations between South Africa and its neighbours will now be based on mutual trust in a shared project of regional peace and development.

This "new optimism" is leading the discourse on Southern Africa's security problematique toward what Nathan and Honwana (1995: 4) term "new thinking" on security[3]: "In contrast to the traditional preoccupation with the security of the state and the military aspects of security, the new model emphasizes the security of people and non-military dimensions of security."[4] Its appropriateness for the Southern African region, as Southall suggests, stems fundamentally from apartheid's demise. For, in the absence of apartheid, Southern Africa's states face no threat of military invasion. Rather, "many of the major threats to the countries of the region are political, social, economic and environmental rather than military in character, and derive more from internal than external factors" (Nathan 1993: 5; also, Bardill 1994, for an overview of these "threats"). It is for this reason, states Nathan, that

[w]hat is required at conceptual and strategic levels is a new approach to security, concerned not only with defence but also with the pursuit of democracy, sustainable economic development, social justice and protection of the environment (1993: 5).

But how capable are Southern Africa's states of banding together in the name of "common security"? What kinds of "threats" exist to pull them apart and perhaps place them at odds with each other in future? Now that the glue of the liberation struggle has come unstuck along with apartheid, what new challenges to the region will serve to bind these states together and keep them from drifting apart? And if regional security cooperation is to be forged, who gets to define the agenda and terms of agreement?

These are significant and vexing questions which fly in the face of optimistic moods and analyses. In this chapter we examine the potential for emerging regional security mechanisms to foster "common security" in the face of numerous unconventional threats—increasing poverty and economic underdevelopment, rapid population growth, migration and refugee movements, AIDS, and environmental crises—to the security of the individual, state and region. We situate this analysis within the context of historical approaches to regional "security," specifically the emergence of regional schemes and institutions designed to enhance security, and through an examination of the so-called "new thinking" on security. While we, too, are hopeful for the region, in the end we counsel caution especially regarding the ability of existing regimes, institutions and bureaucracies to "rethink" their approaches to security in a region riven by historical and contemporary forms and causes of inequality and instability.

"Old Thinking" on Security: Drawing the Frontline

New approaches to regional security depend, in large part, on the ability of state makers in the Southern African Development Community (SADC) to remake regional relations along more inclusive lines. This is no small task. For, in the context of the Cold War and struggles against colonialism and apartheid, Southern Africa's regional relations were conflictual, divisive, and exclusive (Hanlon 1986; Johnson and Martin 1989). Battle lines were drawn clearly between forces for political and economic change (i.e., independence movements, many of which later became pro-communist or -socialist) and forces for the *status quo* (i.e., neo-colonial and settler groups using Cold War rhetoric to maintain exploitative race-based power). Uneven capitalist development, which led to South Africa's hegemonic position in the region, served to exacerbate regional inequalities and heighten animosities.[5]

These were state-centric struggles: either for control of the state (as in Angola, Mozambique, Namibia, South Africa and Zimbabwe); or of one coalition of states (e.g., the Frontline States, formed in 1976, or the Southern

African Development Coordination Conference, formed in 1980) against another (e.g., Rhodesia and/or South Africa). Each side offered up visions of peaceful future regional relations. Each side was dependent on competing and carefully constructed myths about the sources of tension in the region. So, whereas apartheid-fuelled "destabilization" was the cause of regional instability in the eyes of SADCC and the FLS, a "total communist onslaught" necessitating "total strategy" and therefore the militarization of South African society was the cause of instability in the eyes of Pretoria's power wielders (see, for example, Amin et al 1987; Geldenhuys 1984; Grundy 1986).

It was not until shortly after 1980, however, that the use of coercive rather than cooptive force came to dominate Pretoria's strategy. 1980 was a watershed year in regional relations for three inter-related reasons. First, Zimbabwe came to independence under the leadership of an avowed Marxist, Robert Mugabe. South Africa's preferred candidate, Bishop Abel Muzorewa, had been soundly defeated in the pre-independence elections. Second, the independence of Zimbabwe marked the culmination of five years of activity on the part of the Frontline States coalition. At independence, Zimbabwe became yet another radical member of that group—with Botswana the lone democratic and capitalist state—whose activities now turned to the liberation of South Africa. Third, the nine majority-ruled states of the region formed SADCC, clearly rejecting Pretoria's Constellation of Southern African States (CONSAS) proposal.[6]

Zimbabwe's independence was thought to be crucial to the future of the SADCC states. It gave to the idea of regional economic cooperation beyond South Africa "a new kiss of life because of the strategic importance of Zimbabwe for countries like Botswana and Zambia" (Tsie 1989: 8). Not only was SADCC to be centered around the industrial power of Zimbabwe—thus posing a threat, in theory at least, to South Africa's economic domination of the region—it also included as members those states previously considered most dependent upon and/or aligned with South Africa (i.e., Lesotho, Malawi and Swaziland), thus giving the impression that Pretoria was losing control of its destiny.

For South African policy makers, SADCC's mandate, though couched in economic terms, was clearly and correctly perceived as political. In light of the extended nature of this perceived threat, South Africa's military-oriented policy makers saw regional destabilization as, quite possibly, their last resort.

The main point to be drawn from this discussion of regional organization and political response is that both the South African state and the SADCC states defined the major threats to their respective securities as each other. Yet, in the end, neither SADCC nor South Africa was made more secure. Almost every step of the way the basis for future inter-state cooperation was undermined. Regional schemes (e.g., CONSAS) and institutions (e.g., SADCC) were created not with "co-prosperity" in mind, but out of contending "needs" for state-based survival.

This legacy has cost the region dearly. Military "solutions" not only killed thousands and displaced millions (Johnson and Martin 1989), they also served to exacerbate the structural deformities of these countries' political economies entrenched since colonial times (Stoneman and Thompson 1991). The focus on regional military confrontation has severely reduced the capacities of Southern Africa's states to deal with continuing crises brought on by the region's declining importance in the global economy; in Mozambique and Angola, for example, military spending was absorbing "as much as 40 percent of total state expenditure by the end of the 1980s" (SADCC 1991a: 13; also Steiner 1993). This has, in turn, heightened domestic and transnational sources of instability, forcing political and economic elites into more and more defensive modes of survival (see Bardill 1994). This, also in turn, inhibits the emergence of a shared sense of regional identity and limits the ability for "new thinking" on regional security to emerge. In Ohlson and Stedman's (1994) words, "the new is not yet born."

The Need for Common Security

"Common security," simply put, is the recognition by state makers that the protection of neither the state nor its citizens is possible through unilateral, particularly military, means. In an increasingly interdependent world order, states "share an interest in joint survival and should begin to organize their security policies in cooperation with each other" (Nathan and Honwana 1995: 5). In addressing wider, non-region specific security questions *The Bonn Declaration* arrived at the concepts of "global commons" and "global human security," i.e., "the absence of threat to human life, lifestyle and culture through the fulfilment of basic needs" (*The Bonn Declaration* 1993). This broader, non-state centric conception of "security" is echoed in the UNDP's *Human Development Report 1993* (UNDP 1993: 1) and has been further articulated in the recent Commission on Global Governance report, *Our Global Neighbourhood*. According to the Commission, "global security must be broadened from the traditional focus on the security of states to include the security of people and the security of the planet" (1995: 11).[7]

This perspective is particularly important in Southern Africa. Given the arbitrariness of state formation, the history of migration, and the legacy of uneven capitalist development there, state-centric approaches to security are likely to be unsustainable—even in South Africa (see Vale, Chapter 4).

In the absence of apartheid, current "threats" "are as much developmental as they are security challenges" (Southall 1995a: 4; also Cheru 1992: 8-20). Prior to either apartheid's or the Cold War's end, however, raising questions about the meaning and objects of "security" or the nature of long-term "threats" was pointless. The contours of security were clear. The importance of regional events rose and fell with the high politics of the global system. Now, with the emergence of a "new" South Africa in a "new" world order these security contours demand redefinition. South African policy makers, in particular, have a unique opportunity to re-imagine their role in the regional community (cf. Anderson 1981): i.e., to live with and among rather than "up against" their neighbours. As an integral part of the region, South Africa can use its comparative economic, political and military might in constructive ways, to contribute to regional growth and redirection in the name of common security.

Locating the "New" Frontline: New Threats to Security

Regional cooperation is needed now more than ever. Not only do states and peoples in the region face similar developmental and transnational threats to their security; the region also suffers from what might be termed the residuals of apartheid. For example,

> [f]ollowing the years of liberation wars, destabilization and a full-scale conventional war in southern Angola, the region is awash with arms, especially small arms, distributed by entrepreneurs. The smuggling of weapons into South Africa, probably through Swaziland, Lesotho, Botswana and perhaps even Zimbabwe, is a case in point (Breytenbach 1994: 54).

Whether state makers in the region will be up to the task remains to be seen. Before discussing some of the proposed mechanisms for managing regional security, we first turn to a brief discussion of several "unconventional" threats to security: (i) poverty and economic marginalization; (ii) refugees; (iii) rapid population growth and environmental degradation; and (iv) AIDS. What will be clear from this discussion is the fluidity of the new "frontline": no longer can threats be minimized by amassing strong armies along clearly defined borders. Rather, they require the careful construction of regional approaches to security cooperation on many fronts, at "home" and "abroad."

Poverty and Economic Marginalization

The Southern African region has not been exempt from the general crisis facing the continent (Chege 1995).[8] According to the African Development Bank,

> In Southern Africa, as in the rest of the continent, domestic policy shortcomings, an adverse external environment, the collapse of prices of primary commodities, mounting external indebtedness and declining net flows of investments all contributed to the weak or declining economic performance of countries in the region. The net result has been persistence of

poverty, deterioration of the productive and infrastructural facilities, and rapidly declining standards of social services and human welfare (1994: v).

Throughout the region, small internal markets, unequal income distributions and high tariff walls have limited competitive production for wider regional and global markets. Highly subsidized and inefficient industries have long been producing for constricted markets (Stoneman 1991: 2). According to Buzan,

> Weak states may find themselves trapped by historical patterns of economic development and political power which leave them underdeveloped and politically penetrated, and therefore unable to muster the economic and political resources necessary to build a stronger state (1991: 99).

These inherited developmental weaknesses also inhibit the capacity to build a stronger region. Given this legacy of economic underdevelopment, Human Development Index (HDI) indicators reveal a high level of poverty in the region. On the HDI scale nine of the eleven SADC states are classified as having a low level of human development (i.e., less than 0.50). These are Angola, Lesotho, Malawi, Mozambique, Namibia, Swaziland, Tanzania, Zambia, and Zimbabwe. South Africa and Botswana are considered as having medium levels of human development (i.e., between 0.50 and 0.799). South Africa, however, has a very skewed domestic pattern of human development based along both racial and regional lines. Whites enjoy a quality of life comparable to countries with a high HDI while a majority of Blacks endure levels of poverty in line with least developed country standards.

According to a recent Development Bank of South Africa study, HDI indicators vary widely from province to province within the "new" South Africa. For example, Western Cape, Northern Cape and Gauteng (formerly the PWV) provinces had HDI ratings of 0.76, 0.73 and 0.71 respectively. At the other end of the scale were the Eastern Cape at 0.48 and the North-West at 0.57 (see Southall 1995b: 9-10).

The state was supposed to be the prime mover in the eradication of poverty in Southern Africa. Not only has it failed in this task, it has subsequently declined even further (Bayart 1993). Its legitimacy, more often regime legitimacy, continues to be challenged. In many rural, peri-urban, and urban situations, especially those with one form or another of war-lordism, "government" has come to mean anyone who can deliver or provide personal and/or community security. Poverty breeds and heightens personal insecurity and, in the case of Southern Africa, people are very insecure indeed.

Refugees

Another non-traditional security issue clearly related to poverty and the state concerns refugees and their movements. We are used to defining refugees politically, i.e., as persons forced by various circumstances to flee from their places of origin for fear of losing their lives. Historically, Southern Africa has had several types of refugees. Today, in addition to political and economic refugees, environmental and internal refugees—or displaced persons—must be added to this list. Not only have conflicts in Angola and Mozambique "led to almost two million people fleeing across international borders in search of sanctuary," but economic and ecological devastation have displaced "millions more" within national borders (Whiteside 1994: 240).

Sudden large-scale population movements are a problem of long-standing in Southern Africa. The consequences, too, are long-lasting. To the host country, refugees often come like a fast-striking natural calamity: at an unknown time, leaving little if any opportunity for preparation. This should not be surprising. The host country may know from various signals the existence of problems that may cause refugees but it cannot prevent or preempt such problems. It may also know that the only possible refugee destination is itself. There is hardly anything the host country can do, and international conventions and humanitarian considerations basically force the host country to accept refugees regardless of their numbers.

Refugees, like those found in Eastern and Southern Africa, place enormous strains on host countries. Thousands of them flock in a matter of hours and days, normally entering at crossing points far away from the capital. Tanzania's recent experience with refugees from Rwanda and Burundi is a case in point.

Screening facilities are poor or non-existent. The problem becomes exacerbated since there are few or no resources to prepare for this eventuality. There are no tents, food, water, sanitation facilities, and medicines. Incoming peoples are forced to share already scarce resources with the host population, thus engendering conflict at a local level. Refugees also destroy the environment—e.g., through rapid deforestation from the use of trees for shelter and as fuelwood; pollution of waterways and resources; and depletion of game stocks in the struggle for survival. Epidemic diseases, like cholera, often arise and encompass everybody, including the host population. Under such circumstances the government of the host country is forced to stretch its meagre resources, and assistance from the international community is usually slow in coming.[9]

Refugee movements also impact upon traditional "security" issues. Social tensions arise between host and refugee populations. These, in turn, affect inter-state relations between the country of origin and the host. This includes, among other things, border closures, weapons infiltration, drug trafficking, poaching of protected wildlife, and in the future, children (citizens) with multiple nationality. The recent case of the refugee influx from Burundi and Rwanda to Tanzania and its impact on local populations and inter-state politics exemplifies this point.

Rapid Population Growth and Environmental Stress

Rapid population growth is a looming threat, particularly to economic development and environmental sustainability, in the Southern African region. A recent World Bank study estimates that Southern Africa's population will reach approximately 273 million by 2025. This marks a tripling of the population in a mere 45 years (World Bank 1995: 20).[10] "After another 100 years, the population might stabilize at about 560 million. Population growth is considered to be the single most important environmental issue facing the region" (ADB 1994: 38; Moyo et al 1993: 36, 92, 167, 205).

Population growth rates vary inversely with a country's level of socio-economic development (see UNICEF 1994). This is the case in both Sub-Saharan (see, for example, Kalipeni 1994: 4-7; Mhone 1994; UNICEF 1994) and Southern Africa. With the obvious exception of Botswana—which experienced real growth of 8.1 percent over the 1985-92 period in spite of an extremely high population growth rate of 3.3 percent—all SADC countries combined low rates of economic growth (between 1.4 percent and -2.1 percent) with high rates of population growth (on average 2.9 percent) (World Bank 1994: 18-19; and 1992: 268-69 as quoted in Van Wyk 1994; also, ADB 1994: 38).

Mhone (1994: 198) identifies two "ominous" trends in population growth patterns of Southern Africa's countries. The first is that the population will be expanding at a rapid pace over the next two decades. The second is that the demographic structure of these societies is likely to place an enormous burden on their economies—initially because of the large youthful population and later, over the next two decades or so, because of the expanding and aging adult population that will need jobs and health services.

The impact of rapid population growth, and of rapid urbanization in particular, is sure to be devastating. The combined and increasingly unsatisfied demand for jobs, housing, health care, sanitation and clean water, education, and even food[11] is already leading to serious social problems, including high crime rates and increased incidences of communicable disease, particularly in urban areas (Bardill 1994; Percival 1995; Whiteside 1994).[12]

At the same time, rapid population growth places great pressure upon the region's natural resource base. In the estimation of the World Bank, this base (defined as "natural capital") is said to be "rich in terms of biodiversity and production potential, although large areas are under semi-arid and arid conditions with a moderate to high risk of drought" (World Bank 1995: 20). The region faces numerous environmental threats, both natural and human made.[13] A survey of environmental "hot spots" in the region reveals not only their similarity of form (e.g., soil erosion, deforestation, industrial pollution, resource depletion) but also the similarity of circumstances leading up to these problems (e.g., population growth, rural poverty, dualistic economies and attendant pressures on the land) and their unvarying intractability (due, in part, to a wide variety of state incapacities, e.g., lack of data, finances, trained personnel, institutional coordination, monitoring and enforcement capabilities, and political will).[14]

To be sure, this is an eclectic and selective list of environmental stressors in Southern Africa. However, they each have important conflict-making potential. For changes to the environment tend to exacerbate social inequalities (see Swatuk, Chapter 7). Moreover, according to Percival (1995: 1):

> The social effects of renewable resource scarcities may endanger the stability of the post-apartheid period [for] [e]nvironmental scarcity in some areas of South Africa has reached a critical threshold; [and] in some cases the ecosystem has been irreversibly damaged.

So, the coincidence of rapid population growth and increasing environmental degradation are leading toward future struggles over resource scarcity. It is doubtful that, in the absence of significant levels of external financing, existing regional institutions can meet these myriad challenges. To be sure, SADC "as a regional body is beginning to address these issues" (Moyo et al 1993: 3); in addition, there is increasing concern and moral support for environmental policy-making at national and international levels. Yet, as Moyo et al (1993: 3,4) point out, "[T]here has been little political action to resolve environmental problems ... At present, there is significant institutional under-capacity in the environment sector." There are many who feel the regional "peace dividend" can assist in heading off environmental threats (IUCN 1993). This is an issue to which we return below.

AIDS

AIDS is a worldwide tragedy, and has affected and infected different parts of Southern Africa such that the region is said to be at "special risk" (see Whiteside 1994). Whiteside identifies nine inter-related factors which serve to exacerbate HIV and AIDS in Southern Africa (1994: 239-41):

- cross-border migration
- refugees
- conflict and civil war
- militarization
- drought
- poverty
- high levels of sexually-transmitted diseases (STDs)
- rural-urban linkages
- status of women

These factors combine in a deadly mix of mass population movements (both forced and voluntary), government incapacity (due to structural adjustment, poverty and war), female disempowerment (due to their "low status and comparative lack of power"), and human misery which serves as a breeding ground not only for sexually transmitted diseases but other forms of disease, like tuberculosis, which is said to be on the rise in Southern Africa (Whiteside 1994: 238-9).

Most rural populations in Southern Africa are not even aware of the disease, its causes and consequences. Educational campaigns touch limited segments of the population, primarily urban elites. In rural areas the disease is still associated with taboos and customs that encourage its spread. In most Southern African countries there are no mechanisms to control those who consciously or unconsciously spread the disease.

Available data suggest AIDS primarily affects the most economically active population, i.e., those between the ages of 18 and 45. It is no exaggeration to say that it is increasingly the most dangerous social problem of our time. In some parts of Southern Africa the figures are particularly alarming, with one to three percent of national populations said already to be infected.[15] One study suggests that "in the absence of significant behaviour change, the HIV epidemic is likely to peak at a prevalence rate below 30 percent of the adult population while with some change peak prevalence may be below 20 percent" (Doyle 1993: 109 as quoted in Whiteside 1994: 242). This is a threat to personal security and regional stability against which no amount of military spending can defend.

Institutional Responses in the "New" Southern Africa

It should, by now, be clear that Southern Africa faces myriad threats, almost all of which demand coordinated, regional responses and almost none of which can be considered "state-centric" problems. The achievement of "common security" requires more than a collective act of political will, though that too is an important variable. It also requires significant financial resources and adequate institutional responses. According to the World Bank (1992: 2),

> Improving the environment for development may make it necessary to raise investment rates in developing countries by 2-3 percent of GDP by the end of this decade. This would enable stabilization of soil conditions, increased protection of forests and natural habitats, improved air and water quality, doubling of family planning expenditures, sharply improved school enrolment for girls and universal access to sanitation and clean water by 2030.

However, as Steiner points out, even if the will is there in abundance, "the search for such resources in the Southern African context will be extremely difficult" (Steiner 1993: 9). At the same time, it is not clear what formal institutional arrangements will be necessary to tackle these problems, or how they will interact with the many and various groups in civil society already actively engaged in "common security."

Political Will

At present, state makers in Southern Africa are preoccupied with countless challenges, to both their societies and their own right to rule. Nevertheless, it is important to get political and other elites thinking in terms of common security. The "democratic moment" provides some hope for developments of this kind. Members of civil society, community-based organizations, less coherently formed social movements, and other associational groupings acting alone, in concert, or in alliance with international non-governmental and inter-governmental organizations are now more willing to articulate their needs and grievances (see Swatuk, Chapter 7). This development suggests that any movement toward a "common regional security regime" need not be exclusively elite-driven. At the same time, however, coordinated rapid responses to crises in Lesotho and Mozambique during 1994 suggest that, if nothing else, state makers may be willing to cooperate in the name of regional political stability. Despite shades of "gunboat diplomacy" (see Nathan and Honwana 1995), one cannot deny that these interventions were made to restore (in the case of Lesotho) or ensure the continuation of (in the case of Mozambique) democratic processes in the region (see the June 1995 issue of *Southern Africa REPORT*).[16]

Though largely symbolic, these actions nevertheless show the region's leaders' determination to pursue peaceful mechanisms to end regional conflicts, be they intra- or inter-state in nature. Zimbabwe's (former) Foreign Minister, Nathan Shamuyarira, called the action on Lesotho the beginnings of regional security cooperation to ensure stability and peace—"an arrangement to defend democratic trends in our region and to ward off the dictatorship and militarism present in other regions of the world" (Southscan 1994). Zimbabwean President Robert Mugabe added that the FLS would be setting a very dangerous precedent if it allowed the reversal of democracy in any Southern African country:

> If a country that has some democratic order is experiencing a situation where that order is being threatened by forces beyond its control, and that country appeals to its neighbours to assist, that is not a reversal of democracy (Martin 1994).

Symbolic or not, such actions have their own dangers, especially as they suggest that sabre-rattling and direct intervention can only work in Lesotho-type countries, i.e., those which are small and weak compared with the regional giants.[17] But as Minister Shamuyarira noted, these collective actions, taken in response to a perceived common regional threat, form the basis of a sustainable regional security regime.[18]

It is important not to lose sight of the fact that Southern Africans are attempting to create a "common front" among old and bitter adversaries. Ironically, it is the region's militaries which seem most keen on cooperation. For, it is the military which clearly recognizes the potential for "new" threats, if left unattended, to develop into "old" challenges to regional stability. Fortunately, as Southall (1995a: 6) notes,

> One of the most encouraging aspects of these developments has been the leading role played by South Africa, in particular the commitment displayed by senior figures in the South African National Defence Force (SANDF), most of whom have been retained from the former SADF.

Institutional self-preservation cannot be ruled out as a motivating factor in the military's "new thinking" on security. Early thinking on the proposed "peace dividend" for the region involved, first and foremost, disarmament and severely slashed defense budgets. Nervous militaries, their institutional credibility on the line, have therefore been working hard to redefine their own roles in a post-apartheid Southern Africa (CISS 1995).

Financial Resources

Clearly, one of the most pressing obstacles to regional security cooperation is lack of money. New funds were initially thought to be forthcoming from the region's "peace dividend." The militarization of societies and regional relations throughout the 1980s consumed vast amounts of resources better spent elsewhere. As Steiner points out (1993: 5-6):

> While South Africa was able to produce an increasing proportion of its own conventional weapons—and indeed earn export revenues in due course—the other states in the sub-region had to rely on imported arms from the world's arms producers and suppliers. Even during 1990, when detente had set in, South Africa still spent more than twice the amount on its military establishment than the entire SADC region put together ... [T]here can be little doubt that, given the need to import all military hardware, most countries in the region suffered severe "developmental setbacks," irrespective of the actual damage to infrastructure and the environment which resulted from the subsequent use of these weapons.

Yet, the "peace dividend" has been surprisingly slow to materialize, particularly in the "new" South Africa. Nathan and Honwana (1995: 8) illustrate the potential boost to regional cooperation to be given by unilateral South African moves toward disarmament and demilitarization. However, though in agreement with Nathan and Honwana, Steiner (1993) also describes the numerous barriers within militaries, military bureaucracies and society itself to such moves. Chief among these are (i) the inability of society to absorb and provide productive employment for tens of thousands of demobilized soldiers; (ii) loss of status and prestige; and (iii) an inability to rethink, let alone restructure, the military's role in society.

Each of these points bears some elaboration. First, there is anecdotal evidence from Angola, Namibia, Mozambique and South Africa that the rapid demobilization of forces does more harm than good. Former soldiers become rural and township-based warlords, and active participants in drugs, small arms and endangered wildlife trades (Bardill 1994). Yet, as Steiner points out, demobilization may not be so important as redeployment. This leads to the second and third points listed above.

The World Conservation Union (IUCN) suggests that the region's militaries need not unequivocally turn their swords into ploughshares. Rather, military resources have "dual uses" particularly where the conservation of nature is concerned. As can be seen in Table 5.1 below, there are numerous ways in which military personnel, hardware and financial resources can contribute to sustainable development in the region. Moreover, once militaries have been turned toward constructive, developmental tasks, funds normally designated for traditional "defence" expenditures may be released for alternative investments.

Steiner (1993), the IUCN (1993), Nathan (1993) and Nathan and Honwana (1995) all emphasize the need to be realistic when considering construction of a regional security regime. Turning former military adversaries toward sustainable development efforts may seem to be a reasonable beginning. However, such efforts and ideas run headlong into the military "ego." There remains considerable resistance on the part of the military being given tasks deemed unbefitting of trained fighters. There is a loss of prestige associated with conservation efforts. Many soldiers do not want to be seen as "garbage men" or "turtle sitters" (personal communication, Pretoria 1994). Moreover, this perceived loss of prestige combines with the inability of the military in particular, and society at large, to re-conceive of the military's place and role in society (Cock and Nathan 1989). It is for this reason that efforts at reorienting the military away from traditional roles toward "new security" issues should proceed cautiously, avoid radical departures, and pursue very specific programs of action:

> In order for such a process to take place there needs to be a concerted effort by government departments, the armed forces and the international donor community that would provide both a conceptual and logistical framework for such an initiative ... [S]uch a peace dividend needs to be based on a carefully assessed matrix of specific requirements and actual resources available. This needs to be complemented by political dialogue, technical expertise and financial assistance from the international donor community, which has a critical role to play as a catalyst (Steiner 1993: 16).

TABLE 5.1 An Overview of Potential Military Contributions to Natural Resource Management

Natural Resource Management	Activities	Medium to Long Term Tasks for Demobilized Soldier	Short to Medium Term Tasks for Elements of the Armed Forces
Protected Areas Management	- rehabilitation of infrastructure	x	x
	- surveys/assessments	x	x
	- employment as scouts/guards	x	x
	- anti-poaching assignments		x
Forestry Related Activities	-surveys/ assessments	x	x
	-plantation programs	x	
	-fire prevention	x	x
	-control/ supervision tasks	x	
	-utilization of forest products	x	
Wildlife Utilization Management	-establishment of wildlife management areas	x	x
	-surveys/ assessment tasks	x	
	-supervision of conservancies	x	x
	-wildlife management programs	x	x
Urban Environment	-urban rehabilitation activities	x	x
	-reestablishment of cityparks/facilities	x	x
	-refuse collection/ pollution control	x	x
	-city plantation (green lungs)	x	x
Coastal Areas and Wetlands	-rehabilitation/ clearing up tasks	x	x
	-survey/assessment tasks	x	x
	-protection/ supervision (e.g., mangrove forests, turtle nests, fisheries)	x	x
	-development/ supervision of artisanal fishing enterprises/ monitoring/ coastal patrols	x	x
	-provision of facilities for marine research	x	x

Land/Watershed Management	-erosion control measures	x	x
	-construction of small dams (e.g., water harvesting)	x	x
	-survey/assessment tasks		
	-watershed management/plantations	x	x
		x	x
	-mines and ammunition clearing in rural road networks and agricultural areas		x

Source: Adapted from Steiner 1993.

Framing Institutions

International support is presently available in many forms. For example, the IUCN continues to pursue its research program on the "peace dividend" in Southern Africa; the Nordics are supporting a number of peace-building initiatives, for example, a SIPRI-directed study of new security issues in Southern Africa; and the European Union is assisting SADC in developing a regional capacity for dealing with conflict resolution.[19] At the same time, there seems to be an opportunity to further involve the West in spite of proclaimed "aid fatigue." Conservation and other environmental issues, particularly as they constitute potential sites of future conflict, are hot topics for Western governments, academic institutions, international financial institutions, non-governmental and inter-governmental organizations. Moreover, the United States in particular is keen on pursuing sustainable democratic governance in the region.

The onus now seems to be on SADC state makers to decide how they will begin to deal with the new regional context of security and how international capital and expertise can be put to best use.

Not surprisingly, initial moves toward developing a regional security regime came, and continue to come, from existing regional organizations. For example, from its seeming decline in the first half of the 1980s (Omari 1991), partly caused by the erosion of its original mandate, the FLS, at the beginning of the 1990s, perceived its continued existence to be essential in overseeing the process of change in South(ern) Africa. To this end, the FLS increasingly moved into the complex area of regional security and development.

At the same time, SADC began moving along a parallel track. The SADC Program of Action for 1993 included new ideas for promoting regional peace and security.[20] In July 1994, SADC convened a Ministerial Workshop on Democracy, Peace and Security at Windhoek. According to Nathan and Honwana, the meeting was a watershed event for two reasons. First, it went beyond inter-ministerial discussions to include a wide range of individuals and institutions from the region. Second, it began to articulate a framework upon which to build a regional security regime.

It recommended the formation of a Human Rights Commission headed by judges and eminent persons; a Conflict Resolution Forum comprised of foreign ministers; a Security and Defence Forum composed of ministers responsible for defence, policing and intelligence; a SADC sector on security and defence; and an autonomous institute for strategic studies.

At the August 1994 SADC Summit in Gaborone, the organization welcomed South Africa as its eleventh member, absorbed the FLS, and approved the creation of a new sector on Politics, Diplomacy, International Relations, Defence and Security. Initially, it was felt that the new sector would be an integral element of SADC. Given the highly sensitive nature of its subject matter, however, it was decided at the March 1995 SADC Foreign Ministers Meeting in Harare that the "new security" agenda would be better dealt with by a separate but parallel organization known as the Association of Southern African States (ASAS).

ASAS is an inter-ministerial grouping which is to operate independently of the SADC secretariat but will report directly to the SADC summit. According to Southall (1995a: 4), ASAS is to be the "primary mechanism for dealing with conflict prevention, management and resolution in Southern Africa," and is meant to complement, not replace the Organization of African Unity (OAU) mechanism for conflict resolution. In reality, ASAS is the Inter-State Defence and Security (Ministerial) Committee of the FLS.

Indeed, one area in which the FLS, under the rubric of an expanded SADC, has shown propensity for new thinking on regional security has been its deliberate and forceful resuscitation of its Inter-State Defence and Security (Ministerial) Committee (ISDSC). After the impasse of 1993 and 1994, partly caused by debates in the region centering on the relevance of the Committee,[21] the FLS decided in late 1994 to strengthen it. At its meeting in Arusha in November 1994 the Committee was tasked with finding expression for its continued and revised role *within the SADC framework*. It is now urged to promote cooperation for collective security through the eradication of poverty and enhancement of regional development and integration.

Despite the emerging notion of new thinking about regional security, SADC has a long way to go to realize this objective. One problem that may hinder development is the proliferation of regional organizations. For example, the informality of the FLS, its "incorporation" into SADC, the reinvigoration of the ISDSC, the development of an ASAS which may legitimately be considered a continuation of the FLS, and countless proposals to set up research institutions and think tanks throughout the region each dealing with similar subject matter is confusing and saps regional energy. It may be feasible for the region to look into the possibility of consolidating the existing many into a functional few, which presumably will become more regional and more efficient over time. In theory, this is what SADC has accomplished with the formal ratification, in January 1996, of ASAS/ISDSC as the political/security arm of the Community. This "new" security "organ" will stand apart from SADC's sectors, operate at ministerial level, and act to advise members on defense and security matters. ASAS/ISDSC, it seems, is intended to be the operational arm of SADC's Politics, Diplomacy, International Relations, Defence and Security sector. In reality, however, it is not yet clear how this organization is to function, what its specific mandate is, or how it differs from its forerunners.

While this multiplication of regional organs and institutions is tolerable to some extent, the main problem is the region's continuing preference for high politics. Almost all regional organs are centered around summits of heads of state and government. This has several implications. Most of these groupings are catalyzed by summit meetings. On the one hand, this may stall their day-to-day operations should state bureaucracies find regional decisions at odds with "national" interests, or simply find no appeal in carrying out summit directives. In other words, regional cooperation in Southern Africa has never been a response to popular demands. As explained earlier, this is partly the result of regional history itself. On the other hand, such elite-pacting tendencies could hamper the growth of civil society in the region. So, whereas the welcome if moderate inclusiveness of the July 1994 Windhoek meeting suggests a willingness to involve informed publics, the reemergence of the FLS in the form of the ASAS/ISDSC signals a continuing preference for traditional roles, approaches to and definitions of "security." If a genuine regional security and development regime is to be established, people-to-people relations must be encouraged, strengthened, and viewed as integral and necessary elements in the process of regional cooperation and integration. Efforts like those taken by the IUCN need to be nurtured if "new thinking" on security is to translate into policy and practice.

In short, successful human security looks like an antithesis to high politics, particularly in a region where "high politics" has so often translated into high casuality rates. At the same time, a continuing preference for high politics may breed a host of new problems. For example, SADC-state leaders might simply protect each other even when they err. Some observers fear that the proposed regional task force may become an instrument to this end.

Conclusions

Clearly the parameters of security in Southern Africa have changed. No longer does emphasis lie on individual state preservation of sovereign rights. It is increasingly being realized that there is little room for a strong preoccupation with a "national interest" not enmeshed in a greater regional good. However, it should be underscored that Southern Africa is passing through difficult times. The region is in transition. It is rediscovering itself.

SADC state makers are learning how to live with South Africa; their South African counterparts are doing likewise. The region has to learn how to move smoothly from the politics of confrontation of the past era into the new development-focused politics of cooperation in which all Southern Africans may play an active role. Regional security will only be achieved if short-term goals match short-term capabilities. Exaggerated expectations will only breed contempt for the process of peacebuilding and, ultimately, for each other.

Notes

1. See, for example, Dalby 1992; Tuchman-Mathews 1989. For the Third World case, see, for example, Ayoob 1986; Acharya 1994; Acharya and Swatuk 1996; and Thomas 1987. For an early, trenchant discussion of the need to redefine "security" in Africa, see Luckham 1983.

2. According to Nathan and Honwana (1995: 5), "The main criticism of the new model is that it creates so broad a security agenda as to be unmanageable ... [However], the strength of new thinking on security is precisely the fact that it sets a broad agenda. Defining problems like poverty, environmental degradation and abuse of human rights as security issues raises their political profile. There may be times when military considerations are paramount but at other times they need to be balanced against non-military threats."

3. See, also, Breytenbach (1994), Cilliers (1994), Nathan (1992 and 1993), Southall (1995a), Steiner (1993), and Van Wyk (1994). This "new thinking" parallels quite closely the theoretical developments in post-Cold War security studies referred to above (see, for example, Tickner 1995).

4. A great deal of this "new thinking" has come out of United Nations-sponsored forums and commissions. Some of the seminal texts on alternative conceptions of and approaches to security are, the Carlsson and Ramphal Commission report *Our Global Neighbourhood* (1995); the Bruntland Commission report *Our Common Future: The World Commission on Environment and Development* (1987); the Palme Commission report *Common Security: A Programme for Disarmament* (1984), and the Brandt Commission report *North-South: A Programme for Survival* (1980). In the African case, the most significant document on "new security" is the Africa Leadership Forum's *The Kampala Document: Towards a Conference on Security, Stability, Development and Cooperation in Africa* (1991).

5. There is an enormous literature on the "crisis" in Southern Africa. For a succinct overview, see Shaw 1986.

6. On the genesis and performance of SADCC, see Amin, Chitala and Mandaza, eds., 1987. On the genesis of the Frontline States, see Omari 1991.

7. According to the Commission, global security requires the following six principles to be "embedded in international agreements and used as norms for security policies in the new era": (i) all people, no less than all states, have a right to secure existence, and all states have an obligation to protect those rights; (ii) the primary goals of global security policy should be to prevent conflict and war, and maintain the integrity of the environment and life-support systems of the planet, by eliminating the economic, social, environmental, political, and military conditions that generate threats to the security of people and the planet, and by antici-

pating and managing crises before they escalate into armed conflicts; (iii) military force is not a legitimate political instrument, except in self-defence or under UN auspices; (iv) the development of military capabilities beyond that required for national defence and support of UN action is a potential threat to the security of people; (v) weapons of mass destruction are not legitimate instruments of national defence; and (vi) the production and trade in arms should be controlled by the international community (1995: 11).

8. "Southern Africa is responsible for a major part of the African continent's productive activity," with SADC (7.3 percent) and South Africa (21.5 percent) combining for approximately 28.8 percent of continental GDP (SADCC 1991a: 8-9). In global terms, however, the contribution of the region is relatively insignificant, with SADC's (including South Africa) total output approximating that of Finland.

9. There are two districts in Tanzania which border Rwanda and Burundi, where the number of refugees has surpassed the number of the host population.

10. "The fast pace of medical progress and, hence, population growth, has not been matched by equivalent progression in the adoption of production technologies, thereby increasing poverty. Doubling time of the population is between twenty and thirty years in most African countries—a demographic explosion unprecedented in human history. Across Sub-Saharan Africa, almost half of the total population is below sixteen years of age" (World Bank 1995: 7).

11. According to the World Bank, "Starting from a current deficit, food production needs to grow faster than the population. Assuming a consumption growth rate of 3.3 percent per year, the demand for food would more than triple from 1990 to 2025." However, the Bank estimates that, at best, "food supply could be increased about 60 percent until 2025" (World Bank 1995: 24).

12. For an enlightened discussion of the obstacles to national and regional health care programs, see Beattie and Rispal 1994, and Shaw 1995.

13. For a more comprehensive discussion of environmental threats to security in Southern Africa, see, for example, ADB 1994; Moyo et al 1993; Van Wyk 1994; and World Bank 1995.

14. In its 1991 special report to the UNCED Secretariat, SADCC outlined its key environment and development policy issues for the 1990s as: managing demographic change and pressures; achieving food security; security of water supply and quality; maintaining forests and wildlife resources; making efficient use of energy; ensuring sustainable industrial development; preventing and reversing desertification; and combatting coastal erosion and pollution (SADCC 1991b: 9).

15. This threat has been exacerbated by the appearance of a new quick- killer virus, "ebola," in Zaire in 1995.

16. In January 1994, the members of the Frontline States (including South Africa) threatened to send a regional force into Lesotho in response to intra-force fighting. In late August 1994, the leaders of these same states issued an ultimatum to King Letsie III of Lesotho to restore the democratically-elected government he dismissed there (see Swatuk 1995). In October 1994, the FLS sent representatives at the eleventh hour to pressurize the Renamo leader, Mr Afonso Dlakhama to participate, face reality, and accept the results of the Mozambican elections. This was after Dlakhama had threatened to pull out of the process. The FLS were determined to avoid the so-called "Savimbi" syndrome, i.e., "the elections can only be considered free and fair if I win."

17. Suggesting that if Zimbabwe, for example, had problems similar to those in Lesotho, regional states would have behaved differently.

18. Nathan and Honwana (1995: 9) interpret these events quite differently, regarding such "gun-boat diplomacy" as undermining rather than reinforcing regional efforts toward the peaceful resolution of conflict.

19. The European Union and SADC recently concluded the Berlin Declaration which "set out principles for supporting democracy, human rights and good government, disarmament and integrated economic development." The agreement states, in part, "The effective exercise of human rights and fundamental freedoms is the legitimate concern of the international community and inseparable from the pursuit of international peace and security ... [Peace and security are] essential prerequisites for sustainable economic and social development" (*Business Day*, 5 September 1994).

20. Nathan and Honwana (1995) provide an excellent overview of these and subsequent deliberations. The authors suggest that among competing and armed former antagonists, the risk of conflict can be minimized through pursuit of a common security regime. This would involve, among other things: creation of an early-warning mechanism; development of confidence-building measures; promotion of collaborative decision-making; a preference for multilateralism; and active pursuit of peaceful conflict resolution. Nathan and Honwana also suggest that SADC states pursue a flexible security regime along the lines of Europe's CSCE (as opposed to the formal alliance system of NATO).

21. Especially following the decision to disband the African Liberation Committee of the Organization of African Unity (OAU) in mid-1994.

References

Acharya, Amitav. 1994. "Regional Approaches to Security in the Third World: Lessons and Prospects," in Larry A. Swatuk and Timothy M. Shaw, eds., *The South at the End of the Twentieth Century: rethinking the political economy of foreign policy in Africa, Asia, the Caribbean and Latin America.* Pp. 79-94. London: Macmillan.

Acharya, Amitav and Larry A. Swatuk. 1996. *Reordering the Periphery: Third World Security After the Cold War.* London: Macmillan.

African Development Bank (ADB). 1994. *Economic Integration in Southern Africa: Executive Summary.* Harare, mimeo.

Africa Leadership Forum. 1991. *The Kampala Document: Towards a Conference on Security, Stability, Development and Cooperation in Africa.* Ogun State, Nigeria: Africa Leadership Forum.

Amin, Samir, Derrick Chitala, and Ibbo Mandaza, eds. 1987. *SADCC: prospects for disengagement and development in Southern Africa.* London: Zed/UNU.

Anderson, Benedict. 1983. *Imagined Communities: reflections on the origin and spread of nationalism.* London: Verso.

Ayoob, Mohammed. 1986. "Regional Security and the Third World" in Mohammed Ayoob, ed., *Regional Security in the Third World: Case Studies From Southeast Asia and the Middle East.* London and Sydney: Croom Helm.

Bardill, John. 1994. *Sources of Domestic Instability in Southern African States, a conference report*. Backgrounder No. 12. Bellville: Centre for Southern African Studies, University of the Western Cape.

Bayart, Jean Francois. 1993. *The State in Africa: the politics of the belly*. London and New York: Longman.

Beattie, Allison, and Laetitia Rispel. 1994. "Improving health in the southern African region through regional cooperation," in Minnie Venter, ed., *Prospects for Progress*. Pp. 211-24.

Bowman, Larry. 1968. "The Subordinate State System of Southern Africa," *International Studies Quarterly* 12:3.

Brandt Commission. 1980. *North-South: A Programme for Survival*. London: Pan.

Breytenbach, Willie. 1994. "Types of conflicts in southern Africa and mechanisms for their resolution," in Minnie Venter, ed., *Prospects for Progress*. Pp. 52-9.

Buzan, Barry. 1991. *People, States and Fear: an agenda for international security studies in the Post-Cold War era*. Boulder: Lynne Rienner.

Canadian Institute of Strategic Studies (CISS). 1995. *South Africa: Problems and Prospects, conference report*. Toronto: CISS.

Carlsson and Ramphal Commission. 1995. *Our Global Neighbourhood*. Geneva: Commission on Global Governance.

Carter, Gwendolen M., and Patrick O'Meara. 1982. *Southern Africa: The Continuing Crisis*. Bloomington: Indiana University Press.

Chege, Michael. 1995. "Sub-Saharan Africa: underdevelopment's last stand," in Barbara Stallings, ed., *Global Change, Regional Response: The Next International Context of Development*. Cambridge: Cambridge University Press.

Cheru, Fantu. 1992. *The Not So Brave New World! Problems and Prospects of Regional Integration in Post-Apartheid Southern Africa*. Bradlow Series No. 6. Johannesburg: South African Institute of International Affairs, May.

Cilliers, Jakkie. 1994. "National and regional stability: expectations versus reality," in Minnie Venter, ed., *Prospects for Progress*. Pp. 40-51.

Dalby, Simon. 1992. "Security, Modernity, Ecology: The Dilemmas of Post-Cold War Security Discourse," *Alternatives* 17: 95-134.

Cock, Jacklyn and Laurie Nathan, eds. 1989. *War and Society: the militarization of South Africa*. New York: St. Martin's.

Geldenhuys, Deon. 1984. *The Diplomacy of Isolation: South African foreign policy making*. New York: St. Martin's.

Grundy, Kenneth W. 1986. *The Militarization of South African Politics*. Bloomington: Indiana University Press.

——. 1973. *Confrontation and Accommodation in Southern Africa: the limits of independence*. Berkeley: University of California Press.

Halpern, Jack. 1964. South Africa's Hostages. Harmondsworth: Penguin.

Hanlon, Joseph. 1986. *Beggar Your Neighbours: apartheid power in Southern Africa*. London: James Currey.

IUCN (World Conservation Union). 1993. *The Peace Dividend in Southern Africa: Options for Utilizing Military Resources in Environmental Management, program proposal*. Harare: IUCN-ROSA.

Johnson, Phyllis and David Martin, eds. 1989. *Apartheid Terrorism: the destabilization report*. London: James Currey for the Commonwealth.

Kalipeni, Ezekiel. 1994. "Introduction: Southern Africa's Expanding Population," in Ezekiel Kalipeni, ed., *Population Growth and Environmental Degradation in Southern Africa*. Pp. 1-15. Boulder: Lynne Rienner.

Luckham, Robin. 1983. "Security and Disarmament in Africa," *Alternatives* 19(2): 203-28.

Martin, David. 1995. "Frontline States assume a new role," *Daily News* (Tanzania), 6 January.

Mhone, Guy C.Z. 1994. "The effect of population growth on regional economic development," in Minnie Venter, ed., *Prospects for Progress*. Pp. 194-210.

Moyo, Sam, Phil O'Keefe and Michael Sill, eds. 1993. *The Southern African Environment: profiles of the SADC States*. London: Earthscan.

Nathan, Laurie. 1993. "'With Open Arms': Confidence- and Security-Building Measures in Southern Africa," paper prepared for the "Seminar on Confidence- and Security-Building in Southern Africa," United Nations Office for Disarmament Affairs, Windhoek, February.

——. 1992. *A Framework and Strategy for Building Peace and Security in Southern Africa*. Unpublished manuscript, Centre for Intergroup Studies, Cape Town, October.

—— and Joao Honwana. 1995. *After the Storm: Common Security and Conflict Resolution in Southern Africa*. The Arusha Papers: A Working Series on Southern African Security No. 3 (February).

Ohlson, Thomas and Stephen Stedman with Rob Davies. 1994. The New is not yet Born: Conflict Resolution in Southern Africa. Washington, DC: The Brookings Institution.

Omari, Abillah H. 1991. *The Rise and Decline of the Front Line States of Southern Africa: 1975-1990*. Unpublished Ph.D Thesis, Dalhousie University, Halifax, Nova Scotia.

"Opening Remarks by H.E. President Ali Hassan Mwinyi to the Ministerial Committee of the Inter-State Defence and Security," Arusha, Tanzania, 10 November 1994.

Palme Commission. 1984. *Common Security: A Programme for Disarmament*. London: Pan.

Percival, Val. 1995. *Environmental Scarcity and Violent Conflict: The Case of South Africa*. Draft manuscript, University of Toronto, April.

"Regional breakthrough as South Africa invited to help Lesotho Mutiny task-force," *Southscan* (London), 9(4) (28 January 1994): 2-3.

SADCC. 1991a. *SADCC: Towards Economic Integration*. Gaborone: SADCC Secretariat.

——. 1991b. *Sustaining Our Common Future: Special Report for the UNCED Secretariat*. Maseru: SADCC-ELMS, October.

Shaw, Amanda K. 1995. *Towards a Healthier South Africa: A Critical Examination of the ANC Health Plan*. Unpublished honours thesis, University of Waterloo, Canada, May.

Shaw, Timothy M. 1986. *Southern Africa in Crisis: an analysis and bibliography*. Halifax: Centre for Foreign Policy Studies, Dalhousie University.

Southall, Roger. 1995a. "Regional Security: the 'New Security' in Southern Africa," *Southern Africa REPORT* 10(5) (July): 3-6.

——. 1995b. "Levels of Understanding: Towards a Differentiated Canadian Perception of South Africa," paper presented to the international workshop on "South

Africa and Africa After Apartheid: Canadian Connections and New Foreign Policy Directions." 19-21 October 1995, Halifax, Canada.

Southern Africa REPORT (Toronto), various.

Steiner, A.M. 1993. "The Peace Dividend in Southern Africa: prospects and potentials for redirecting military resources towards natural resource management," paper presented at the UNDP Conference on Military and Environment "Past Mistakes and Future Options," New York, 22-23 February.

Stoneman, Colin. 1991. "Future Economic Policies in South Africa and Their Effects on Employment: some lessons from Zimbabwe," paper prepared for presentation at the International Conference on South Africa, Copenhagen, 21-23 February.

—— and Carol Thompson. 1991. *Southern Africa after apartheid: economic repercussions of a free South Africa*. Africa Recovery Briefing Paper No. 4. December.

Swatuk, Larry A. 1995. "Lesotho: Troubled Monarchy, Troubled Country," *Southern Africa REPORT* 10(4) (June): 30-2.

The Bonn Declaration, European Parliamentarians Conference: Building Global Human Security. 1993. Bonn: 17-18 September, mimeo.

The LUPOGO Report, The Southern African Institute: A Forum for Security and Development Concerns. 1993. mimeo.

Thomas, Caroline. 1987. *In Search of Security: The Third World in International Relations*. Boulder: Lynne Rienner.

Tickner, J. Ann. 1995. "Re-visioning Security," in Ken Booth and Steve Smith, eds., *International Relations Theory Today*. Pp. 175-97. Cambridge: Polity Press.

Tsie, Balefi. 1989. *Destabilization and its Implications for Botswana*. Roma: National University of Lesotho.

Tuchman-Mathews, Jessica. 1989. "Redefining Security," *Foreign Affairs* 68(2): 162-77.

United Nations Development Programme (UNDP). 1995 and 1993. *Human Development Report*. New York: Oxford University Press for the UNDP.

United Nations Children's Fund (UNICEF). 1994. *State of South Africa's Children: An Agenda for Action*. Johannesburg: UNICEF/UNHCR, June.

Van Wyk, J.J. 1994. "Regional Security in Southern Africa After the Cold War," paper presented at the 35th annual meeting of the International Studies Association, 28 March - 1 April.

Venter, Minnie, ed. 1994. *Prospects for Progress: critical choices for Southern Africa*. Cape Town: Maskew Miller Longman.

Whiteside, Alan. 1994. "AIDS and its impact on the economic, social and political environment," in Minnie Venter, ed., *Prospects for Progress: critical choices for Southern Africa*. Pp. 235-49.

World Bank. 1995. *Toward Environmentally Sustainable Development in Sub-Saharan Africa: A World Bank Agenda*. Washington, DC: World Bank.

——. 1992. *World Development Report: Development and the Environment*. New York: Oxford University Press.

6

Promoting Regional Integration in Southern Africa: An Analysis of Prospects and Problems from a South African Perspective

Robert Davies

In the period leading up to South Africa's first democratic elections in April 1994, there were high expectations in some quarters that the country's entry into regional organizations would be a major catalytic event driving a process of regional cooperation and integration forward. Sceptics, on the other hand, argued that preoccupation with domestic problems would lead to a sidelining by a democratic South African government of the regional issues, and to no serious effort being made to contribute to a regional program.

Surveying the scene in the nearly two years since the installation of South Africa's Government of National Unity (GNU), it is evident that neither of these expectations has been borne out. There has been neither a great leap towards a more integrated region, nor has South Africa turned its back on its neighbors. On the contrary, the GNU moved with some speed and decisiveness in taking organizational decisions intended to lay the basis for a new relationship with the Southern African region. Two decisions stand out in this regard: the accession in August 1994 to the Treaty of the Southern African Development Community (SADC), and the initiation in November 1994 of negotiations for a revised Southern African Customs Union (SACU) Agreement.

This chapter will look at the prospects for, and some of the problems being encountered in promoting, regional integration in Southern Africa from a specifically South African point of view. Through surveying both the state of the policy debate and some of the practical issues that have been encountered by South African officials in the past few months, it will argue that there are conceptual, strategic and practical problems that will have to be addressed not only by South Africa, but by the entire region if regional integration is to become a reality in the Southern African region.

Conceptual Issues and Approaches to Regional Integration: An Unfinished Debate

The policy debate on regional cooperation and integration can in no sense be considered to have arrived at a point of firm conclusion by the time South Africa took its place as a partner in regional organizations. A number of studies commissioned by regional organizations (SADCC 1992; SADC 1993), NGOs (SAFER 1992) and important extra-regional organizations (African Development Bank (ADB), 1993) had broadly concurred with the main conclusion of one of the most important of them all: that "all SAR (Southern African Region) countries have much to gain from various forms of regional cooperation and from launching a determined effort to integrate the regional market (ADB 1993: 171).

Within South Africa itself, while several influential voices in business and other circles continued to question whether the region should be a priority at all, the democratic movement led by the ANC had broadly come to accept the following propositions:

- That greater involvement in regional trade, involvement in regional projects, obtaining access to regional resources and infrastructure, and cooperation in various sectors could all be of great significance to efforts to promote growth and development in a democratic South Africa.
- That existing economic relations in Southern Africa were characterized by great unevenness and by acute imbalances and disparities. South Africa's visible exports to the rest of the region exceeded imports by a factor of more than 4:1, a product not only of the stronger productive base of the South African economy, but also of protective tariffs and non-tariff barriers of various kinds that kept goods produced in regional states out of the South African market.
- That the overall regional ambient would be of considerable significance for a democratic South Africa, that a region characterized by relative growth and stability would have very different implications than one plagued by stagnation and crisis, and that South Africa could not hope to become an island of prosperity in a sea of poverty.
- That Southern Africa should thus command top priority in South Africa's foreign policy and that the country should act together with

its partners to promote growth and development throughout Southern Africa.
- That South Africa was already part of a region, in which there is a significant degree of economic integration, being a member of a customs union with four other countries, and part of a monetary union with three of these.

While no very firm conclusions on integration as such had been agreed, there was general support for the idea of exploring the prospects of a program of mutually-beneficial cooperation and integration based on a general recognition that the real question was not whether there should be cooperation or integration, but rather to identify that combination of cooperation, coordination and integration which was realistic and feasible under prevailing conditions, and which could thus best advance the goals of contributing to growth and development.

One of the issues that was far from resolved in the policy debates taking place either in South Africa or the rest of the region, was the approach or paradigm to adopt in promoting integration. In fact, both in the literature and underlying various concrete proposals for integration programs in the Southern African region, several distinct approaches could be recognized.

For much of the period until the early 1990s the debate was dominated by proponents of one of three paradigms. One of these was the conventional *trade or market integration* paradigm which is recognizable as having informed much of the practice of the Eastern and Southern African Preferential Trade Area (PTA), now known as the Common Market for Eastern and Southern Africa (COMESA). This essentially viewed integration as a process in which tariff and non-tariff barriers to trade between cooperating partners were progressively removed and in which the external trade regimes and eventually fiscal and monetary policies of cooperating partners are harmonized. Progress up what might be termed "the ladder of integration" was conventionally seen as moving in linear succession from a Preferential Trade Area through a Free Trade Area, Customs Union and Common Market to an Economic and eventually, perhaps, Political Union.

Strong emphasis was placed in this approach on the distinction between *trade creation* and *trade diversion*. Trade creation refers to a situation in which the production of particular goods in country A, which does not have a comparative advantage in that area, is replaced by the purchase of cheaper goods from country B which does. Trade diversion, on the other hand, takes place if country A turns from lower cost suppliers in country C to what are in reality higher cost suppliers in country B, now enjoying an "artificial" advantage because of a preferential tariff arrangement. Under the trade integration paradigm, economic integration is held to be economically desirable in cases where the trade creation effects are greater than trade diversion. In the literature, this is seen as most likely to occur in situations where: a) trade among cooperating partners is either currently or potentially a large proportion of their total trade; or b) there is a high level of complementarity in productive structures, i.e. A produces what B needs and vice versa.

This approach has been subject to a number of criticisms in the Southern African debate (see, for example, Saasa 1991). The Ricardian "comparative advantage" theory on which it is based was criticized as presenting an unrealistic vision of the mechanisms and power relations in contemporary international trade. The approach to the issue of "trade creation" versus "trade diversion" has been seen as static in that it refers to existing comparative advantages without considering the potentiality of regional cooperation to overcome obstacles and create new comparative advantages. More particularly, for these and other reasons, critics have seen it as inappropriate in "Third World" regions where the above described conditions justifying the formation of customs unions generally do not apply.

An alternative approach, recognizable as that which informed the practice of the Southern African Development Coordination Conference (SADCC) during its first decade was described as *functional integration* or *integration through project cooperation*. This set out from the premise that cooperation in the formulation and execution of joint projects aimed at overcoming underdevelopment-related deficiencies in the spheres of production and infrastructure should have first priority in programs in Third World regions. Not only was this viewed as essential to remove immediate barriers to regional trade, it has also been seen as a means of generating a regional identity and consciousness which would set in train processes of interaction which would lay the ground for a more secure integration than would overly hasteful trade liberalization. The latter, it was argued, would under conditions of underdevelopment tend to benefit stronger partners disproportionately and could thus lead to a polarization ultimately prejudicial to the whole integration effort.

A more ambitious model proposed at various times is known as *development integration*. Like the project coordination approach, it too set out from a critique of a conventional laissez-faire trade-driven approach as either not leading to effective integration or else creating unacceptable polarization in underdeveloped regions. In contrast to the project cooperation approach whose initial focus at least is largely micro, development integration stresses the need for both macro- and micro-coordination in a multi-sectoral program embracing production, infrastructure and trade. It thus stresses the need for close political cooperation at an early stage of the integration process in contrast to the market integration approach under which this only emerges at a rather late stage. The development integration approach also emphasizes the need for an equitable balance of the benefits of integration, and argues that trade liberalization measures need to be accompanied by compensatory and corrective measures oriented particularly toward the least developed member countries. It thus sees a need for trade integration to be complemented by:

- efforts to promote coordinated regional industrial development;
- the establishment of regional funds or banks giving special priority to the least developed members;
- measures to give less developed members greater preference in access to regional markets and facilities and a longer period to reduce tariffs; and
- some coordination of macro-policies at a relatively early stage, particularly in relation to fiscal incentives for investment.

As argued elsewhere (Davies 1994), changes in the global political economy and in fashions in economic theory led, by the early 1990s, to significant modifications in the paradigms most influential in informing efforts to promote integration in Southern Africa. On the one hand, factors such as the ascendency of neo-liberal discourse and the lack of success of many earlier integration projects in region in the South fuelled efforts to refine and adapt the conventional trade integration approach to bring it more into line with the current preoccupations of the "structural adjust-ment" agenda of the international financial institutions (the IMF and World Bank).

The World Bank and IMF, it should be noted, are relatively recent converts to regional integration. Both institutions stood aloof from integra-tion efforts in Africa and elsewhere in the past. The structural adjustment programs (SAPs) adopted by a succession of African countries at the behest of the Bank and Fund were partly premised on a view that the fundamental requirement as far as a country's external economic relations is concerned is to undertake "unilateral trade reform" which will "open up" the domes-tic economy and integrate it more closely with the world economy at large. Regional integration was seen as an irrelevance at best and, at worst, a diversion from the fundamental goal of lowering tariffs toward the world at large.

The Bank's shift towards supporting a new round of regional integration efforts in Africa dates from around 1991. It was partly based on the reality that most countries on the continent had already embraced SAPs and a perception, in this context, that an integration program of a certain type could reinforce efforts to promote unilateral trade reform. In studies un-dertaken to give substance to its new found support for regional integration programs, a significant attempt to modify the conventional trade integra-tion paradigm to make it compatible with "unilateral trade reform" was discernible.

Neo-classical customs union theory on which the trade integration approach is based had, as indicated earlier, always cautioned against measures which would artificially divert trade from third parties with comparative advantages. It was, however, relatively silent about the type of trade regime the union as a whole should maintain with the outside world: whether the common external tariff which comes into existence when a customs union is established should be high or low, relatively protective of intra-regional trade or more "open." This derived from the focus of the theory, which was always on relations between members of the union rather than on relations between the union and the rest of the world.

It is precisely toward this perceived lacuna in the conventional neo-classical paradigm that officials in the World Bank sought to address themselves. Side by side with the Bank's new found support for a new round of regional integration efforts was thus an attempt to refine and adapt conventional customs union theory to bring it more into line with the perspectives underlying "unilateral trade reform." An example of this approach can be found in a 1991 World Bank study on integration in sub-Saharan Africa (World Bank, 1991).

The main argument of this study is that the Bank should support a new round of integration projects in sub-Saharan Africa but that these should be "consistent with an outward orientated strategy that 'promotes incentives which are neutral between production for the domestic market and export'" (para. 2.08). Regional integration should thus not become a means of salvaging failed import substitution industrialization programs but should be harmonized with ongoing structural adjustment programs.

This required, the study argues, some modification of the conventional goals of integration. "Customs Unions, with their potential for trade diversion behind a high CET [Common External Tariff], should not be the primary objective of integration efforts" (para. 2.09). The "ultimate objective" should rather be "to create conditions which would allow the private sector to freely work, trade and invest across African borders and *with relative low barriers against third parties*" (Executive Summary, para. 10; emphasis added).

Integration should then be seen as a process of "'mutual regional liberalization' which would strengthen and extend on-going adjustment efforts by adding another dimension" (para. 11). While "temporary increases in regional preferences are acceptable" this should be within a framework of a "general and significant lowering of external protection" which would guarantee that "regional preference would indeed be temporary" (para. 15). Regional integration as a process of regional liberalization is accordingly "an intermediary stage towards general liberalization" (para. 14). Its essential driving force would be "a private sector constituency that would benefit from the focus on creating conditions conducive to legalizing and enhancing private cross-border economic activity" (para. 13).

It was such an approach that largely informed the IMF, World Bank, ADB, and European Union (EU)-sponsored "Cross-Border Initiative" (CBI) which began to be implemented in a number of PTA/COMESA countries in 1993. The "concept paper" on which the initiative is based indicated that it was premised on "accelerated economic liberalization with respect to external payments and domestic regulatory environment" and sought to "build on the progress achieved in national structural adjustment programs." The initiative involves a series of core measures in the areas of trade: payments and exchange systems and investment. In the trade area the program envisages eliminating all tariffs on intra-regional trade on a reciprocal basis by 1996 and removing a range of non-tariff barriers on imports from all countries. On payments, the program aims at "complete non-discriminatory elimination of all restrictions on current account transactions and relaxation of certain types of capital account transactions." In the area of investment, the program envisages harmonization of investment incentives and simplification and liberalization of cross-border investment procedures. The emphasis on this initiative is on "unilateral action and self-selection" (CBI 1993). Although based on extensive interactions with the PTA/COMESA and consultations with SADC and the Indian Ocean Community (IOC), the CBI did not simply seek to reinforce efforts of these organizations but to encourage a self-selecting group of countries to proceed on a faster track. Goaded on by an offer of US $30 million on average, a number of PTA/COMESA, SAC and IOC member states signed on to this initiative.

Critics of this approach focus on a number of aspects:

- First, the underlying assumption that the fundamental requirement of a successful externally-oriented growth strategy is a unilateral and pre-emptive liberalization of domestic tariff and regulatory regimes was seen as not taking adequate account either of the experiences of the East Asian NICs or of the acute unevenness and inequities of the current phase of "global liberalization"—where countries of the South have made significant moves towards opening up their domestic economies only to be confronted with an increasing range of non-tariff barriers in countries of the North (see UNDP 1992: 63-4).
- Second, such an approach was rooted in an assumption that what's good for business is good for the community as a whole. Its essential thrust is towards accommodating the demands of capital, without taking account of the interests of other stakeholders.
- Third, it took little heed of, and indeed appeared to be relatively indifferent to, the potentiality for polarization in laissez faire approaches to integration. It also said little or nothing about such critical questions as how to overcome the barriers to integration

deriving from underdevelopment, inadequate infrastructures and other deficiencies, or how to empower the most impoverished and least developed partners to become more effective in regional trade.

- Fourth, while conceding that an integration and cooperation agenda may proceed at different paces and that within either there may be a need to take account of "variable geometry" and accepting that subsets of countries may move at different paces, initiatives like the CBI appeared to be based on an almost total isolation of the integration from the cooperation agenda with a near exclusive focus on the "fast track" group.

The alternative to this type of approach is seen by many as continuing to lie in the overall direction of the basic concerns and thrust of the development integration approach outlined above. SADCC's 1992 theme document, for example, concluded that "the Development Integration approach, providing for investment, production and market or trade integration, is appropriate for SADCC and that it [should] be accorded priority in the overall integrative framework" (SADCC 1992).

However, it was also conceded that an alternative development-oriented integration strategy will have to take account of both changes in the global conjuncture and weaknesses or failures demonstrated in past practice. In particular, such a strategy will need to take account, *inter alia*, of:

- The unlikelihood that import substitution industrialization financed by foreign exchange earned from the sale of primary products on world markets would be any more successful, under prevailing circumstances, on a regional basis than similar policies were at national level.
- The fact that project cooperation had been shown to be an insufficient basis for promoting regional integration. This appeared to be a major lesson that SADC drew from its own self critical review in the early 1990s. Cooperation in infrastructural projects was important in its own right and could contribute towards the creation of a regional identity and common sense of purpose, but an integration program needs to reach beyond this and embrace trade issues as well as such "thorny questions" as currency convertibility.
- The need to find ways to promote the political commitment necessary to drive an integrated regional program. This was widely seen as a key lesson from the experience of the EU, but was seen as a complex question with several elements. On the one hand, it depends on governments seeing concrete benefits flowing from what is generally perceived as a "surrendering" of some degree of sovereignty to regional institutions. On the other hand, it depends on

creating a degree of overall legitimacy, popular support and a sense of involvement by peoples and non-governmental institutions.

While such points have been widely acknowledged, there has been no further major development at the conceptual or strategic level of an approach towards promoting development-oriented integration in the Southern African context. The reality is that there remains a little noticed, still unresolved debate between different approaches or paradigms towards promoting integration in Southern Africa. As will be argued later, this reflects itself, *inter alia*, in some of the current debates about a SADC trade protocol.

Steps Taken by South Africa's GNU and Problems Ahead

Trade with the rest of Southern Africa is of considerable importance to South Africa. Officially published South African trade statistics have historically referred to the trade of the whole of the Southern African Customs Union with the rest of the world, thus obscuring the trade that takes place between South Africa and its partners in the Customs Union and understating the full significance to its economy of trade with other African countries. A calculation undertaken by officials of the Department of Trade and Industry after the 1994 elections attempted to unpack these figures and thereby indicate the full significance of South African trade with the region. This calculation revealed that exports to other SACU countries amounted to more than R15 billion in 1993, more than the country's exports to either Asia or America. Trade with all other African countries amounted to 31.7% of total trade if SACU countries are included and 12.8% if they were not (DTI 1995). The remaining non-SACU SADC member countries as a group stand second only to the SACU countries in terms of their importance as trading partners on the African continent.

Figures published by the Commissioner for Customs and Excise (which refer to the entire SACU area and not just South Africa) show that these countries totalled R1.4 billion. The figure for exports represented 71% of all exports from the SACU area to the rest of Africa. Expressed as a proportion of total trade, the aggregate figures for this group remained fairly modest. Non-SACU SADC countries accounted for just 6.8% of total exports and only 1.8% of total imports. However, when disaggregated by product categories the figures clearly show that this trade has a much greater significance for manufacturing industries. The figures for 1994 thus show that the non-SACU SADC group was the destination of over a third of total exports of machinery and appliances, of more than a quarter of vehicle exports, 21% of chemical products, 39.1% of plastics and rubber products, 16.9% of foodstuffs and beverages, and 13.8% of textiles and clothing (Republic of South Africa 1994).

The GNU's approach towards trade integration issues has set out from an implicit if not explicit recognition of a point made in several policy studies, *viz.* that the region is characterized by "variable geometry" with different arrangements at different levels of integration applying among different groups of countries within the broader region. As indicated earlier, two important organizational decisions stand out as having created a framework for developing a new approach to regional trade policy—the renegotiation of the SACU agreement, and membership in SADC.

SACU has operated as a customs union between South Africa and Botswana, Lesotho, Namibia, and Swaziland (BLNS) for many decades and is governed at present by an Agreement negotiated in 1969. The main provisions of this are that the tariff regime in force in South Africa applies to the other countries (i.e., serves as a common external tariff), that customs and excise revenue collected in member countries is paid into a common pool and distributed according to a formula weighted in favor of the BLNS countries. This weighting is intended to compensate the smaller SACU countries for the polarization and price raising effects of being drawn behind South Africa's protective tariff regime and for the loss of sovereignty over tariff and trade policy issues.

The BLNS countries have complained over the years that the revenue sharing formula does not, in fact, fully compensate them even for the price raising effects, that there is a lack of consultation by South Africa of its SACU partners, and that there have been various alleged non-tariff barriers preventing their access into the South African market. South Africa has complained in turn that the weighted allocation of excise as well as customs duties to BLNS has become an increasing burden on the South African fiscus, and that SACU has become unaffordable to it (see Davies, 1994a).

Despite such problems, there remains broad support both in South Africa and the other SACU countries for maintaining a customs union arrangement among the five while making SACU itself a less South African-dominated and more equitable arrangement. Indeed, some have argued for SACU to be upgraded into a common market by introducing free movement of labour, as well as of goods and capital in the SACU area (Maasdorp 1993: 245).

The SACU renegotiations now underway are addressing such critical questions as the creation of new structures and mechanisms for joint decision-making in tariff setting bodies (instead of, as under the current agreement, the tariffs in force in South Africa simply applying to other SACU members) and the possibility of achieving a greater degree of coordination in such areas as industrial and competition policy, as well as the long-standing "hot potato" of the revenue sharing formula.

Another major issue that has arisen is whether SACU should be enlarged by admitting selected SADC member countries who are not currently members or be restructured as a "subset" arrangement which needs to be harmonized with broader regional organizations like SADC. Enlargement of SACU appeared to be a policy objective of the former South African regime (which saw this as a means of extending South African hegemony and undercutting organizations like SADC). There are also a number of SADC countries (Malawi, Mozambique, Zimbabwe) that have been mentioned from time to time as inclined to seek membership in SACU.

A number of problems can be identified with any proposal to enlarge SACU at least in the short run. In the first place, the very specific history of the close integration of BLNS into the South African political economy cannot be ignored. These countries were at one time all administered from South Africa as virtual economic regions of the country and were, indeed, destined in the colonial scheme of things to become incorporated politically as well. SACU was thus formed not to promote integration as such, but rather to manage trade relations among a group of countries already highly integrated with South Africa in a specific, one-sided way. The level of integration between SACU countries has, moreover, tended to lessen rather than deepen over the years. There was, for example, at one time virtual free movement of labour across borders (although once in South Africa apartheid influx control regulations applied). South African currency was also at one time legal tender in all SACU countries—in other words they were once members of a tight monetary union. This history and background clearly does not apply to the rest of Southern Africa. Other SADC member countries, while having significant ties to South Africa and, in some cases, among themselves, all have different practices, institutional arrangements and levels of development—all of which would require significant adjustment and time—before they could become part of Customs Union arrangement.

Second, the implications of the democratization of decision-making processes, widely expected to result from a new SACU agreement, have had to be taken into account. Democratization will almost certainly mean that the SACU Common External Tariff (CET) will cease being, as it is under the 1969 agreement, the tariff "in force in South Africa" and become instead a tariff set in negotiation by all member countries. Bringing in new members would thus very probably imply highly complex negotiations with countries with very different levels of development and interests over the CET.

The Marrakesh General Agreement on Trade and Tariffs (GATT) Agreement, concluded after the Uruguay Round, has, moreover, introduced an important clarification in the interpretation of Article XXIV of the GATT which is relevant in this regard. Article XXIV, which governs the acceptance by the World Trade Organization (WTO) of regional integration schemes amounting to a departure from the Most Favorable Nation (MFN) principle supposed to apply to all other member countries, states that these arrangements are acceptable provided that the tariff applying to external parties is not, on the whole, higher than the tariffs previously in force. The Uruguay Round "Final Act" states that "the evaluation ... of the general incidence of duties and other regulations of commerce before and after the formation of a customs union shall in respect of duties and charges be based on an overall assessment of weighted average tariff rates and customs duties collected" (GATT 1993; Interpretation of Article XXIV, p. 1). It goes on to indicate that the Secretariat of the WTO will itself make such computations in accordance with the methodology used in assessing offers made during the Uruguay Round. What this means is that merely extending a CET already in force and accepted by GATT to other countries may not be acceptable to GATT—even if it were to potential new members. A new tariff would have to be no higher than the weighted average of the existing SACU CET and the tariffs in force in potential new members.

Third, the admission of new members would raise huge questions in respect of the revenue sharing formula. While there are signs of flexibility on the part of some BLNS countries about adjusting some aspects of the present formula, there is also a strong consensus among them that any new formula should include a weighting in favor of the less developed member countries. Several potential new members could well have levels of exports and imports higher than those of the BLNS countries. They would almost certainly press for a significant weighting to compensate for the potentially major effect on their domestic industries of the duty free entry of South African goods. Extending a weighted formula to new members would thus have important fiscal implications for South Africa as well as hugely complicating negotiations on revenue sharing.

For these and other reasons, the alternative perspective of viewing SACU as an important subset arrangement within a broader regional program appears much more viable. This would see SACU as having an important role to play in its own right and in reinforcing efforts to promote an equitable deepening of integration in the region at large. But, it would not, as an organization embracing only some countries in the Southern African region, seek to abrogate to itself any exclusive or privileged role in this regard. Rather it would seek to harmonize its actions to an increasing extent with those of organizations like SADC. This appears to be the approach of South Africa's negotiating team in the SACU negotiation.

The other major regional trade issue has, of course, been the type of trade relationship to work towards with the broader non-SACU SADC region. A major question which immediately confronted the South African GNU in this regard was whether to work towards a new relationship on a bilateral or multilateral basis. The new government found itself bombarded with proposals from several individual SADC countries to either renegotiate existing, or negotiate new, preferential bilateral trade agreements. At the same time, the SADC Secretariat, which had been working on a regional trade protocol, tabled for discussion a draft protocol to establish a Free

Trade Area in the SADC region shortly before South Africa's accession to the organization.

South African officials have expressed their preference for a multilateral, regional approach. Several reasons appear to underlie this, including the desire to avoid duplication, an expressed commitment to reinforcing efforts to promote regional cooperation, and a sense that the new rules created by the Uruguay Round of GATT could pose problems for a purely bilateral route.

With regard to the last point, legal opinion in South Africa (Blumberg 1994) has suggested that provisions of the Marrakesh Agreement appear to be much more receptive than previous GATT rules to claims by classes or groups of countries to have preferences granted to similar countries extended to them on the grounds that not to do so would constitute discrimination. Any substantially new bilateral agreements could, it has been suggested, find themselves either rejected or compulsorily extended to other countries in the region (i.e., multilateralized) through WTO intervention. Moreover, to secure a waiver for a bilateral agreement from the WTO under Article XXV, South Africa would probably have to present itself as a developed country making concessions to developing countries. This completely contradicts the stance it is taking in negotiations with major trading blocs where the advantages of it being seen as a developing country are apparent.

Current thinking within the GNU appears to be in favor of seriously working toward a viable multilateral framework agreement that would also allow for some bilateral flexibility. It has been suggested that a SADC trade protocol should focus on defining a process of negotiating a new regional trade regime, rather than specifying its content and, in particular, doubts have been expressed about whether a Free Trade Area would be a beneficial arrangement for the rest of the region in the short term at least.

A "quick and dirty" study by staffers of the South African Industrial Development Corporation has suggested that the SACU countries (and mainly South Africa) would benefit to the extent of a 1.1% increase in GDP, a 4.6% increase in total exports and an 8.0% increase in manufactured exports from the removal of all tariffs within the SADC area. The same study, however, concluded that the resulting increased competition to domestic manufacturing industries from South African imports would have a net negative impact on GDP of four of the remaining six SADC countries (IDC 1995).

The conclusion that would appear to follow from this study, which in fact merely repeats that of several of the policy studies in the years before 1994, is that further South African access to these countries' markets would need to be carefully structured and phased. On the other hand, the IDC study identified a range of agricultural and industrial products (including textiles and clothing, footwear, furniture, and ferrous products) produced in the non-SACU SADC member countries which would be competitive in the South African market at lower tariff rates (IDC 1995). This would suggest that an asymmetrical Preferential Trade Area, in which South Africa opened up its market to a greater extent than would be required by other countries, and which operated on a somewhat differentiated basis country by country, would be the optimum arrangement in the short term.

Such proposals have, however, come up against strong counter-arguments from other countries. One line of argument that is being increasingly encountered is that neighboring countries have already liberalized and that South Africa should simply follow suit. Where this argument has a point is that existing South African tariff arrangements do, indeed, still display features of the historical protectionism towards the rest of the region. This issue has loomed largest in discussions with Zimbabwe and Zambia. Zimbabwe had a bilateral preferential trade agreement with South Africa which dated back to 1964. Attempts to update it in negotiations with the previous South African regime broke down and the existing agreement was allowed to lapse at the end of 1992 with serious implications for Zimbabwe's clothing and textile industry among others. A partial reinstatement at the end of October 1995 against strong lobbying by South African clothing manufacturers has been dismissed as inadequate by Zimbabwe which has from time to time threatened to retaliate by increasing tariffs on South African imports (*Business Day*, 24 August 1995; also, see Swatuk, Chapter 7). Zambia, which has had no trade agreement with South Africa, has complained that it has "progressed far in liberalizing markets and opening up its economy," but that this has not been matched by the strongest economy in the region (*Business Day*, 12 October 1995).

What calls for reciprocal liberalization, like those made by Zambia, fail to highlight is that the liberalization exercise in which they themselves were involved was undertaken within the context of SAPs, was spurred on by their signing on to the CBI, and was thus oriented toward external liberalization in general. Brought into the regional integration debate, and it is here that the unfinished debate over paradigms of integration has relevance, they amount (probably unselfconsciously) to a call for an integration program based on the World Bank CBI-type approach, with all that entails.

Another major challenge to the development of an appropriate regional program in Southern Africa is the pressure for South Africa to become involved in cross-continental Free Trade Area agreements with advanced industrialized regions. This has been most evident to date in the current negotiations for a long-term agreement with the European Union. South Africa's application to be admitted to the Lomé Convention has not been accepted as far as the trade chapter of the convention is concerned. Instead, the EU has proposed that South Africa's desire for greater access to the EU market could be accommodated by a reciprocal, but asymmetrical Free Trade Area agreement. Negotiators from the two sides have agreed to explore the possibilities of such a FTA on the condition that "nothing is agreed until everything is agreed."

In the proposal forwarded to the Council of Ministers by the European Commission in October 1995, a Free Trade Agreement with a coverage of at least 90% and implemented in tranches over a maximum of ten years was proposed. On the commission's own figures this would give South Africa increased duty free access to the EU market for about seven percent of its mainly agricultural products while requiring South Africa to liberalize more than 40% of its current imports from the EU (European Commission 1995). Apart from the implications for the South African domestic economy, it has been pointed out that such proposals could have major repercussions for any program of regional integration.

For a start, any agreement with tariff implications reached with South Africa would automatically have to apply to the rest of SACU if the customs union is to be maintained. The BLNS countries are all members of Lomé, whose trade relations with the EU are currently governed by the convention and its protocols. Since the EU is bound to exclude from an FTA a range of South African agricultural products, the question of on the basis of which agreement—Lomé or South African FTA—similar products produced in BLNS would enter the EU would arise. If it were to be the latter, significant losses would be experienced by BLNS (ERO 1995). Moreover, the elimination of duties on 40% of EU imports into South Africa would be bound to have significant implications for customs revenue, and hence on the negotiations over the revenue sharing formula.

As far as relations with the rest of the region are concerned, if, as was argued earlier, the appropriate arrangement at this point is something more like a preferential than a free trade area, then the economic and political implications of South Africa moving further with Europe than with Southern Africa would arise as a serious issue. Indeed, it is a moot point more generally what space the pressures of post-Uruguay Round globalization (of which the proposed EU agreement is an example) will allow for regional integration.

Conclusions

South Africa has now taken its place as a fully legitimate partner and member of at least two of the major Southern African regional organizations. In the short period of time since the installation of South Africa's GNU, it has begun to work with the rest of the region toward developing a program of increasing sectoral cooperation and restructuring trade relations to promote a more balanced pattern of trade and a more integrated regional market.

A Memorandum of Understanding to establish a Southern African Power Pool and an agreement on Shared Watercourses were signed at the

SADC summit in August 1995. Discussions on a multimodal transport agreement to develop road, rail, port and tourism facilities in the Maputo corridor are underway with Mozambique. And South Africa is now participating in meetings of appropriate SADC sector coordinating units or commissions. There have also been, as this chapter has indicated, negotiations aimed at creating new trading relationships in the region. These have taken place against the background of an increase in exports from the SACU to other SADC member countries equivalent to 24.5% of the 1993 total in 1994 and an increase in imports of 45.8% (Republic of South Africa 1994).

While these developments are all positive, and perhaps all that could be expected in the short space of time since the process of democratic transition in South Africa, expectations as to what South Africa can bring to a new partnership with the region need to be kept in perspective. Although South Africa's GDP is nearly three times that of the rest of SADC (excluding Mauritius), figures released by the Central Statistical Services indicate that the Human Development Index for the country's African population in 1991 (0.500) was below that of either Botswana or Swaziland and was only marginally above that of Zimbabwe (CSS, n.d.)

Many challenges lie ahead for Southern Africa. The region still has to produce a comprehensive strategy for regional cooperation and integration which fully takes account of the new opportunities and realities facing it. It also still has largely to define how it sees its efforts at regional level fitting in with and complementing those at the broader African continental level and how the region of Southern Africa should position itself in a global context still characterized by acute divisions between the underdeveloped South and developed North.

Progress toward a more integrated regional market in particular requires developing greater clarity about what integration is intended to achieve, how it fits into a broader program including also sectoral cooperation and coordination, and of the significance of post-Uruguay Round pressures of globalization. In this context, taking forward the unfinished debate about approaches or paradigms of integration in a way which places equitable and mutually-beneficial development oriented growth firmly at the top of the regional agenda is becoming increasingly urgent.

References

African Development Bank (ADB). 1993. *Prospects for Economic Integration in Southern Africa*. Oxford: Oxford University Press.

Blumberg, Leora and Webber Wentzel. 1994. *Trade Relations with Southern Africa: A Preliminary Legal Analysis*. Halfway House: Development Bank of Southern Africa.

Business Day (Johannesburg). various issues.

Central Statistical Services (CSS). n.d. "The Socio-Economic State of South Africa as Reflected by: a) The Results of the October Household Survey (OHS) according to the nine provinces; b) the Human Development Index (HDI)." Pretoria.

Cross Border Initiative (CBI). 1993. "Concept Paper - Initiative to Facilitate Cross-Border Private Investment, Trade and Payments in Eastern and Southern Africa and the Indian Ocean," mimeo of project supported by the World Bank, African Development Bank, IMF and Commission of the European Communities. Brussels.

Davies, Robert. 1994. "Approaches to Regional Integration in the Southern African Context," *Africa Insight* 24: 1.

——. 1994(a). "The SACU: Background and Possible Negotiating Issues Facing a Democratic South Africa" in Max Sisulu, Morely Nkosi and Rosalind Thomas, eds., *Reconstituting and Democratizing the Southern African Customs Union.* Braamfontein: National Institute of Economic Policy.

Department of Trade and Industry (DTI). 1995. Text of Presentation to Parliamentary Portfolio Committee on Trade and Industry. Cape Town. 7 June.

European Commission. 1995. "Communication from the Commission to the Council: Recommendation for a Council Decision on complementary negotiating directives for an Agreement for Trade and Cooperation between the European Community and the Republic of South Africa." Brussels. mimeo.

European Research Office (ERO). 1995. "EU-South Africa Free Trade Area Negotiations: Regional Implications." Brussels. mimeo.

GATT. 1993. *Final Act Embodying the Results of the Uruguay Round of Multilateral Trade Negotiations.*

Industrial Development Corporation (IDC). 1995. "Impact of Trade Liberalization on Intra-Regional Trade in SADC." presentation to Workshop on SADC Trade Protocols organized by Department of Trade and Industry. Pretoria. June.

Maasdorp, Gavin. 1993. "The Advantages and Disadvantages of Current Regional Institutions for Integration" in Pauline Baker, Alex Borraine and Warren Krafchik, eds., *South Africa and the World Economy in the 1990s.* Cape Town. David Philip.

Republic of South Africa. 1994. *Monthly Abstract of Trade Statistics: Foreign Trade Statistics of the common customs area of Botswana, Lesotho, South Africa and Swaziland released by the Commissioner for Customs and Excise of the Republic of South Africa January-December 1994.* Pretoria.

Saasa, Oliver S. 1991. "Economic cooperation and integration among developing countries: an overview" in Oliver S. Saasa, ed., *Joining the Future: Economic Integration and Cooperation in Africa.* Nairobi. African Centre for Technology Studies.

SADCC. 1992. *Towards Economic Integration.* Theme Document for 1992 Consultative Meeting. Gaborone.

SADC. 1993. *Southern Africa: A Framework and Strategy for Building the Community.* Harare.

Southern African Foundation for Economic Research (SAFER). 1992. Papers presented at conference held at Africa Institute of South Africa. Pretoria. July.

World Bank. 1991. *Intra-Regional Trade in sub-Saharan Africa.* Economics and Finance Division: Technical Department: Africa Region. Washington, D.C. May 23.

United Nations Development Program (UNDP). 1992. *Human Development Report 1992*. New York. Oxford University Press.

7

The Environment, Sustainable Development, and Prospects for Southern African Regional Cooperation

Larry A. Swatuk

Southern Africa is undergoing a massive transformation... [T]he people of Southern Africa are creating a landscape much as they created the agricultural landscape of the past. Yet such a process of development brings new problems—not just of pollution and resource exhaustion but, significantly, of renewable resources. Energy requirements, wood consumption and, more importantly, water demand will be critical resource issues to address in the 21st century.
—Sam Moyo et al (1993: xiii)

"All changed, changed utterly," the poet W.B. Yeats wrote of his beloved Ireland in 1916. He might well have been referring to South Africa in 1990, when President F.W. de Klerk set the country on a changed course. South Africa now stands on the threshold of a new century and of a more just and equitable future for all its people. But to achieve that future will mean huge new demands on limited natural resources.
—Jonathan Yeld (1993: 13)

Raising the challenge of sustainable development can help the South African policy debate go forward in new directions. At the heart of the problem is how best to move from separate development to sustainable development.
—Barry Munslow and Patrick Fitzgerald (1994: 1)

The Southern African region faces common problems which derive in part from historical patterns of uneven and inconsistent capitalist development. These problems have been exacerbated by decades of liberation struggle, South African state-directed interventions based on political criteria, the presence of predatory or status-quo-oriented regimes and, more recently, over a decade of economic structural adjustment programs (Ohlson and Stedman 1994). The list of pressures is increasingly well known:

- unchecked urbanization;
- mis- and over-use of diminishing communal lands;
- virtually unregulated commercial agricultural and large-scale industrial practices;
- the incapacity and/or unwillingness of government to deal with any or all of the aforementioned pressures.

The social and environmental outcomes of such pressures are also familiar: reassertion of diseases such as tuberculosis, cholera, and bilharzia; desertification due to overgrazing, overstocking, and heightening uses of fuelwood; siltation of dams and riverbeds due to soil run-off; water and air pollution due to improper use of pesticides, toxic waste dumping and inadequate controls on industrial emissions (Moyo et al 1993).

At the same time, in response to political and economic instability, new threats have emerged throughout Southern Africa. The feelings of alienation from and abandonment by the state on the part of the majority of the region's peoples, exacerbated in some cases by the negative impacts of structural adjustment, have given rise to sub- and supra-national redefinitions of "security" and "community": from Islam and ethnicity to crime networks and cooperatives (Bardill 1994). Economic disparities are increasing and increasingly visible.[1]

Everywhere there seems to be increasing incapacity of the state to take remedial actions. As a result, unemployment is on the rise throughout the region, and a majority of Southern Africans find themselves engaged in some form of informal sector activity in order to make ends meet (Bardill 1994; also Swatuk and Omari, Chapter 5).

The costs of ignoring or failing to deal with these problems are beginning to be recognized, however. And if the language of "sustainable development" remains more rhetoric than reality (see Cole 1994: 227), at least policy makers have begun to discuss the practicalities of cooperation on some of these issues (SADCC 1991; IUCN 1993).

This chapter explores some of the obstacles to and incentives for increased regional cooperation. It locates the majority of these obstacles and incentives within prevailing forms of regional state formations and economic interactions (Cheru 1992; Stoneman and Thompson 1991). It emphasizes the long-term unsustainability of the region's political economies on these bases, and points to areas of potential cooperation (Moyo et al 1993; on cooperation see African European Institute 1992; Johnson 1994; and PRODDER 1994). If left unexplored, however, these areas may ultimately lead the region toward conflict and continual decline (Bardill 1994; Homer-

Dixon 1994 and 1991; Kaplan 1994; Percival 1995). If addressed systematically and seriously, on the other hand, they may form the basis for potential cooperation and renewal (Swatuk 1994 and 1995). Economic cooperation, water resource use and the relevance of community-based organizations are three areas requiring fuller exploration.

Regionalism and Sustainable Development

This chapter takes as its philosophical starting point the nine principles for sustainable living articulated by the International Union for the Conservation of Nature (IUCN), the United Nations Environment Program (UNEP) and the World Wildlife Fund (WWF) in *Caring for the Earth: a strategy for sustainable living* (IUCN 1991). Those principles are as follows (see Yeld 1993; also Lawson 1991; and Munslow and Fitzgerald 1994):

- respect and care for the community of life
- improve the quality of life
- conserve the Earth's vitality and diversity
- minimize the depletion of non-renewable resources
- keep within the Earth's carrying capacity
- change personal attitudes and practises
- enable communities to care for their own environments
- provide a national framework for integrating development and conservation
- create a global alliance

These criteria point toward the need to view "conservation" and "development" both as mutually constitutive processes and central components of sustainable development.[2] Moreover, they suggest that sustainable development is more than technological problem solving; rather, it is part of a holistic, historical process based on the accumulated knowledge and participation of average people, especially those in rural areas (Lawson 1991). In other words, for development to be "sustainable" it must move away from top-down, overly-technocratic and scientific processes, toward more inclusive forms of policy-making and cooperation (see, Group for Environmental Monitoring, 30 September-2 October 1994; and Webster and Cock 1994).

This perspective does not discount or underestimate the strength of extant (particularly Western, modernist and capitalist) social, productive and ideological forces in shaping our world. To be sure, what is possible in terms of sustainable development is in part determined by pre-existing structures of hegemony and domination (see Cox 1981; Mittelman 1995). Clearly, sustainable development is a long-term project fraught with struggle. Nevertheless, there is both scope and need for action. This chapter now turns to a discussion of some of the more pressing obstacles to cooperation before discussing both incentives for and evidence of enhanced cooperation.

Obstacles to Cooperation

South Africa First

According to the Reconstruction and Devleopment Program (RDP), "The South African economy is in a deep-seated structural crisis and as such requires fundamental reconstruction" (1994: 75; also, see Shaw, Chapter 2 and Gelb, Chapter 3). In light of the mammoth tasks of reconstruction and development within South Africa, it will be exceedingly difficult to convince South African policy makers that their primary interests lie in a regionally focused, sustainable development-oriented socio-economic policy. As the African Development Bank (ADB) states in a recent policy document, "What is clear is that for South Africa national interests are paramount, while regional issues are secondary and likely to remain so" (ADB 1994: 16). At present, there is growing pressure from South Africans themselves for a "South Africa-first" approach to economic growth and development. The forces within South African society arrayed against regional/continental cooperation are legion and varied: from cement cartels and textile producers who are keen to see tariffs maintained and labour protected, to local NGOs, the media, and ordinary citizens who foresee increased contact with the continent not in terms of benefits to be derived from trade and investment, but as costs to be incurred from meddling in too many Rwandas, Liberias, and the like. In spite of African National Congress (ANC) statements about the long-run importance of regional cooperation (1994: 116), short-term, domestic pressures may prove too formidable for the most regionally-committed government to ignore, let alone transcend.

Mutual Fears of Regional Economic Exchange

At the same time, many policy makers and producers in the region and the continent remain sceptical of the "benefits" to be derived from increased economic cooperation with South Africa (see, in particular, Mugyenyi and Swatuk, Chapter 8). Freer movement of capital and goods, if not labour, suggests a hardening of neo-colonial relationships and uneven development. Worse, this eventuality is less easily resisted in the absence of apartheid and in the presence of debt and Bank/Fund ultimatums. Post-apartheid regional relations have already resulted in a number of trade policy disputes (E.R. Tillett, interview, 24 July 1994, Harare; John Makumbe, interview, 21 June 1994, Cape Town).[3]

Clearly, in areas as important to national policy makers as textiles and automobiles, i.e. in those areas where thousands of people are traditionally employed and whose jobs are presently threatened, cooperation is highly unlikely. As the ADB points out, regionally "the fear is that expanding trade in manufactured goods with South Africa could lead to significant deindustrialization in importing countries or that it could halt efforts of individual countries to rehabilitate their industrial sectors" (ADB 1994: 16). At the same time, South African labour fears the loss of jobs in those areas where SADC and other African states hold a distinct comparative advantage: Kenya in wood, furniture and paper products; Zimbabwe in foodstuffs, leather and footwear; and Kenya and Zimbabwe in textiles.[4]

Indeed, rather than quickly or willingly comply with the demands of the World Trade Organization (WTO) for the removal of the General Export Incentive System (GEIS),[5] many "experts" within South Africa's textile industry are arguing for increased protection prior to WTO-agreed liberalization so as "to reestablish [sic] a reasonable domestic base from which to meaningfully launch a committed export drive" (*Weekly Mail and Guardian*, 11-17 July 1994).

With South Africa's recent accession to full SADC membership, the ongoing debates within state-houses and IFIs regarding the utility of SADC versus COMESA, the desire of Africa's larger states to reach bilateral trade agreements with South Africa and the worries this engenders in smaller states fearing increased marginalization, these disputes are only the beginning of a very difficult period in regional economic relations.

Perils of Short-Term Success

In the short- to medium-term, should South Africa appear to successfully "go it alone," there will be little inclination for policy makers to alter course. Its comparatively well developed economic infrastructure—which includes, among other things, ports, road, rail and air transport networks; global telecommunications linkages; physical plant; an increasingly capital-intensive manufacturing sector; finance capital; and human resources—may tempt policy makers to seek a manufactures-for-export-oriented development strategy at the expense of all else. This would see South Africa aim for international markets beyond both the region (e.g., Kenya, Nigeria) and the continent (e.g., Europe via Lomé, the Far East, and trans-Oceanic trade with India, Australia and New Zealand).

Indeed, this NIC-bound approach meshes well with the prevailing global orthodoxy as put forward directly and rather forcefully to the new government by members of the World Economic Forum at a June 1994 meeting in Cape Town. It would also fit well with South African business priorities which emphasize the larger and decidedly more affluent markets of Asia, Europe, and North America.

(Re)Imagining Identity

The above are practical and tangible obstacles, however, and as such may ultimately be amenable to mutually beneficial solutions. There are, at the same time, equally serious but less tangible barriers to regional cooperation. One of these is a resurgent "nationalism," which remains a powerful concept by which most of the world's peoples orient themselves and their thinking in terms of "place" and "identity" (see Anderson 1983; Denham and Lombardi 1995; Walker 1994; Shapiro 1989). "Nationalism" is particularly problematic in the South African case, where the "state" has been not only a major site of conflict, but the major prize to be won during the course of the last half-century.

Black South Africans have only recently gained political power and therefore the capacity and the freedom to re-imagine both their state and their personal place within it. They are unlikely, therefore, to quickly or willingly adopt a unified national, let alone regional,[6] focus. Ongoing problems between Inkatha and the ANC offer testimony in this regard; efforts to establish an independent white "homeland," too, suggest that questions of "nationalism" and "identity" undermine the myth of white, particularly Afrikaner, "unity" fostered under apartheid ideology. In addition, for many South Africans the "region" remains a dark "other," conditioned as they have been by apartheid education to think that anything north of the Limpopo is something to be feared, subdued and overcome (see also Vale, Chapter 4).[7]

At the regional level, in spite of the fact that the majority of SADC states are unsustainable political economies (Jackson 1992; Moyo et al 1993; Bayart 1993), policy makers remain committed to "independence."[8] "Sovereignty" remains the ultimate prize in international relations. To attain, by ballot or bullet, the right to call one's self "Prime Minister" or "President," and one's allies "the government" is to increase exponentially the capacity for self-enrichment and self-aggrandizement: "sovereignty" as means of accumulation, if not production. This is a serious drawback to regional cooperation in Southern Africa. If regional cooperation can be built in other areas utilizing both traditional and non-traditional means, however, perhaps issues of sovereignty and identity will work themselves out over time.

Economic Incentives for Cooperation

The Myth of Neo-Autarchical National Development

It is true that South Africa's manufacturing sector possesses many advantages over its continental counterparts, and "tends to be internationally competitive in a range of capital-intensive lines of production" (ADB 1994: 14). However, South Africa's economy suffers from a number of embedded structural weaknesses that, if left unattended, will only worsen in the longer run (see Shaw, Chapter 2; and Gelb, Chapter 3).

One serious constraint lies in an economy structured around the extraction of wasting assets (principally gold) combined with a "continuing raw materials mentality in the South African mining industry that has restricted creative thinking about alternatives to traditional mineral and metal exports" (van Heerden 1991: 16). Moreover, in terms of the manufacturing industry of South Africa:

> The price of capital in South Africa is significantly greater than in OECD countries. South Africa's capital/labour ratios are more than twice as high as those of newly-industrialized countries, and its incremental capital output ratios far higher. Its labour costs are half of the level of those in the US and the European Community, but twice those in NICs; hourly wage rates have risen faster in South Africa than in the United States, Japan or Germany since 1970; yet labour productivity is considerably lower than in OECD countries and the major NICs. Except for power costs, most intermediate input costs are significantly higher than world price levels. Moreover, industrial production occurs behind a relatively high level of tariff protection (ADB 1994: 14).

As stated earlier, South Africa must abide by WTO trade liberalization provisions by early in the 21st century. This means that South African manufacturers stand to lose many of the cultivated advantages they have enjoyed in both the country and the continent. South African exporters currently receive comprehensive assistance under the GEIS. This system costs the state R2 billion per year and is rife with problems, most notably corruption. As reported by Hirsch and House (*Sunday Times*, 3 July 1994), "[a]ccording to the World Bank, it is doubtful that South Africa can sustain its level of manufactured exports without GEIS."

Positive-Sum Regional Economic Cooperation

While South Africa stands to lose out among foreign competition beyond the region, there remains scope for increased cooperation with SADC states. For Rob Davies, "[t]he markets of Africa will be of considerable importance to a future democratic, non-racial South Africa's efforts to become a significant exporter of manufactured goods" (*Weekly Mail and Guardian*, 30 November - 6 December 1990; see also Davies, Chapter 6). Africa absorbed 8.4% of total South African exports in 1992; this is virtually double the figure of 4.3% for 1985. According to the Africa Institute of South Africa (1994: 66),

> [b]etween 25% and 30% of all South African exports of manufactured goods go to Africa... No less than 45.8% of South Africa's exports of plastics, resins

and rubber products went to African destinations in 1992. The corresponding figures for machinery and chemicals were 43.0%, and 25.5% respectively.

Given the high value-added on end products, Africa holds great potential as a market for post-apartheid South African goods.

Significantly, 91% of South Africa's exports to and 92.7% of its imports from the African continent were with the SADC states. This fact serves to highlight the centrality of the regional market for South African goods and services (see Table 7.1). Given the existence of numerous economic institutions in Southern Africa—SACU, SADC, COMESA, MMA[9]—there also exists the possibility that a common tariff policy could be put in place which would further encourage emerging regional complementarities while maintaining some barriers to the entry of cheaper foreign goods. In other words, within SADC (which seeks enhanced production in the region), COMESA (which seeks a liberalized regional trade regime), SACU (which allocates customs revenues based on a negotiated formula) and the MMA (which links the currencies of Lesotho, Namibia and Swaziland to South Africa) lies the foundation for enhanced regional cooperation on a wide variety of economic issues.

The most immediate priority for the region is a common approach to structural change and adjustment.[10] There seems to be a number of areas in which structural adjustments can take place. First and foremost would be the removal of national and the establishment of regional export licensing arrangements. Similarly, tariff and non-tariff barriers (particularly those resulting from poor infrastructure) to trade would have to be lessened. Capital flows could be freed via the ending of exchange controls, and the welcoming of South African banks, insurance companies and other financial institutions into the region. This would need to be complemented by relatively stringent fiscal measures throughout the SADC states in order that confidence in and therefore stability of regional currencies would lessen the "financial dualism" which so hinders the ability of states to advance formal economic development on a regional basis.

TABLE 7.1 South Africa's Trade with Africa (1990 and 1992) (R millions)

Region	Exports		Imports	
	1990	*1992*	*1990*	*1992*
Total Africa	13,292.0	17,348.0	3,012.0	4,120.0
SACU	9,437.0	11,372.0	2,285.0	2,814.0
Rest of SADC	2,576.4	4,434.8	575.0	1,004.5
Rest of SEA	1,083.4	1,223.8	75.4	62.2
Rest of Africa	317.9	77.3	238.7	195.2

Source: Africa Institute of South Africa 1994: 64.

To entice cross border investment, labour policies would have to be standardized; total or partial privatization of parastatals, perhaps via entry into joint ventures with South African capital, would become a priority; and trade and investment packages would need to be regionalized (including a drastic reduction to the GEIS). The focus would be on enhancing regional industrial development, with designated centres perhaps operating solely as export processing zones (EPZ). Profits from the EPZs could be channelled into a regional industrial development fund.

Policy makers would need to coordinate responses to the demands of foreign lenders and bilateral donors, including maintaining pressure to accept the regional mandate and to treat the region as a whole.[11] Leading development institutions, like the Development Bank of South Africa, would work closely with other development banks like the ADB (of which South Africa is now a member), particularly those from the region, to act as a clearing house for bilateral donor projects and capital.

To be sure, the barriers to a successful transition to regional trade integration are formidable. A key factor is the ability of South African policy makers to resist the myriad pressures pushing toward both niche development (the prevailing global orthodoxy) and the pursuit of South African job creation at all costs. In a sense, these positions are antithetical: big capital keen to be assisted in the drive to global competitiveness; big labour, in particular, keen to preserve jobs that may be lost in the process. South African policy makers must be made to see that a nuanced approach to regional development can be a win-win situation. Economic growth within South Africa can be pursued via selective support for enhanced access to regional and continental markets.

Regional partners can also be encouraged if South Africa lowers trade barriers to SADC goods—e.g., Zimbabwe textiles—and if South African business begins to see the region as a place in which to buy goods as well as sell them. This is by no means an easy transition in thinking. As can be seen in Table 7.2, however, there is much room for increased two-way trade with the continent beyond SACU member states. Global markets can be accessed via the development of EPZs, as well as through Lomé, the Commonwealth, and bilateral arrangements.

States must recognize that the kinds of structural changes or adjustments suggested here are not the sweeping, one-dimensional package offered by the Bank and the Fund. To the contrary, there will be a need to be selective, e.g., to pursue currency devaluations on a "crawling-peg," periodic control-led basis rather than the one-shot shock therapy measures that so destabilized the economies of Zambia (see Loxley 1990; Young 1988) and Sierra Leone (Weeks 1992: 107-145), among others, in the mid-1980s; and to forge ahead with Zimbabwe-South Africa, Kenya-South Africa, and Nigeria-South Africa linkages, because that is where increased trade, investment and industrial development are most likely to bear immediate

TABLE 7.2 South Africa's Trading Partners[a]

Partner	Imports	Exports	Total Trade	Trade Balance
Continent				
Europe	26,357,129,118	26,018,548,866	52,375,677,984	(338,580,252)
Asia	15,609,055,322	14,539,690,035	30,148,745,357	(1,069,365,287)
Americas	9,257,487,317	7,118,223,767	16,375,711,084	(2,139,263,550)
Africa	1,629,498,966	6,827,346,200	8,456,845,166	5,197,847,234
Oceania	771,941,414	594,288,740	1,366,230,154	(177,652,674)
Region/Bloc				
UE	23,827,489,162	16,466,916,388	40,294,405,550	(7,360,572,774)
EFTA	2,207,766,144	8,649,857,562	10,857,623,706	6,442,091,418
Southern Africa	961,510,520	4,875,970,557	5,837,481,077	3,914,460,037
Africa Rest	667,948,681	1,950,475,297	2,618,423,978	1,282,526,616
Europe Central	202,396,518	283,565,936	485,962,454	81,169,418
Europe Rest	117,919,445	617,029,129	734,948,574	499,109,684

[a] Table adapted from Government of South Africa, Ministry of Trade and Industry, *South Africa's Trading Partners According to Total South African Imports from the Specific CoUntries, Continents and Regions/Trade Blocs* (January-December 1993), mimeo.

TABLE 7.2 South Africa's Trading Partners, continued

Partner	Imports	Exports	Total Trade	Trade Balance
Africa				
Zimbabwe	664,292,004	1,747,722,879	2,412,014,883	1,083,430,875
Zaire	262,188,230	313,659,189	575,847,419	51,440,959
Malawi	159,606,099	593,119,246	752,725,345	433,513,147
Zambia	76,158,641	1,307,155,962	1,383,314,603	1,230,997,321
Mozambique	60,323,624	964,576,504	1,024,900,128	904,252,880
Côte d'Ivoire	58,900,043	97,920,491	156,820,534	39,020,448
Kenya	30,757,524	36,865,795	67,623,319	6,108,271
Togo	29,984,888	14,516,074	44,500,962	(15,468,814)
Tanzania	21,831,951	58,562,889	80,394,840	36,730,938
Chad	19,719,676	0	19,719,676	(19,719,676)
Mauritius	19,223,919	470,932,209	490,156,128	451,708,290
Benin	16,286,203	8,021,236	24,307,439	(8,264,967)
Cameroon	8,997,007	41,082,399	50,079,406	32,085,392
Mali	8,724,209	5,549,503	14,273,712	(3,174,706)
Egypt	6,581,617	54,541,319	61,122,936	47,959,702
Sudan	6,278,305	31,037,137	37,315,442	24,758,832
Ghana	5,780,235	49,911,632	55,691,867	44,131,397
Morrocco	5,076,206	21,816,053	26,892,259	16,739,847
Gabon	4,660,110	21,965,657	26,625,767	17,305,547
Nigeria	3,684,141	40,657,946	44,342,087	36,973,805
Burkina Faso	3,310,900	2,899,538	6,210,438	(411,362)
Congo	2,217,900	48,806,224	51,024,124	46,588,324
Senegal	2,150,166	2,549,470	4,699,636	399,304
TOTAL	1,476,733,598	5,933,869,352	7,410,602,950	4,457,105,754

fruit (see Chapters Eight through Eleven in this volume). At the same time, however, the larger state and non-state actors must recognize that the rest of the region may have something to offer as well, if only skilled (Batswana technocratic) or semi-skilled (Basotho mine) labour.

The ADB (1994) calls this "variable geometry": not seeking a sweeping, once and for all attempt at regional integration; rather, seizing the advantage wherever it lies and learning to think regionally by doing things regionally. Clearly, the opportunity exists for extensive regional cooperation. Given the strength of business and labour lobbies throughout the region, however, it is unlikely that movement in the directions suggested above will occur with any kind of speed or coordination. Nevertheless, as the RDP makes clear,

> [i]n the long run, sustainable reconstruction and development in South Africa requires sustainable reconstruction and development in Southern Africa as a whole ... The democratic government must negotiate with neighbouring countries to forge an equitable and mutually beneficial program of increasing cooperation, coordination and integration appropriate to the conditions of the region. In this context, the RDP must support the goals and ideals of African integration as laid out in the Lagos Plan of Action and the Abuja declaration (RDP 1994: 116-17).

Environmental Issues as a Locus for Regional Cooperation

Increasingly, policy makers in the region have been looking toward individual (mega-) projects as panaceas. Many of these revolve around the desire to exploit natural resources, particularly water, for domestic use and for sale in the form of hydroelectric power to South Africa (Coetzee 1994; Environmental Monitoring Group: Western Cape 1992; O'Keefe and Kirkby 1994; SARDC 1994g; and van Horen 1994). Angola, Lesotho, Mozambique, Namibia, Zambia, Zaire, and Zimbabwe have entertained or are pursuing such ideas. Clearly, water—both intentionally and accidentally—is being pushed as a primary source and incentive for regional cooperation in the not too distant future. Water provides a useful focal point, then, for a discussion about potential and/or actual regional cooperation on environmental issues.

According to the Water Research Commission, "South Africa will run out of water between 2020 and 2030 unless measures to combat the shortage are taken" (SAIRR 1994: 1). Most countries or parts of countries in the region are prone to drought. Moreover, existing forms of water resource use have everywhere given way to a multitude of related environmental problems: e.g., serious overgrazing around boreholes in Botswana; erosion along the banks and siltation of the Zambezi River due to inappropriate farming practices and small-scale gold panning; severe siltation and pollution of the region's dams, lakes, rivers and wetlands; coastal erosion and destruction of shrimp nurseries in Mozambique and Tanzania due to unchecked exploitation of mangrove forests; declining fish stocks due to over-exploitation of the resource and/or eutrophication of water bodies (Moyo et al 1993; SARDC/SADC 1995).

Water, Conflict and Security

Both the need for "water security" and actions taken to assure it highlight the potential for increased conflict (in addition to cooperation) over water resources in the near future. Moreover, these conflicts may be inter-state and/or intra-state in nature, and may involve both state and non-state actors at local, national, regional, continental and global levels.

In terms of inter-state relations, many types of water resources and their uses have transboundary characteristics: proposed upstream interventions, like the Namibian National Eastern Water Carrier (NNEWC) or the proposed Pungwe River dam in Zimbabwe can have serious downstream consequences. Whereas the NNEWC proposes to "extract a limited $3m^3$/sec from the Okanvango River early in the next century, which is less than one percent of the present inflow," the Pungwe River dam will cut off the traditional water supply for many rural people in the Beira area of Mozambique (van der Heiden in Matiza and Chabwela 1992: 113; also interview with Matiza, Harare, July 1994). Similarly, Botswana's use of the Chobe impacts on riverine communities along the Zambezi. Lesotho and South Africa cooperate on the Highlands Water Project which is designed to bring water to South Africa's industrial heartland. South Africa and Mozambique, and South Africa and Zambia cooperate on supplies of hydro-electrical energy (Africa Institute 1994: 40-6).

The electrical parastatals of Zimbabwe and Zambia cooperate via the Zambezi River Authority (ZRA) on potential future use of the Zambezi. The ZRA excludes Mozambique, though actions taken upstream clearly have downstream effects. Similarly, recent plans by Zimbabwe for construction of a new hydropower station at Batoka Gorge, which runs between Victoria Falls and Kariba along the Zambezi River, have raised the interest of state and non-state actors around the world. Many people are concerned about the impact of this project on the Falls (see *Sunday Mail*, 17 July 1994; also, *IPS Environmental Bulletin* 1994: 7; Environment 2000 1994a). Clearly, water resources transcend national boundaries. It is in the interest of all those involved to sit down and discuss shared use of these resources.

The potential for conflict at the local level is no less severe. The legacy of the Tonga (see Machena in Matiza and Crafter 1994: 27-42), who inhabited and were displaced from their traditional lands in the Gwembe Valley, has left a bitter taste in environmentalists' mouths. Yet, these kinds of top-down decisions continue to be handed out. The recent commissioning of the Osborne Dam, situated on the Odzi River 30 km northwest of Mutare, has displaced 1,600 families (*Herald*, 15 July 1994). A similar pattern has marked developments around the construction of the Katse Dam in Lesotho (see Massinga in Matiza and Chabwela 1992: 43-57 for a general discussion of costs and benefits of dam construction).

The desire for hydro-electric power is compelling and indeed over-whelming, however. The provision of power for industrial development, the prospect of a steady source of foreign exchange deriving from, for example, the sale of hydroelectric power, fish exports, and tourism, among other things, in addition to the creation of numerous jobs in seriously debt distressed national economies, is clearly hard to resist. Large-scale dam construction, in spite of localized negative effects and the controversy it continues to generate, is likely to continue into the foreseeable future. The option for civil society, therefore, is one of engagement not disparagement.

Dam construction is but one small, if important, element of inter- and intra-state cooperation on water issues. Wetlands, too, are of increasing concern. Ironically, the Wetlands Program for Southern Africa was started by SADC in recognition of the negative impact haphazard and uncoordinated developments in the region had on wildlife. It was, therefore, neither a water resource or sustainable development/sustainable livelihood issue.

According to Thabeth Matiza, the International Union for the Conservation of Nature was invited by SADC to coordinate its Wetlands Program primarily in recognition of the IUCN's diverse state, (I)NGO, and business membership base. Given this base, the organization was seen to be well placed to deal with conflict/cooperation in the area of transboundary water resource issues (interview, Matiza, Harare, July 1994). The Wetlands Program seeks to integrate all aspects of water resource utilization and management: from ocean fisheries and mangrove cultivation, to hydropower, tourism and national parks management along lakes and rivers, from dambo-based, small-scale agriculture, to groundwater borehole construction and their use. In other words, it attempts to begin to treat water resource issues as part of a wider, ecologically-integrated process of regional development.

The importance of water for regional cooperation, then, is manifold. Its use involves people and institutions that transcend state boundaries and narrow, usually overly-scientific, perspectives. Increasingly, people are reluctant to leave resource management to government (Cock 1994; Group for Environmental Monitoring, 30 September-2 October 1994; Koch 1995). To avoid conflict and enhance cooperation it is therefore imperative that a broad-based dialogue be encouraged around various forms of resource use.

Beyond "Conservation"

A related potential flashpoint concerns national and regional approaches to "conservation," which since the mid-19th century in Southern Africa has been associated with racially-exclusive needs and practises. According to Koch (1995: 5), during the colonial period,

[C]onservationist legislation was diametrically opposed to the holistic relationship between people and their environment that had generally characterized the culture of most indigenous African societies. Crop and livestock farming by local peoples were seen as "unnatural" and ecologically unsound... [S]ubsistence hunters became defined as "poachers"—often by the very same settler population that had once relied on this form of economic activity for its survival. The emergence of paramilitary conservation authorities, funded by the state and devoted to the armed policing of protected areas under their control, was a logical outcome of this preservationist way of conceiving the relationship between man and nature.

Approaches to resource conservation in the late-20th century must recognize that (i) economic growth is a driving concern of business, labour and government; (ii) as populations grow and make more demands on government, scarce resources will be utilized; and (iii) conservation in its "traditional" sense is therefore outdated and unrealizable. Indeed, given the historical legacies of racial-domination in Southern Africa, it is essential that historical approaches to conservation be rejected as viable forms of natural resource management.

Ecological conservation has too long been associated with the marginalization of local communities from their lands and their resources.[12] This has been particularly so in the South African case:

> If conservation means losing water rights, losing grazing and arable land and being dumped in a resettlement area without even the most rudimentary infrastructure and services, as was the case when the Tembe elephant park [near Kosi Bay] was declared in 1983 ... this can only promote a vigorous "anti-conservation" ideology amongst the rural community of South Africa (*Weekly Mail and Guardian*, 6-12 October 1989).[13]

Increasingly, where governments take decisions without consulting local communities, conflicts ensue and, in the cases of conservation area or national parks creation, resource poaching continues.[14]

Popular Participation and Community-Based Organizations

Nevertheless, debates over natural resource use continue to be dominated by those with the time and money to devote to these issues. The multi-year debate over proposed mining of the dunes north of St. Lucia along South Africa's east coast is one example. Involved in this dispute were, on the one hand, Richards Bay Minerals, which sought to mine titanium in an area considered by many to be worthy of World Heritage Site status; and, on the other hand, a number of environmental and labour groups either permanently or temporarily opposed to the plan.[15] Ultimately, an independent tribunal headed by Justice R.N. Leon found in favour of the environmentalists and decided to ban mining from St. Lucia.

While this decision obviously pleased many environmentalists, David Fig, Director of the Group for Environmental Monitoring (GEM), lamented

the absence of communal groups from that decision-making body. According to Fig:

> Unless local communities are given a full say, right from the start, in decisions
> about the different ways in which their land can be used for economic
> development it will be impossible to promote popular support for these
> projects (*Weekly Mail and Guardian*, 17-22 December 1993).

The local community had sought return of the land for their own
designated purposes, with many favouring development of the proposed
mine and the jobs it would create. In the absence of popular participation
in the decision-making process, Fig warned,

> There is no doubt [the tribunal's decision on St. Lucia] ... will be seen by these
> people as yet another autocratic decision to protect the rights of animals and
> wealthy tourists before those of ordinary people. They will resist it—and
> there is a grave possibility of violence.

Ironically, new land dispensations introduced under the Government of
National Unity (GNU) suggest that those communities forcibly removed
from the area in the 1960s may possess title to the affected land. The GNU
is being "asked to reopen the Environmental Impact Assessment (EIA)
process and to widen the scope of participation" (IDRC/ANC/et al 1994:
42).

A similar case emerged in the Western Cape where Iscor is to build a
R4.7 billion steel mill at Saldanha Bay. There are numerous parallels with
the proposed mine at St. Lucia. First, the proposed site for the mill is "barely
a kilometre away from Saldanha harbour" and environmentalists are concerned about the project's impact on the region's sensitive "Langebaan
lagoon, the delicate wetlands ecology and the local tourist industry" (*Cape
Times*, 30 June 1995). Second, the proposed project pits politicians and
industrialists against environmentalists and local property owners concerned about groundwater pollution, the establishment of a serious eyesore
in the form of a steel mill, and other conservationist issues.[16] Third, policy
options have been articulated in an either/or fashion, i.e., either development of the steel mill and pollution of the environment, or preservation of
the environment and loss of over 4,000 temporary and several hundred
permanent job opportunities (*Weekly Mail and Guardian*, 2-8 June 1995).
Fourth, the initial decision was taken at the top levels of business and
government and was shrouded in secrecy; broad-based discussion and
transparency were not initially on the agenda. Lastly, like the St. Lucia case,
a court injunction postponed construction of the mine and provided opportunity to discuss the merits of the steel mill in a more inclusive and
systematic way. Ultimately, the decision was taken to go ahead with the
mill; jobs and the interests of poor and working class people, it seems, won
out in this case.[17]

Each of these South Africa-specific cases suggests there to be both space
and hope for community-based organizations (CBOs) to effectively partici-

pate in decision-making processes on issues vital to their survival.[18] By extension, such developments bode well for similar kinds of dialogue to emerge regarding other cases of regional and trans-national resource development.[19]

International Coalition Building

Fortunately, CBOs do not stand alone in their struggle for empowerment. Many international NGOs and inter-governmental organizations (like the IUCN, UNICEF, UNEP, UNDP, and the WWF), which now endorse conservation strategies based on sustainable utilization of resources for sustainable livelihoods, are actively assisting formerly-marginalized groups (see Makombe 1994: 4-5, 10). Sustainable utilization recognizes that conservation is not possible unless the people who live within these various eco-systems are themselves given a voice regarding preservation of the natural environment and use of the resources therein (see Munslow and Fitzgerald 1994 for a discussion of sustainable livelihood).

Programs like CAMPFIRE in Zimbabwe (Communal Areas Management Program for Indigenous Resources), the Selous Conservation Program in Tanzania, and Pilanesburg National Park in South Africa are examples of peoples' empowerment at the local level, as are game farms and commercial hunting (see, also, GEM 1994).

Dialogue has become a key element in these endeavours, with international, high profile groups like IUCN and UNDP supporting lilliputian-like CBOs by pushing Gulliverian states and companies toward inclusion and negotiation rather than exclusion and confrontation; and by lobbying for direct participation of CBOs at all levels of the policy-making process, including, in many cases, a central position for rural women (interview, Moyo-Mhlanga, Harare 1994).

For example, in 1994 the IUCN convened a seminar on the Save River catchment area. The IUCN argued for a regional management project centered on resuscitating the river. Like most environmental issues, however, action on the Save has been marred by an elitist, exclusivist approach with governments perceiving other "stakeholders" as competitors or obstacles, not partners (interview, Moyo-Mhlanga, Harare 1994). According to Matiza, this is exactly why the Zambezi River Action Plan (Zacplan) is, in her view, a failure: in its formulation, it was a UN-initiated, government-controlled project regarding management of the Zambezi River Basin; NGOs had no voice and stakeholders were not consulted.[20] At the Save River seminar, in contrast, 86 groups were represented, including many representatives from Zimbabwean-based local communities.[21]

At the same time, high-profile INGOs like IUCN are beginning to listen to government as well. Perhaps having learned from mistakes made during its handling of the EIA contracted by the government of Botswana for the proposed Southern Okavango Integrated Water Development Program, the IUCN now emphasizes communication and consensus. The IUCN coordinated the EIA from Switzerland, overlooked the feelings and interests of many Batswana, including those in the area, and approached the project from a very traditional definition of conservation. Given this approach, it is not surprising that the IUCN argued for total rejection of the program.

At present the IUCN is working on an integrated management project for the Makgadigadi Pan. And, like a reformed pugilist now preaching the virtues of pacifism, the IUCN is highly critical of those NGOs which are quick to criticize without offering alternatives (interview, Matiza, Harare, February 1996).

Conclusion

Recognizing that resource use, particularly water resource use, will be a major *casus belli* in the region in the 21st century, it is incumbent upon all groups interested in conservation, sustainable utilization, sustainable livelihoods, economic growth, and sustainable development to communicate openly and regularly with each other. It is imperative that the pressures under which governments operate be recognized, not trivialized: problems of debt, structural adjustment, burgeoning populations that increasingly live in poverty, and within a decaying environment, ensure that these resources will be used. It is imperative that stakeholders and other members of civil society, both in the region and internationally, be made aware of the issues, the stakes, and the proposed options, and take an active role in discussion.

This chapter has sought to highlight several options and opportunities for increased regional cooperation on selected economic and environmental issues. It has emphasized the role to be played by civil society in building a regional identity based on principles of sustainable development, particularly in the area of water resource use. There are many other hopeful signs as well: IGO and (I)NGO pressure on business to practise and participate in sustainable development (interviews, Hewatt, Chiuta, Tillet, Harare, July 1994); business's willing participation in sustainable development practises (Burns and Hobbs 1992; Environmental Forum of Zimbabwe n.d.; Nelson 1991); attempts by civil associations to foster indigenous NGOs, link them regionally and perhaps build a core in each group to deal with commonly shared problems (interview, Kachingwe, Johannesburg, January 1996; also MWENGO and AACC 1994); the commitment of some IGOs—like the UNDP's Africa 2000—to environmental education, resource training, popular participation and peoples' empowerment at village level; and the clever use of limited resources by NGOs like Earthlife Africa and Environment 2000 to heighten peoples' environmental awareness on both basic (e.g., litter, recycling) and complex but key issues, like nuclear power, thermal pollution, and toxic waste (interviews with Knil, Cape Town, June 1994; Hewatt, Harare, July 1994).

What is important is that these issues in every case transcend class, race and state. It is imperative that they continue to be portrayed as such, and that proposed solutions seek to avoid zero-sum scenarios, and search for variable and equitable pay-offs. Stakeholders have different preference curves, so consensus and enhanced cooperation may be possible.

Notes

1. In South Africa "the white share of total personal wealth has been estimated to be more than 80%" (Munslow and Fitzgerald 1994: 12); in Namibia, 5% of the population is responsible for 70% of the GDP, whereas the bottom 55% contribute a mere 3%; in Zimbabwe, 4,600 farmers (of which an estimated 350 are black) control 75% of the land (interview with Makumbe, Harare, July 94); in Malawi, Banda's economic interests are said to account for 30% of the country's GDP, and his economic investments include controlling interest in all Malawi's banks (interview with Chipeta, Cape Town, June 1994); and in Botswana, the seeming incontrovertible and tangible "success" of having $3 billion in forex reserves is tempered by recent UNICEF/UNDP findings that of Botswana's 1.3 million people, 45% live in absolute poverty, and 60% in relative poverty (UNICEF/UNDP 1994).

2. "Sustainable development" here follows the World Commission on Environment and Development's definition, i.e., "Development that meets the needs of the present without compromising the ability of future generations to meet their own needs."

3. Zimbabwe is one country which stands to lose a great deal in any free trade arrangement with South Africa. According to Iden Wetherell, writing in the *Weekly Mail and Guardian*, though South Africa has enjoyed a positive balance of trade with Zimbabwe for decades, "in the past three years [1992-1995] a floodtide of South African goods has swamped local manufacturers." (SAFTO reported a trade surplus with Zimbabwe of R1.5 billion in 1994.) In the words of Confederation of Zimbabwe Industries (CZI) Acting Chief Executive, Joe Foloma, "If we erode our industrial base, we will never catch up again. We do not want to become a commercial shop window in an extended Customs Union." To counter the effects of cheap South African goods, CZI is asking for trade sanctions against South Africa.

4. When Lonrho Zimbabwe attempted to export textiles to South Africa, the South African Textile Association cried for increased tariffs against Zimbabwean producers; this in spite of the fact that Lonrho's exports would barely make a ripple in the South African market (E.R. Tillett, interview, 24 July 1994, Harare). For Lonrho, this seemed to be not so much a rational reaction on the part of South African producers as a knee jerk response from a sector too comfortable and complacent behind state protection.

5. Under WTO concessions, GEIS provisions are allowed to operate until 2003. At the same time, customs duties in several key areas (e.g., on built-up cars, commercial vehicles, minibuses; on component parts; and on textiles—clothing, household textiles, fabrics, yarn, polyester fibre) are to be significantly lowered by 2002 (see *Weekly Mail and Guardian*, 15-22 June and 23-29 June 1995).

6.   According to Laurie Nathan, this applies no less to members of the ANC-in-exile who spent years living within the region: "In spite of years of exile, South Africans are not one bit concerned about the region" (interview, 4 June 1994; see also Mugyenyi and Swatuk in this volume).

7.   The persistence of this "prejudice" has been remarked upon time and again by representatives of business, government, inter- and non-governmental organizations from the SADC states (various interviews, Cape Town, 21-23 June and Harare, 13-27 July 1994).

8.   Perhaps the most trenchant recent example is that of Lesotho, a small "country" whose major export is labour, and whose major contributor to GNP lies outside the state, i.e., remittances from that labour. In the run-up to Lesotho's 1992 elections, the leader of the Basotho Congress Party (BCP), Ntsu Mokhehle, stated that integration with post-apartheid South Africa was both reasonable and possible. Once political power was attained, indeed with his party winning every seat in the national assembly, Mokhehle's position reversed. Rather than voluntarily give up sovereignty—and Kenneth Waltz (1979: 137) reminds us that "the death rate for states is remarkably low"—Mokhehle's government would now pursue the return of the so-called "lost territories" (see Weisfelder 1992 for a lucid discussion of these issues; also Southall 1991). One can only speculate on the motives underlying this policy turnaround. The point to be made is clear, however: not even the least viable state in the region is willing to contemplate the loss of sovereignty.

9.   These acronyms stand for the Southern African Customs Union (SACU), the Southern African Development Community (SADC), the Common Market of Eastern and Southern Africa (COMESA) which was formerly known as the Preferential Trade Area for Eastern and Southern Africa (PTA), and the Multilateral Monetary Area (MMA), formerly known as the Rand Monetary Area (RMA) or Rand Zone.

10. SADC economists have argued in favour of a coordinated approach to SAP for years with little positive result (Charles Hove, interview, 17 November 1989, Gaborone).

11. There is some evidence that donors are moving in this direction via, for example, the US-sponsored Cross Border Initiative (CBI). Similarly, CIDA's "Africa 21" program recognized the importance of regional solutions to Africa's various and ongoing crises (CIDA 1991).

12. Webster and Cock (1994), have recently been theorizing ways around this fact. One proposed solution is to introduce "social impact assessments" alongside "environmental impact assessments" when considering resource use.

13. Anti-conservationism or -environmentalism goes beyond the individual or community level. According to Barney Desai, senior member of the Pan-Africanist Congress (PAC), "[F]or the majority of black states whose lives and aspirations are dictated by the struggle for survival, environmental considerations are regarded with indifference or hostility" (*Weekly Mail and Guardian*, 16-22 November 1990).

14. See the sectional, country-based discussions on "Resource Use Conflicts" in Moyo et al, *The Southern African Environment* 1993.

15. See Swatuk (1996) for an extended discussion of these issues.

16. Among the groups opposed to construction are Cape Nature Conservation, National Parks Board, Wildlife Society, Earthlife Africa, the National Union of Metalworkers of South Africa, and the World Wildlife Fund. See the ongoing coverage of this issue in, for example, *The Argus*, 26 May 1995; *Weekly Mail and*

Guardian, 2-8 and 15-22 June 1995; *Business Day,* 8 June 1995; and the *Cape Times,* 30 and 31 May, 29 and 30 June, and 5 July 1995.

17. For an extended discussion of this case, see Larry A. Swatuk, "Learning the Hard Way: Environmental Policy-Making in Southern Africa," in Dan Nielson and Marc Stern, eds., *Environmental Policy Making in Latin America Compared* (San Francisco: Westview, 1996).

18. See the extended and informed discussions of community-based struggles around ecological problems in, for example, Abugre 1994: 121-34; Koch 1991: 20-31; Ramphele with McDowell 1991; and the Group for Environmental Monitoring (GEM) National Conference Proceedings from its 1994 *People and Parks National Conference.*

19. There is much concern regarding the viability of creating trans-border national parks, however. For example, South Africa, Zimbabwe and Botswana have agreed to the establishment of a trans-frontier reserve area along the Limpopo Border. Similar discussions have taken place regarding extension of the Kruger National Park into Mozambique. On paper these seem to be relatively simple ways to enhance regional cooperation. In reality, however, the creation of such "super parks" impinges on the living spaces of indigenous peoples, a problem also experienced at national level. For example, a recent decision to establish the Vhembe/Dongola National Park, which comprises 2,000 ha of land at the confluence of the Limpopo and Shashe Rivers and is to be jointly administered by the Natal Parks Board and the Northern Transvaal provincial government, has run into a serious snag. Farmers who played a key role in support of the South African government during the total onslaught era are refusing to sell and vow they will not be moved (see *Weekly Mail and Guardian,* 15-22 June 1995).

20. To this day, small-scale gold panning by those marginalized by large-scale development processes continues virtually unchecked along the banks of the Zambezi River causing serious problems of erosion, pollution, AIDS, and social conflict.

21. However, Mozambican-based CBOs were not involved in spite of their feeling the down-stream impacts of actions taken in Zimbabwe.

References

Abugre, Charles. 1994. "NGOs, Institutional Development and Sustainable Development in Post-Apartheid South Africa," in Ken Cole, ed. *Sustainable Development for a Democratic South Africa.* Pp. 121-34. London: Earthscan.

Africa 2000 Network Zimbabwe. 1993. *It's Ours: Ndezvedu/Ngokwethu.* 1(5) (September/October).

Africa Institute of South Africa. 1994. *South Africa in Sub-Equatorial Africa: Economic Interaction.* Pretoria: Africa Institute of South Africa.

African Development Bank (ADB). 1994. *Economic Integration in Southern Africa: Executive Summary,* mimeo, Harare.

African European Institute (AEI). 1992. *Post-Apartheid Regional Cooperation: International Support for Transforming Southern Africa,* Conference Report, 27-29 April, Gaborone, Botswana. The Hague: AEI.

African National Congress (ANC). 1994. *The Reconstruction and Development Program.* Johannesburg: Umanyano Publications.

———. 1993. *Foreign Policy in a New Democratic South Africa,* a discussion paper. ANC Department of International Affairs, October.

Anderson, Benedict. 1983. *Imagined Communities: Reflections on the Origin and Spread of Nationalism.* London: Verso.

Bardill, John. 1994. *Sources of Domestic Instability in Southern African States,* a conference report, Backgrounder No. 12. Bellville: Centre for Southern African Studies, University of Western Cape.

Bayart, Jean Francois. 1993. *The State in Africa: The politics of the belly.* London and New York: Longman.

Burns, D.G. and J.C.A. Hobbs. 1992. *Business and Environment in South Africa—Opportunities and Constraints.* Johannesburg: ENGEN and ESKOM.

Cheru, Fantu. 1992. *The Not So Brave New World! Problems and Prospects of Regional Integration in Post-Apartheid Southern Africa.* Bradlow Series No. 6. Johannesburg: South African Institute of International Affairs, May.

Canadian International Development Agency (CIDA). 1991. *Africa 21: A vision of Africa for the 21st Century.* Hull: CIDA.

Cock, Jacklyn. 1994. *The Potential Contribution of Social Scientists to Environmental Management in South Africa.* A GEM Discussion Paper, GEM Monitor 3/94, Social Impact Assessment Seminar, 20 May.

——— and Eddie Koch. 1991. *Going Green: People, politics and the environment in South Africa.* Cape Town.

Coetzee, Henk. 1994. "Southern African water issues," in Minnie Venter, ed. *Prospects for Progress: Critical choices for Southern Africa.* Pp. 142-51. Cape Town: Maskew Miller Longman.

Cole, Ken, ed. 1994, *Sustainable Development for a Democratic South Africa.* London: Earthscan.

Cox, Robert W. 1983. "Gramsci, Hegemony and International Relations: An Essay in Method," *Millennium* 12(2) (Summer): 162-75.

Denham, Mark and Lombardi, Mark, eds. 1995. *Problems Without Borders: Perspectives on third world sovereignty.* London: Macmillan.

Environment 2000. 1994a. *Zambezi River Environment Project,* mimeo, (Harare).

———. 1994b. *Greenline: The Newsletter of the Environment 2000,* No. 4, January.

Environmental Forum of Zimbabwe. n.d. *Code of Conduct.* Harare.

Environmental Monitoring Group: Western Cape. 1992. *Towards Sustainable Development in South Africa: A discussion paper.* Cape Town: EMG:WC.

Group for Environmental Monitoring. 1994. *National Conference Proceedings: People and Parks.* 30 September - 2 October.

Herald (Harare), various.

Herald (Port Elizabeth), various.

Homer-Dixon, Thomas. 1994. "Environmental Scarcities and Violent Conflict: Evidence from Cases," *International Security* 19(1) (Summer): 5-40.

———. 1991. "On the Threshold: Environmental Changes as Causes of Acute Conflict," *International Security* 16(2) (Fall): 76-116.

IDRC/ANC/COSATU/SACP/SANCO. 1994. *Environment, Reconstruction and Development in the New South Africa.* Mission on Environmental Policy Report, 15 August.

Interviews, various, June/July 1994, September-December 1989, Cape Town, Gaborone, Johannesburg, Pretoria and Harare.

IUCN/UNEP/WWF. 1991. *Caring for the Earth: A Strategy for Sustainable Living*. Gland, Switzerland: IUCN.

Jackson, Robert H. 1992. "The Security Dilemma in Africa," in Brian L. Job, ed. *The Insecurity Dilemma: National Security of Third World States*. Pp. 11-35. Boulder: Lynne Rienner.

Johnson, Phyllis. 1994. "Special Report: SADC: Encouraging the Concept of Community," *Southern Africa News Features*. Harare: SARDC, 29 March.

Kaplan, Robert. 1994. "The Coming Anarchy," *The Atlantic Monthly* (February): 44-76.

Koch, Eddie. 1995. "War and Peace: Changing Conservation Patterns in Southern Africa," *GEM Discussion Document*. March. Johannesburg.

———. 1991. "Rainbow Alliances," in J. Cock and E. Koch, eds. *Going Green*. Pp. 20-32.

Lawson, Lesley. 1991. "Sustainable Development for Beginners," *GEM Discussion Document*. Johannesburg: October.

Loxley, John. 1990. "Structural Adjustment Programs in Africa: Ghana and Zambia," *Review of African Political Economy* 47 (Spring): 8-27.

Makombe, Kudzai. 1993. *Sharing the Land: Wildlife, People and Development in Africa*. IUCN/ROSA Environmental Issues Series No. 1. Gland: IUCN.

Matiza, T. and H.N. Chabwela, eds. 1992. *Wetlands Conservation Conference for Southern Africa: Proceedings of the SADCC wetlands conference held in Gaborone, Botswana 3-5 June 1991*. Gland: IUCN.

——— and S.A. Crafter, eds. 1994. *Wetlands Ecology and Priorities for Conservation in Zimbabwe: Proceedings of a seminar on wetlands ecology, Harare, 13-15 January 1992*. Gland: IUCN.

McCarthy, C.L. 1988. "Structural Development of South African Manufacturing Industry: a policy perspective," *South African Journal of Economics* 56(1) (March): 1-23.

Mittelman, James H. 1995. *Globalization: Opportunities and challenges*. Boulder: Lynne Rienner.

Moyo, Sam, Phil O'Keefe and Michael Sill, eds. 1993. *The Southern African Environment: Profiles of the SADC States*. London: Earthscan.

Munslow, Barry and Patrick Fitzgerald. 1994. "South Africa: The Sustainable Development Challenge," *Third World Quarterly* 15(2), prepublication draft.

MWENGO and AACC. 1994. *Civil Society, the State and African Development in the 1990s*. Report of a Workshop on the Receding Role of the State in African Development and Emerging Role of NGOs. Nairobi: Central Graphics Services.

Nelson, Jane. 1991. "The Financial Sector and Sustainable Development," paper prepared for presentation to the South African Industrial Environmental Forum.

Ohlson, Thomas and Stephen John Stedman. 1994. *The New is Not Yet Born. Conflict and Conflict Resolution in Southern Africa*. Washington, DC: The Brookings Institute.

O'Keefe, Phil and John Kirkby. 1994. "Energy and Sustainable Development in Southern Africa," in Cole, ed. *Sustainable Development*. Pp. 57-67.

Percival, Val. 1995. "Environmental Scarcity and Violent Conflict: The Case of South Africa," draft manuscript. April. Toronto.

Programme for Development Research (PRODDER). 1994. "Southern Africa: The Dawn of a New Era," *PRODDER Newsletter* 6(2) (June).

Ramphele, Mamphela, with Chris McDowell, eds. 1991. *Restoring the Land: Environment and Change in Post-Apartheid South Africa*. London: Panos.

SADCC. 1991. *Sustaining Our Common Future, Special Report for the UNCED Secretariat*. Maseru: SADCC ELMS.

SARDC/SADC. 1995. *The State of Southern Africa's Environment*. Harare: SADC in association with Panos, SARDC and IUCN, pre-publication draft.

SARDC. 1994a. *Southern African Environmental Issues No. 1: Soil Erosion*. CEP Factsheet.

——. 1994b. *Southern African Environmental Issues No. 2: Threats to Wildlife*. CEP Factsheet.

——. 1994c. *Southern African Environmental Issues No. 3: Sources of Pollution*. CEP Factsheet.

——. 1994d. *Southern African Environmental Issues No. 4: Facts About Fish in Southern Africa*. CEP Factsheet.

——. 1994e. *Southern African Environmental Issues No. 5: Deforestation*. CEP Factsheet.

——. 1994f. *Southern African Environmental Issues No. 6: The Human Side of Soil Degradation*. CEP Factsheet.

——. 1994g. *Southern African Environmental Issues No. 7: Water*. CEP Factsheet.

Schapiro, Michael. 1989. "Textualizing Global Politics," in James der Derian and M. Shapiro, eds. *International/Intertextual Relations*. Toronto: Lexington.

Southall, Roger. 1991. "Lesotho and the Reintegration of South Africa," paper prepared for presentation at the annual meeting of the International Studies Association, Vancouver, March.

Stoneman, Colin and Carol B. Thompson. 1991. *Southern Africa after Apartheid: Economic repercussions of a free South Africa*. Africa Recovery Briefing Paper No. 4 (December).

Sunday Mail, (Harare), various.

Sunday Times, (East London), various.

Swatuk, Larry A. 1996. "Environmental Policy Making in Southern Africa: Learning the Hard Way," in Dan Nielson and Mark Stern, eds., *Environmental Policy Making in Latin America Compared*. (San Fransico: Westview).

——. 1995. "Security Beyond Sovereignty: Southern African Social Formations and Prospects for Regional Integration," in Denham and Lombardi, eds. *Problems Without Borders*.

——. 1994. "Prospects for Southern African Regional Integration after Apartheid," *Journal of the Third World Spectrum* 1(2) (Fall): 17-38.

United Nations Development Program (UNDP). 1994. *Africa 2000 Network Zimbabwe: Annual Report 1993*. Harare: UNDP.

UNICEF/UNDP. 1994. *Country Report: Botswana*. Gaborone, mimeo.

Van Heerden, Auret. 1991. *Issues and Trends in South Africa's Economy*. International Labour Organization: Geneva, unpublished.

Van Horen, Clive. 1994. *Household Energy and Environment*. South African Energy Policy Research and Training Project Paper No. 16. Cape Town: EDRC.

Walker, R.B.J. 1994. *Inside/Outside: toward a social theory of international relations*. Cambridge: Cambridge University Press.

Waltz, Kenneth W. 1979. *Theory of International Politics*. New York: Addison-Wesley.

Webster, Eddie and Jacklyn Cock. 1994. "Looking Before They Leap: Environmental Impact Assessments and Social Impact Assessments," unpublished paper, Johannesburg.

Weekly Mail and Guardian, various.

Weeks, John. 1992. *Development Strategy and the Economy of Sierra Leone*. New York: St. Martin's Press.

Weisfelder, Richard F. 1992. "Lesotho and the Inner Periphery in the New South Africa," *Journal of Modern African Studies* 30(4): pre-publication draft.

Yeld, Jonathan. 1993. *Caring for the Earth, South Africa. A strategy for sustainable living*. Stellenbosch: South African Nature Foundation.

Young, Roger. 1988. *Zambia: Adjusting to Poverty*. Ottawa: North-South Institute.

8

Of "Growth Poles" and "Backwaters": Emerging Uganda-South Africa Relations

Joshua B. Mugyenyi and Larry A. Swatuk

The National Party Elite is getting into bed with the ANC to preserve its silken sheets and the leadership elite in the ANC is getting into bed with the NP to enjoy this new-found luxury.

—Winnie Mandela

He who despairs of the human condition is a coward, but he who has hope for it is a fool.

—Albert Camus

South Africa's emerging relations with the rest of the continent are yet one more element in an already difficult and complicated process that Southall (1994: 13) has appropriately labelled "the double whammy": i.e., "having to locate a rapidly changing South Africa in a rapidly changing global environment."

This chapter argues that policy signals emanating from the two year old South African government indicate that, notwithstanding major political changes and emerging democracy, the new government's foreign economic policies will not present a radical departure from those pursued by the previous regime. The Southern African region will certainly reap post-apartheid "dividends" to the extent that regional destabilization, in the form it took during the apartheid era, will cease, allowing those economies to concentrate on the current crises of production, participation and adjustment. But South Africa's overall Africa policy, given the nature of domestic and global environments, as well as the nature and composition of the governing coalition, will be inspired and driven by economic and trade imperatives. As the Uganda case shows, and as confirmed by both Daddieh and Nyang'oro in this volume, ANC allies in harder times will not necessarily receive more "dividends." That is, Uganda and other close allies will reap few rewards for their support of the ANC through the liberation struggle, while the complicity of Kenya and Côte d'Ivoire with the apartheid state will be forgotten in the "new" South Africa's quest for more promising market opportunities. South Africa's Africa policy, therefore, is likely to be characterized by loose multilateral and selected bilateral arrangements in the continent while focusing attention on linkages with other "growth poles" beyond Africa.

While the attainment of majority rule in South Africa was a major post-Cold War "dividend," the "New World Order" environment will pose serious challenges to the political economy of South Africa: new hierarchies in the international division of labour, new forms of control, emerging regional trading blocs with protectionist tendencies, and the increased marginalization of Africa will test the limits of South Africa's capacity to mobilize investment resources and to find markets for its industrial and agricultural products (Daniel 1994: 41; Bienefeld 1994: 31). Indeed, when the new South African regime applied for economic concessions, under the General System of Preferences, to export agricultural products duty-free to the European Market, several community members were quick to deny access. Indeed, France remains determined to do so (*Africa Confidential* 1994: 6; see also Davies, Chapter 6).[1]

In spite of these externally-imposed constraints to growth, domestic expectations of post-apartheid "dividends" remain overwhelming. They include jobs; better education; improved health, housing, water, sanitation, and electricity supplies and services; the establishment of law, order and socio-political stability; and the general dismantling and transformation of apartheid political and economic structures (Cilliers 1994: 41; Daniel 1994: 30; Herbst 1994: 153; also, see the sub-section entitled "redistribution" in Chapter Three above). Simultaneously, South Africa is expected by both the domestic and international environments to continue with the consolidation of the democratic process. While attempting to meet popular demands, the ruling coalition will have to assure white South Africans that the new dispensations will not be put in place at their expense. In the meantime, local corporations and foreign investors will want to check on the "stability indicators" before committing their resources in the country.

In order to confront these daunting domestic challenges, South Africa will certainly need a more robust economic growth than the real rate of 1.2% registered in the 1980s, and -0.2% between 1990-93, i.e., the bottom end of what Gelb in Chapter Three terms "long-run stagnation." For now, however, the ANC is continuing to perform the unenviable task of dampening popular demands in the name of fiscal responsibility, balanced budgets and macro-economic stability. The expected arrival of the IMF and the World Bank on the scene to provide conditional funding may yet see more of the ANC's pre-election policy positions shelved (see Bond and Mayekiso 1996). The resulting social and political discontent will present major challenges to the ANC in the 1999 elections. For all these reasons— Southall's "double whammy"—it is unlikely that the Government of National Unity (GNU) will act charitably toward its continental neighbours. As seen in the recent uproar over Nigeria, South African foreign policy makers were unwilling to take a position against Shell Oil for fear of sending the wrong policy signals to foreign capital, i.e., "potential investors" in the "new" South Africa. As Peter Vale has remarked, "the business of foreign policy is business."

African "backwaters," like Uganda, are unlikely to realize many, if any, benefits from enhanced economic interaction with South Africa, regardless of their roles during the liberation struggle. Indeed, as the Uganda case shows, an unfettered "leviathan" may wreak havoc among Africa's smaller, fragile and less sustainable economies.

Regional and Continental Policy Imperatives

South Africa will be seeking to expand its trade world-wide but also with the other Southern African Development Community (SADC) member-states, as well as those of the Common Market for Eastern and Southern Africa (COMESA). The manner in which South Africa will deal with the rest of Africa, however, seems to be dependent upon several considerations. Will South Africa want to consolidate and assume leadership of the African geo-economic region? Will it use its relatively more diversified and larger economy to dominate or to cooperate with the weak, struggling economies of the continent, some of which previous South African regimes helped to weaken? Will African cooperation go beyond economic links to political and security concerns? Will it prefer comprehensive regional structures or differential and loose multilateral and bilateral structures guided by trade interests? Will it attempt to restructure existing regional organizations, like the South African Customs Union (SACU) and SADC, to its own advantage or toward mutually beneficial relations? Who will lose and who will gain from South African membership in regional and continental organizations? Will South Africa concentrate on more dynamic markets beyond Africa while still benefiting from its captive market in the region? Will it concentrate on global and multilateral mechanisms for enhancing trade (like the World Trade Organization), or will it prefer creative approaches to "regional" integration (like SADC, but also the proposed Indian Ocean Rim)? Several informed speculations have been put forward. Daniel (1994: 36), for example, suggests three likely scenarios for the *Southern African region*: South African domination under failed cooperation; integration under South African hegemony; and non-hegemonic regional cooperation. Clearly, SADC member-states would prefer the latter scenario, but fear the second scenario as, indeed, "second best." Hence, there has been much talk of enlarging SACU to include Zimbabwe (see Davies, Chapter 6).

Cheru (1996), Cilliers (1994: 24), and Maasdorp (1994: 42), among others, have speculated on emerging *continental economic relations*. In recent overviews of sub-Saharan Africa in a globalizing international division of labour, Chege (1996: 309-45) and Cheru (1996: 44-72) highlight the severity of Africa's problems: e.g., declining production, limited popular participation, continuing and debilitating IFI-dictated structural adjustment, high levels of external indebtedness, and marginalization from information-based, global production processes.

Given this situation, South Africa's policy makers may resolve that the country's best options lie not with Africa's predominantly weak and inefficient economies which produce more or less similar products and which have limited domestic markets. Indeed, it is a prudent South African policy maker that resists entering into any sweeping, binding agreements regarding regional and/or continental economic integration. Rather, this scenario suggests a cautious mix of selected bilateral and multilateral agreements as the cornerstone of a "South Africa-first" Africa policy.

Finally, at the *global level*, Daniel (1994: 36) suggests that, among "emerging markets," South Africa will put most of its emphasis on forging linkages with the Gulf states, South and Southeast Asia, India, China, and Latin America. Whether Southern Africa will directly benefit from these efforts remains to be seen, however.[2]

Policy Signals and Shifts

Before the emergence of the new order, South Africa had two foreign policies, the government's and that of the ANC. It may well be that the post-apartheid era still reflects this dual process, but primarily and somewhat ironically at the *national economic* level. Although the ANC's economic policies were not always succinctly stated, the Freedom Charter, which was adopted in 1956, envisaged and advocated nationalization of the commanding heights of the economy and widespread redistribution of wealth. After his release from prison, Mandela appeared to support the growth through redistribution framework when he said that "nationalization is a demand which is reasonable from our point of view. [W]here do we get the capital and resources to tackle the national issues facing us?" (quoted in Nattrass 1994: 343).

Since the unbanning of the ANC, this "growth through redistribution" framework, particularly its "inward industrialization" aspect, has been jettisoned.[3] While the ANC's 1990 *Discussion Document on Economic Policy*

(DDEP) was still in favour of redistribution and state intervention, the document did not squarely address the "tensions between state and market and between strong state intervention and consultation with organizations of civil society" (Nattrass 1994: 346).

The debates within the ANC between moderate leaders, grass roots activists, the South African Communist Party, and the Congress of South African Trade Unions (COSATU) have clearly tilted in favour of moderate leadership, and the ANC is gradually putting COSATU at arm's length while incorporating the leadership of the latter in high visibility government positions. Mandela began to signal the new shift to the effect that the ANC "would follow a mixed economy that would not differ from South Africa's present economic system" (quoted in Nattrass 1994: 352). In other words, South Africa would opt for a "developmental" state, with considerable independence from the labour movement.

Clearly, the ANC must have been under pressure from international forces, particularly the West and International Financial Institutions (IFIs), to moderate its stand. Indeed, post-election policy priorities seem to be redefining the ANC agenda away from popular demands. For example, in the 1994 budget the Reconstruction and Development Programme (RDP), a central ANC policy document, was accorded lukewarm budgetary support of R2,500 million whereas the military was allocated R10,600 million, four times the RDP total (*Africa Confidential*, August 1994). At the same time, the ANC raised salaries of the President, Cabinet Ministers, and Members of Parliament. As indicated in the opening quotation by Winnie Mandela, these actions indicate an increasing sense of self-interest and a growing gap between the historical ANC social agenda and its post-election agenda. This is an alarming and distressing development. For, two short years after the historic April 1994 elections, the GNU seems to have deliberately redefined broad-based, mass organizations into a series of fractured "interest groups" in a "pluralistic" South African political economy. In this way, the interests of township civics groups hold no priority over, and therefore must "compete" with, the major shareholders on the Johannesburg stock exchange. According to Miller (1996: 15):

> In the South African context where the distribution of wealth and resources still retains the old social configuration of apartheid, pluralistic forms of competition over resources will not swing the balance of influence onto the side of civil society. A fragmented and divided civil society constituted as stakeholders will, in the context of a dearth of resources, lead to even greater division in communities.

Pluralism as emergent in the "new" South Africa masks the real configuration of power in society. For Miller, it is imperative that civics, township, and labour organizations come together in order to avoid fragmentation and marginalization. This begins with a willingness to criticize the RDP, and expose its many less than progressive elements.

The concept of community needs to be retrieved from prevailing neo-pluralist versions and reinstated as more than a localized, administrative, participatory unit into a wider, political entity for defence of wider, working class interests. The road of pluralism will lend the divisive schemes of ethnic warlords and other elitists even greater clout.

Certainly the fight over the form and future of the South African state is not settled. Indeed, according to Ben Turok, "the South African state is not yet gelled."[4] Yet, the same may not be said for the form and future of South Africa-Africa relations.

Bilateral, Regional and Foreign Economic and Political Initiatives

The directions in which the governing coalition is pushing economic and political initiatives within Africa and beyond are, indeed, beginning to gel. As expected, the new South Africa has rejoined the United Nations and is already in the fold of the Organization of African Unity and the African Development Bank. In the regional context, South Africa has joined SADC, an organization initially established to reduce the region's dependence on South Africa. It is not entirely clear whether South Africa is seeking to redefine the structure and functions of SADC. At the same time, there are ongoing discussions regarding the reformation and potential expansion of the South African Customs Union. South Africa appears to be in little hurry to join the PTA or its more integrationist and ambitious outgrowth, COMESA (see Davies, Chapter 6).

South Africa has shown considerable interest in the resolution of perennial political crises in Angola and Mozambique. Mandela and senior government officials have put considerable pressure on warring factions in those countries to come to a negotiated accommodation. But the anticipation that Savimbi and his UNITA would be as easily suffocated by the new order as they were generously supplied and supported by the old order has not materialized. It is not entirely clear whether the South African military, always depicted as subordinate to civilian control, has fully adjusted to the new order on issues such as the subtle support of UNITA.

Thus, in continental terms, South Africa seems to be giving considerable attention to political issues focused on the Southern African region rather than Africa as a whole. For example, while it turned down the request to provide peace-keeping forces in Rwanda it has vigorously pursued peace-keeping, -making and -building efforts within the framework of SADC. Aside from simple geographical imperatives, this enhanced political emphasis on the Southern African region can be understood in at least three ways. First, in terms of the historical, primarily economic, integration of the region albeit along uneven capitalist lines. South Africa is, in Dot Keet's words, a "migrant nation."[5] Second, in terms of the immediate legacy of the contemporary "regional destabilization" period. The region is awash in refugees and small weapons, neither of which—unlike Rwanda/Burundi—can be safely ignored. Third, in terms of donor-driven efforts at regional cooperation, particularly in the areas of peace-building and human security. The Nordics and the European Union have provided extensive funding for training, workshops and research on Southern African regional security issues. There are no such pressures operative at the continental level.

Nevertheless, while diplomatic initiatives appear to be low-keyed in the continent, the private sector is vigorously combing the area for export outlets. Many erstwhile supporters of the ANC during the struggle are unlikely to cash in on "post-apartheid dividends" either in forms of bilateral aid or soft financial loans; even were it willing, South Africa possesses no such largesse. Instead the pattern that emerges indicates that the private sector, rather than the state, will be leading the South African charge into Africa, seeking out markets for their manufactured and agricultural products. "Growth poles" in the continent with developed financial and marketing infrastructures will be more attractive to the South African private sector. In the case of East Africa, Kenya, not known for its pro-ANC stance, seems to be upstaging Tanzania, an ardent ANC supporter, in diplomatic and commercial ties with the new order (although trade figures show a decline in imports from and substantial growth in exports to each country over the 1993-94 period; see Tables 8.1 and 8.2).

Overall, however, South Africa seems to have reserved its most energetic economic diplomacy and relations for growth poles and markets beyond the continent. For example, Mandela has been assiduously targeting American government and business communities for financial support and investment respectively. Firms which pulled out of South Africa in the 1980s are being enticed back into the country. It is expected that the IMF and World Bank, still viewed with suspicion by the SACP, certain elements within the ANC, and much of organized civil society (e.g., the civics, labour), will eventually join this "Washington bandwagon" by providing conditional funding. South Africa is also targeting improved relations with the European Union, which accounts for 60% of South African farm trade. Asia, too, is of major interest to both government and the private sector in the "new" South Africa. In early 1996, Japan concluded a R1,300 million aid and trade deal with Pretoria. Trade links with China and India have been strengthened while Thailand and Malaysia have become major markets for South African military equipment and technology. Similarly, South Africa has initiated vigorous commercial links with Eastern Europe, Latin America, and the Pacific (*Africa Confidential* 1994: 6).

Thus, while South Africa will continue to use its influence to attend to more proximate and immediate Southern African political and security issues, and to create a favourable diplomatic climate across Africa to enhance private sector opportunities, the main thrust will be a NICs-inspired, export-oriented strategy targeting the expanding markets of Asia.

Uganda-South Africa

What do African countries, particularly those beyond the SADC regional boundaries, expect from the new South Africa? Will those countries which supported the ANC during the struggle expect favourable diplomatic, political and economic terms from an ANC-led GNU? Are there foreign policy disagreements within the coalition regarding the status of such countries? Do such considerations matter to the South African private sector which will be looking for export opportunities in this area? How will such states sustain trade with South Africa when they may not be in a position to export goods and services to the latter? Will this situation demand South African state intervention or elaborate regional structural arrangements? Many of these questions are pertinent to emerging relations between Uganda and South Africa.

Many countries extended all manner of help to the ANC during the struggle. This included provision of refugee facilities, military and civilian training, as well as financial and diplomatic support. Uganda's contribution involved the accommodation of the bulk of Umkhonto we Sizwe (MK) cadres in the 1980s and early 1990s. At considerable risk, the Uganda government provided the MK with training and other facilities. Chris Hani had just been to Uganda when he was assassinated. To dramatize the bond between Uganda and the new South Africa, the ANC electoral success was celebrated by military parades in the streets of Kampala by hundreds of MK cadres. In the weeks that followed, South African generals arrived in Uganda to organize the airlift of the MK cadres, the majority of whom have since joined the South African National Defence Force.

The Ugandan gesture must have been appreciated by the ANC, and probably did not go down well with the then National Party government, even though the location of MK in Uganda was less of an immediate threat than had those cadres been located nearer South African borders. In essence, Uganda was a "war ally" with the ANC and might reasonably have expected some sort of post-apartheid "dividends": close diplomatic relations, bilateral economic arrangements, preferential trade relations, and South African official aid and low-interest financing.

After the euphoria, the expected bilateral warmth and vigorous relations between the two countries are yet to materialize. While Uganda has expressed a wish to open an embassy in South Africa, the latter's diplomatic priorities seem to exclude small countries like Uganda where full diplomatic ties may seem uneconomical. Nevertheless, the South African business community has taken advantage of the conducive political atmosphere to establish several commercial ventures:

- a South African bank, Stanbic, has bought out Grindlay's Bank and established a presence in Kampala;
- South African Airways and Uganda Airlines have established low level collaborative arrangements;
- elements of the South African private and parastatal sectors are negotiating business deals in the energy, mineral and health sectors;[6]
- South African manufactured goods as well as agricultural products are beginning to emerge on the Uganda market; and
- most probably the South African military is seeking to interest its counterpart in Uganda in purchasing military hardware.

The problem with these emerging relations is that Uganda has almost nothing to export to South Africa. As seen in Table 8.1, Uganda ranked 25th among African countries in terms of total exports to South Africa in 1994. Even though Uganda's exports to South Africa grew by 48.23% (to a total of R1,631,865), this increase came from a very small base (i.e., R1,100,876 or roughly US $302,000). These totals were approximately the same as those for Niger, ranked the least developed country in the world according to the UNDP's 1995 Human Development Index, and Burundi, which managed to export almost as much as Uganda in spite of ongoing ethnic tensions and civil strife.[7]

If there is to be growth in Ugandan exports to South Africa, it would seem that the best hope is in agricultural products.[8] But such products are either grown in South Africa or can be obtained more cheaply in the region and elsewhere. At the same time, there are South African agricultural goods—apples, oranges, pineapples—readily available on the streets and in the shops of Kampala.

The possibility of attracting South African tourists has been suggested, but preliminary results are disappointing. South Africa's magnificent Kruger National Park, plans for an inter-state game park stretching between Zimbabwe, Mozambique and South Africa, and an emerging Southern African regional tourist industry centred on attractions like Victoria Falls in Zimbabwe, the Okavango Delta in Botswana, and numerous opportunities for big game viewing and hunting, not to mention the continent's most well-developed tourism infrastructure, make it unlikely Uganda will be able to compete for precious tourist dollars soon.

South Africa is also unlikely to relocate industrial activities to Uganda, or other small African states, because of the latter's lack of skilled labour, financial and physical infrastructure, small domestic market, and geographical location—landlocked and next to a more diversified and "dynamic" country like Kenya with access to the sea. There are also multiple pressures within South Africa to keep and create jobs at home. If any relocation is to take place in the East African region, Kenya is likely to

TABLE 8.1 South African Imports from Africa by Country (excluding BLNS)
1993 and 1994, Selected Countries

Country	Rank 1994	Rank 1993	Value (R) 1994	Value (R) 1993	% change
Zimbabwe[a]	1	1	1,021,598,763	664,292,004	+53.79
Zaire	2	2	353,575,922	262,188,23	+16.04
Malawi	3	3	185,221,446	159,606,099	+16.05
Zambia	4	4	103,889,697	76,158,641	+36.41
Mozambique	5	5	91,930,751	60,323,624	+52.40
Côte d'Ivoire	6	6	85,704,781	58,900,043	+45.51
Togo	7	8	61,606,735	29,984,888	+105.5
Kenya	8	7	28,118,859	30,757,524	-8.58
Ghana	9	17	22,555,844	5,780,235	+290.2
Nigeria	10	21	21,182,611	3,684,141	+475.0
Tanzania	12	9	15,856,347	21,831,951	-27.37
Senegal	24	25	2,900,307	2,150,166	+34.88
Uganda	25	30	1,631,865	1,100,876	+48.23
Niger	26	-	1,574,874	690,432	+128.0
Burundi	27	39	1,499,777	146,312	+925.1
TOTAL			2,354,027,329	1,629,504,569	+44.5

[a] Exports to and imports from Zimbabwe rank approximately with those to
and from Canada. For example, South Africa exported R864,400,860 worth of
goods to Canada in 1994 while it imported R640,327,120 in the same year.
Given the size and buying power of the Canadian market versus the
Zimbabwean market; and given how the Canadian market was *restricted* while
the Zimbabwean market was *captive* over much of the apartheid era, clearly
South African business see more scope for expansion in Canada than in the
region (data provided by Statistics Canada and converted from Canadian
dollars to Rands).

Source: Government of South Africa, Ministry of Trade and Industry.

emerge as the "growth pole." As can be seen in Tables 8.1 and 8.2, excluding
the South African Customs Union states, Kenya ranked fourth among
African markets for South African exports and eighth in terms of imports.
Among South Africa's top thirteen export markets, including the Customs
Union states, Kenya and Zaire are the only non-SADC member-states.

At the same time, there is a massive drop-off between the top eight
export markets and the rest. The R22 million in goods and services Uganda
absorbed is a paltry sum in comparison to the R8 billion in goods absorbed
by the top eight (excluding BLNS). Yet, even such a seemingly small total
is significant to Uganda's economy. By comparing the data in Tables 8.1
and 8.2, it can be seen that Uganda-South Africa trade results in substantial
surpluses in favour of the latter. In 1994, the trade imbalance stood at
R22,096,610. In 1993, it was only R8,089,467. So, while Uganda's exports to

South Africa increased substantially between 1993 and 1994, imports from South Africa rose much more substantially. This imbalance in the terms of trade between South Africa and Uganda replicates itself throughout the continent. As can be seen in Table 8.3, the ratio of Exports to/Imports from Africa (excluding BLNS) in 1994 was 3.67:1. In 1993 it was 4.19:1. Yet, while the ratio showed a marginal decline, due to the relatively more rapid rise of imports from than of exports to the continent, the absolute total of the trade imbalance increased by more than 1 billion rands: from R5.2 billion in 1993 to R6.28 billion in 1994.

TABLE 8.2 South African Exports to Africa by Country (excluding BLNS) 1993 and 1994, Selected Countries

Country	Rank 1994	Rank 1993	Value (R) 1994	Value (R) 1993	% Change
Zimbabwe	1	1	2,459,440,265	1,747,199,711	+40.76
Mozambique	2	3	1,406,776,271	964,533,925	+45.85
Zambia	3	2	1,158,676,367	1,306,998,553	-11.35
Kenya	4	8	664,772,828	205,414,255	+323.6
Malawi	5	4	622,044,333	593,052,760	+4.88
Mauritius	6	5	541,318,052	470,932,209	+14.95
Zaire	7	6	349,675,991	313,596,091	+11.50
Angola	8	7	311,834,774	263,388,345	+18.39
Tanzania	9	13	183,233,438	58,562,889	+212.88
Reunion	10	9	147,406,619	190,652,814	-22.65
Ghana	12	15	80,922,432	49,477,132	+63.56
Nigeria	15	18	63,640,674	40,657,946	+56.53
Côte d'Ivoire	16	10	52,832,683	97,891,801	-85.29
Burundi	21	24	24,199,720	13,186,881	+83.51
Uganda	22	26	22,728,475	9,190,343	+147.3
Ethiopia	23	34	16,411,269	3,863,290	+324.8
TOTAL			8,631,997,982	6,825,971,272	+26.46

Source: Government of South Africa, Ministry of Trade and Industry.

TABLE 8.3 South Africa's Total Trade with Africa (excluding BLNS) and Export/Import Ratio 1993-94 (value in rands)

	1993	1994	% Change
Exports	6,825,971,272	8,631,997,982	+26.46
Imports	1,629,504,569	2,354,027,329	+44.46
Balance	5,196,466,703	6,277,970,653	
Ex/Im ratio	4.19:1	3.67:1	

Source: Derived from Ministry of Trade and Industry statistics.

In several instances the imbalance is not simply the result of traditional dependency relations, where the metropole exports manufactured goods to the periphery and the periphery exports raw materials to the metropole. As seen in Tables 8.4 and 8.5, South Africa exports the same range of goods it imports from the continent. To be sure, manufactures (particularly machinery, chemicals and transport equipment) head the list of exports. But South Africa also exports base metals, foodstuffs and vegetable products, items it also imports from the continent. South Africa's dominance of two-way trade with the continent is therefore virtually absolute. With "backwater" economies like Uganda, Burundi and Niger, however, South Africa's trade relations resemble more the classical dependency relationship. By the mid-1980s, 95% of Uganda's and 87% of Burundi's export earnings were coming from a single commodity: coffee.[9] In Niger, 85% of its export earnings came from uranium, 12% from livestock. Given debt and structural adjustment conditionalities, these countries have little hope of diversifying production, i.e., of ever "making" anything of value to South African consumers.[10] In addition, whether South Africa buys any coffee at all from Burundi or Uganda (or Brazil or Indonesia) will depend less on the "liberation struggle" and more on market prices.[11] Yet, trade liberalization opens these small markets to South African goods and services; over time, then, already glaring trade imbalances with the "new" South Africa might worsen.

TABLE 8.4 Major Items Exported to Africa (excluding BLNS) 1994

Commodity Group	Value (R)	% of Total
Machinery	1,339,315,872	15.5
Chemicals	1,253,388,171	14.5
Base metals and articles thereof	1,210,545,041	14.0
Transport equipment	833,983,297	9.7
Prepared foodstuffs	719,774,531	8.2
Vegetable products	633,859,667	7.3
Paper and board	597,426,430	6.9
Plastics and rubber	492,473,845	5.7
Textile articles	337,891,545	3.9
Animal products	227,633,423	2.6
Mineral products	226,412,195	2.6
Miscellaneous manufactured Items, including furniture	162,817,823	1.9
Cement, glass	129,717,854	1.5
Measuring, medical/surgical instruments, clocks/watches	103,611,084	1.2

Source: Government of South Africa, Ministry of Trade and Industry.

TABLE 8.5 Major Items Imported from Africa (excluding BLNS) 1994

Commodity Group	Value (R)	% of Total
Precious stones	467,753,395	19.9
Textile articles (including cotton)	403,686,685	17.1
Prepared foodstuffs	277,986,973	11.8
Vegetable products	200,809.003	8.5
Base metals	183,486,427	7.8
Mineral products	156,491,569	6.6
Machinery	134,275,125	5.7
Wood	107,111,096	4.5
Chemicals	58,248,290	2.5
Transport equipment	56,091,259	2.4
Animal products	51,416,297	2.2
Plastic and rubber	45,416,376	1.9
Miscellaneous manufactured items, including furniture	42,391,683	1.8
Hides, skins, leather	36,522,324	1.5
Footwear, headgear	36,391,741	1.5
Animal/vegetable fat	27,942,860	1.2
Measuring instruments, clocks, watches	24,294,631	1.0

Source: Government of South Africa, Ministry of Trade and Industry

It is often said that trade with the continent is important to South Africa. Indeed, the figures most cited in support of this case are that while Africa accounted for only 9.6% of total 1994 South African exports, if one includes BLNS the figure rises to 32%. Of greater importance still is the fact that the continent absorbs over 25% of all South African manufactured exports (see Davies above). These figures are usually cited by those keen on fostering mutually beneficial relations between South Africa and the rest of the continent as sufficient reason for the former pariah state to look to Africa for its economic salvation. However, and as suggested above, such simplistic analyses are to be resisted. It is more important to look at two-way trade, the already vast and still growing imbalances in South Africa's favour, and what these mean for future political and economic stability within and between African states. For, in small, debt-distressed economies like Uganda's, to see such large amounts of foreign currency drained off to South Africa year after year marks a potential flash point in developing Uganda-South Africa relations. It is for this reason that all African states, not merely the *bona fide* "back waters," fear entering into any free trade arrangements with South Africa. In the absence of compensatory mechanisms, like those which exist in the Customs Union, free trade with South

Africa is tantamount to the deindustrialization and perhaps long-term destabilization of already fragile African economies and regions.[12] It seems that more careful thought must be given to this issue if future conflicts are to be avoided.

Beyond the issues of trade and commerce, there are other areas of mutual interest in evolving Uganda-South Africa relations. For example,

- both countries are in the process of developing new constitutional orders that have to come to grips with ethnic and regional rivalries;
- both countries have opted for governments of national unity where power is shared between previously hostile political forces; and
- both countries have been undergoing the teething problems of integrating previously antagonistic armed camps into a single national defence force.

In addition, the two countries have been conducting informal consultations on the Rwanda crisis. Uganda has also been studying the financial institutional framework in South Africa, particularly financial markets.

There are other bases for inter-state cooperation which do not hinge on economics or absolute size of markets. For example, following the overthrow of Obote II, the government of Yoweri Museveni instituted a series of public fora where people could come and talk about the war, confess their roles in it, grieve their losses. In some ways this constituted a kind of national-healing, and therefore an important aspect of post-conflict nation-building. In considering the costs and benefits of their own Truth Commission, South Africans would do well to look at the Ugandan example.

At the same time, Uganda has been given something of a "window of opportunity" by the international financial institutions. Clearly, Western governments, IFIs and IGOs are all keen to see an island of stability develop amid an East/Central Africa sea of chaos. Museveni has recognized this, and used this political space to his and his country's economic and political advantage. To be sure, IFI-determined structural adjustment conditionalities remain in place (including the retrenchment of an estimated 40,000 civil servants). Yet Museveni's government has been able to bargain more effectively and sometimes more to its own satisfaction than other similarly debt-distressed, "gasping states,"[13] certainly more effectively than the size of the Ugandan economy would seem to warrant.

Leadership and good governance, however defined, are key factors in Uganda's relative "success."[14] Mandela would do well to look to Museveni for advice as the GNU edges ever closer to the Bank and the Fund.

Conclusion

The new South Africa appears to have jettisoned the growth through redistribution model in favour of a pro-business, market-led and export-oriented strategy. In order to create jobs and address other urgent domestic concerns, South Africa is likely to conduct an African policy that is animated by trade, rather than political considerations. While South Africa will continue to be interested in regional markets as well as political and security concerns, substantial integration with weak, crisis-ridden African states is unlikely to be entered into just yet. In any case, expanded trade contact between South Africa and individual African states, as the Uganda case illustrates, will be limited by the latter's inabililty to balance their trade with the former. South Africa will deal relatively more intensely with states within the immediate Southern African region as its retention of SACU and entry into SADC indicate. But the expanded SADC, now including Mauritius, will not run away from the original issue of South African economic domination which, in any case, prompted the formation of SADCC in the first place. South African entry into the regional body, however, will present opportunities for bargaining and allocation of economic activities and infrastructures in the region. This will probably present an early opportunity to determine whether South Africa is going to emphasize domination or cooperation in the region.

Beyond SADC, the South African business community will focus on other "growth poles" in Africa, like Kenya. At the same time, small, "backwater" countries like Uganda will continue to do limited business with South Africa. In other words, support for the ANC notwithstanding, Uganda will be further relegated to the margins as the Kenya-South Africa and other similar axes generate momentum.

Notes

1. The problem with the free trade deal does not lie solely with France, however. To be sure, France is reluctant to open up to South African agricultural products. According to French Senator Yves Guéna, "I know that for the [European] commission, free trade areas are a religion. Not for France." Yet, according to the Commission, "which is responsible for negotiating a trade deal with South Africa," the South Africans are not helping their case. The Commission "would like to see South Africa lobbying member countries individually and not just focusing on the heart of the union in Brussels" ("SA must go to trade talks with open eyes," *Cape Times*, 21 February 1996; also "EU slates SA govt for slow trade talks," *Business Day*, 1 February 1996).

2. There seems to be some determination on the part of fellow SADC member-states to not be left out of extra-continental trade and investment arrangements. For example, in January 1996, Botswana played host to a high-level—i.e., mostly inter-ministerial—workshop on developing SADC-East Asia linkages, specifically

with Thailand and Malaysia. While this bodes well for several SADC states, it worries state makers beyond the Southern African region.

3. There is some disagreement on this point. For example, while Ben Turok, ANC Member of National Parliament, states "inward industrialization is a dead issue, we've lost that one" (personal communication to one of the authors, 16 February 1996), Stephen Gelb's analysis in Chapter Three above suggests that the loss may not have been total.

4. Comments made at the international workshop, "South Africa Within Africa: Emerging Policy Frameworks," 24-27 January 1996, Johannesburg, South Africa.

5. Remarks made at the international workshop on "South Africa Within Africa: Emerging Policy Frameworks," 24-27 January 1996, Johannesburg, South Africa.

6. These deals basically involve supply of spare parts, technology and service. However, Eskom enquired about the possibility of buying out the Uganda electricity board.

7. Of the 174 countries ranked in the 1995 UNDP *Human Development Report*, Uganda, Burundi and Niger came in at 158, 165 and 174 respectively. Their HDI ratings are 0.329 for Uganda; 0.286 for Burundi; and 0.207 for Niger. Kenya and Tanzania, Uganda's former East African Community neighbours, have HDI ratings of 0.481 and 0.364 respectively. Of Uganda's 18 million people, 49% have access to health services, 31% to safe water, and 57% to sanitation. Life expectancy in Uganda is 44.9 years (this may be compared with 55.7 in Kenya, 52.1 in Tanzania, 50.2 in Burundi, 46.5 in Niger and 62.9 in South Africa). GNP per capita in Uganda stands at US $180 (Kenya, $330; Tanzania, $100; Burundi, $210; Niger, $290; and South Africa, $2,830). (All data taken from UNDP 1995: 156-9; and World Bank 1995: 182-3.)

8. Fifty-three percent of Uganda's 1993 GDP derived from agriculture; 12% from industry; 5% from manufacturing; and 35% from services (World Bank 1995: 186). At the same time, and also according to the World Bank (1995: 210), in 1993 100% of Uganda's exports were of primary products. This contrasts with 91% of exports in 1970.

9. Uganda's growers specialize in production of *robusta* coffee beans, whereas Burundi/Rwanda's growers specialize in *arabica*. "Of the two main varieties of coffee, the *arabica* grows in the highlands, and gives high quality mild coffee for filtering, the *robusta* from the tropical lowlands gives the stronger tasting coffee for manufacturing the soluble, so-called 'instant' beverages" (Barratt Brown and Tiffen 1992: 41).

10. In 1992, Uganda's total external debt stood at US $3,056 million. Whereas this total amounts to roughly 75% of Zimbabwe's total external debt, Uganda lacks the relative economic diversification that could help not merely service it, but pay it back (World Bank 1995: 220-1). Instead, given its near total dependence on world coffee prices, Uganda continues to lead a very precarious existence in the global economy. At the same time, it is attempting to revive its tea industry to help off-set the overwhelming dependency on coffee. However, "Uganda's tea production last year fell six percent from the previous year because of poor world prices ... Output fell to 12,687 tons from 13,461 tons in 1994, the Uganda Tea Authority said ... 'World prices remained low during the year and, with the ever-increasing costs of produc-

tion, many farmers abandoned some of the farmland'" (*The Star,* Johannesburg, 15 February 1996).

11. Or on the prospects for reciprocal trading arrangements. It may be the case that the South African government will consciously decide to buy coffee from Newly Industrializing Countries (NICs) like Brazil and near-NICs like Indonesia in hope of currying favour and therefore future access to their growing and more prosperous markets.

12. According to Ian Felps, managing director of Chloride (CA), Zimbabwe's leading battery manufacturer, "It was particularly ironic that South African Home Affairs Minister Mangosuthu Buthelezi had been in Zimbabwe last week to discuss the tide of illegal immigrants pouring into his country, when South African trade policies were contributing to de-industrialization and unemployment in the region." Felps made his comments during SADC's annual consultative conference held in Midrand, Johannesburg. "Delegates accused South African manufacturers of 'flooding the region' with their goods—while Pretoria's protective tariffs prevented reciprocal trade—and warned it could have an impact on good relations between South Africa and its neighbours" ("SA trade 'destabilizes' its neighbours," *Weekly Mail and Guardian,* 9-15 February 1996).

13. Unlike Zartman's notion of "collapsed states," Uganda might be seen as a "gasping state," i.e., while some states gasp while they die, Uganda may be catching its second breath toward renewed life. Cf. Zartman 1995.

14. The shine of Museveni's "success" is not without some tarnish, however. "The remarkable economic gains during Museveni's 10-year rule appear to have been undermined by a growing lack of public transparency and accountability. During the past two years, donors encouraged by Uganda's commitment to economic and political reforms have poured millions of dollars into the country for project and budgetary use. But the influx of aid has been matched just as vigorously by millions of Uganda shillings that disappear into the pockets of politicians and greedy bureaucrats" ("Museveni losing credibility as Kampala's banks collapse," *The Star,* 15 February 1996).

References

Africa Confidential. 1994. 35(21).

Barratt Brown, Michael, and Pauline Tiffen. 1992. *Short Changed: Africa and World Trade.* London: Pluto Press.

Bienefeld, Manfred. 1994. "The New World Order: Echoes of a New Imperialism," *Third World Quarterly* 15(1).

Bond, Patrick and Mzwanele Mayekiso. 1996. "Developing Resistance, Resisting 'Development': Reflections from the South African Struggle," *Socialist Register,* pre-publication draft.

Business Day, Johannesburg (various).

Cape Times, Cape Town (various).

Chege, Michael. 1995. "Sub-Saharan Africa: underdevelopment's last stand," in Barbara Stallings, ed., *Global Change, Regional Response: The New International Context of Development.* Pp. 309-45. Cambridge: Cambridge University Press.

Cheru, Fantu. 1996. "Africa and the New World Order: Rethinking Development Planning in the Age of Globalization," in Adebayo Adedeji, ed., *South Africa and Africa: Within or Apart?* Pp. 44-72. London: Zed.

Cilliers, Jakkie. 1994. "National and Regional Stability: expectations vs. reality," in Minnie Venter, ed., *Prospects for Progress*, pp. 40-51.

Daniel, John. 1994. "South Africa's role in the changing world and its impact on the region," in Minnie Venter, ed., *Prospects for Progress*, pp. 28-39.

Herbst, Jeffrey. 1994. "Populist Demands and Government Resources in the New South Africa," *Journal of Commonwealth and Comparative Studies* 32 (2).

Maasdorp, Gavin. 1994. "Models of co-operation in Southern Africa," in Minnie Venter, ed., *Prospects for Progress*, pp. 14-27.

Miller, Darlene. 1996. "The Ambiguities of Popular Participation in Development: A South African Case Study," paper prepared for presentation at the international workshop on "South Africa Within Africa: Emerging Policy Frameworks," 24-27 January, Johannesburg.

Nattrass, Nicoli. 1994. "Politics and Economics in ANC Economic Policy," *African Affairs* 93 (372).

Ottaway, Merina. 1991. "Liberation Movements and Transition to Democracy: the case of the ANC," *Journal of Modern African Studies* 29 (1).

Owoeye, J. 1994. "What can Africa expect from a Post-Apartheid South Africa?" *Africa Insight* 24 (1).

Somerville, Keith. 1994. "Africa: Peace in the South, in the North," *The World Today* 50 (8-9).

Southall, Roger. 1994. "Beyond the 'Double Whammy': The New South Africa in the New World Order," *Third World Quarterly* 15 (1).

The Star. Johannesburg (various).

United Nations Development Program (UNDP). 1995. *Human Development Report.* New York: Oxford University Press.

Venter, Minnie, ed. 1994. *Prospects for Progress: Critical Choices for South Africa.* Cape Town: Maskew Miller Longman.

Weekly Mail and Guardian. Johannesburg (various).

World Bank. 1995. *World Development Report.* Washington: Oxford University Press.

Zartman, I. William. 1995. *Collapsed States: The Disintegration and Restoration of Legitimate Authority.* Boulder: Lynne Rienner.

9

Post-Apartheid Kenya-South Africa Relations

Julius E. Nyang'oro

Introduction

South Africa has identified Kenya, Nigeria, Zimbabwe, and Côte d'Ivoire as sub-regional springboards for its economic thrust in Africa (SARDC 1993: 21). The identification of these four countries as important players in the "new" economic policy of South Africa is based on the perceived strength of these economies relative to the rest of the continent. Significantly, these economies are the most diversified in sub-Sahara and do present potential "growth poles" in a region that has been ravaged by economic decline for almost two decades.[1]

It is particularly interesting that the identification of these four economies by South Africa as important players in the strategy for expansion into the rest of Africa came about fairly early in the newly "liberalized" era in South African politics. By 1992, only two years after the release of Nelson Mandela from almost three decades of incarceration, Pik Botha, South Africa's Minister of Foreign Affairs under the government of President F.W. de Klerk, had visited all four countries to promote a "new understanding" and to prove that South Africa was no longer a threat to the security of other African countries. Henceforth, economic linkages with the rest of the continent would be emphasized. Trade figures were there to prove Botha's point. Exports to African countries, excluding Botswana, Lesotho, Namibia, and Swaziland which are members of the South Africa dominated South African Customs Union (SACU), rose to R5.97 billion in 1992 as compared to R3.86 billion in 1991 (see Table 7.1). Imports rose over the same period from R727 million to R1.31 billion. By 1994 exports had risen to R8.63 billion and imports to R2.35 billion, marking a three-fold increase in just four years (see Table 7.2). A paradox, however, exists in the trade relationship between South Africa and the rest of the continent. In 1992, South Africa's arms industry supplied 16 African countries with arms which earned South Africa R100 million. It may be recalled that during the heyday of apartheid, South Africa's military dominance of the Southern African region and the regime's campaign of political, military and economic destabilization had been one of the most contentious issues in the relations between South Africa and the rest of the continent.

This chapter is an attempt to analyze South Africa's relationship with Kenya, one of the presumed "growth poles" on the continent. One of the drawbacks of this exercise is the paucity of data on bilateral relations between the two countries. Beyond recorded official two-way trade—itself often misleading—the collection of reliable data has long been recognized as a serious problem in Africa (see, also, Vale's comments in Chapter 4, endnote 7 above). In addition to the trade aggregates cited above, however, there are a few obvious activities that can be noted as signifying a growing relationship between the two countries: daily airline service involving the national air carriers and other international carriers, trade missions and diplomatic exchanges. The analysis in this chapter, therefore, takes a broader outlook on the relationship between South Africa and Kenya and contextualizes the relationship in terms of both a dynamic and changing global economy, and South Africa's desire to become the sub-Saharan Africa's economic powerhouse.

The Broader Context: South Africa in Sub-Sahara

South Africa has clearly demonstrated its great desire to become and maintain itself as sub-Saharan Africa's economic leader. The Johannesburg City Council for example has launched what it calls the "Africa Initiative Club" (AIC) whose main objective is to make Johannesburg the "gateway to Africa" by developing the concept of a sub-Saharan trading area with Johannesburg as the commercial capital of the region (*Into Africa*, January 1994: 6). Part of the AIC's activities would be to participate in, or create new joint ventures which will seek to finance South African exports to other African countries.

The drive by the Johannesburg City Council to engage in these commercial activities comes on the heels of tremendous economic problems faced by South Africa in spite of the fact that its economy remains the most diversified and dynamic on the continent. Economic sanctions of the 1980s certainly took their toll. The General Agreement on Trade and Tariffs (GATT), for example, estimated that international trade and financial sanctions imposed on South Africa between 1985 and 1991 cost the country almost R40 billion—US$12.6 billion at the 1993 rate of exchange (SARDC 1993: 18). Unemployment running up to 50 percent—mainly affecting the black population—continues to be a drag on the economy. Even after the tremendous events leading to the April 1994 elections, relatively little foreign investment has come in. South Africa is coming out of the longest recession in its history—four long, painful years—and the worst since the world depression of the 1930s (see also Shaw, Chapter 2 and Gelb, Chapter 3). The non-farm economy has continued to struggle with total production essentially stagnant. Mining is slightly up and for the first time in many years, manufacturing output is climbing.

This is the context which informs South Africa's desire and strategy in dealing with the rest of the continent. But as South Africa maps out its Africa strategy, several issues need to be identified as playing an important role in the equation—issues that must be resolved if the new expansionism is to succeed: the state's role as a long time and central player in economic organization as part of the grand apartheid strategy for white welfarism; the inefficiencies created by state intervention at various levels; a black labour market that seeks to liberate itself from bureaucratic controls but with no guarantee that the "market" will deliver where the apartheid state failed due to its inherent inequalities based on race; the need to address serious inequities and maldistribution of resources within the South African political economy; and the structural constraints created by the historical development of South Africa's capital and its relationship and response to globalism. Thus, South Africa-Kenya relations cannot be understood unless these other dynamics are brought into the picture.

The other context of course is Kenya's political economy. Even though Kenya is still the most diversified of the East African economies, there has been a steady decline in performance in the last few years. According to Swamy (1994), Kenya started the 1980s with many economic advantages over other sub-Saharan countries. He attributes the structure and dynamism of the economy in the late 1970s to "the favourable policy environment" (1994: 193). But economic management deteriorated in the late 1970s resulting in the intensification or the emergence of a number of major distortions. Thus, during the 1980s, progress was significant in only a few areas. By the late 1980s and early 1990s, most of the gains of the mid-1970s had been lost.

Swamy (1994: 193-4) argues that the deterioration of the Kenyan economy can be traced to three basic factors. First, the stated policies of efficiency and budget balancing were undermined by implementation that was often lethargic and sometimes contrary to the stated policies. Second, the lack of transparency in the implementation of reforms often dampened or nullified the structural reforms that were undertaken. Here the problems associated with corruption and rent-seeking are of significance. Third, a lack of commitment to full liberalization of the economy was manifest in the continuation of state controls of pricing structure, especially in the agricultural sector, and the state's inability to escape political pressure.

Michael Chege (1994) argues that the poor implementation of economic reforms under the regime of President Moi has largely been due to the perceived need to redress some of the ethnic inequities benefiting the Kikuyu under the Kenyatta regime. Moi's government has systematically favoured the so-called Kalenjin ethnic group in its quest to counterbalance early Kikuyu domination.

To achieve Kalenjin dominance while maintaining the hegemony of the Kenya Africa National Union (KANU) has proven difficult for Moi. Since December 1991 Kenya has regained the status of a multi-party polity but only after foreign donors threatened to or did terminate their economic assistance. Significantly, in November 1991, Kenya's leading donors (the Paris Club) froze US$100 million in program aid, pending improvements in its human rights record and economic management. The repeal of the single-party provision in the constitution in December 1991 was partly a result of this external pressure. The other side of the equation was the pressure mounted by domestic proponents of multi-partyism, many of whom form the opposition in parliament today. In any case, by 1990, Kenya's economy was on a downward path, with a constant per capita GDP growth rate officially estimated at -0.9 percent between 1980 and 1987. As Chege has concluded, Kenya's

> political climate was unlikely to allow external grants and loans to take agriculture's place. Despite heroic attempts to liberalize international trade and establish duty-free "export-processing zones", British, American and other Western capital was divesting from Kenya. And although the country had a high (20 percent) domestic investment rate, new capital was channelled increasingly into construction and non-tradables rather than manufacturing or agriculture. Tourism, the leading foreign exchange source, was extremely vulnerable to political unrest and adverse international publicity (1994: 265).

Both Swamy and Chege ignore the structural inequalities embedded in Kenya's political economy since the time of independence and the contribution of resource maldistribution to the current crisis (Kitching 1980). The two authors instead put emphasis on the failure of the current regime to undertake political and economic reforms which would put Kenya in the good stead of International Financial Institutions (IFIs) with the assumption that once reforms are successfully implemented, Kenya's economy will dramatically improve. Of course this is a highly debatable assumption given the experience of other African countries (Callaghy and Ravenhill 1993) and given trends in the global political economy away from primary to manufacturing and service exports (Brown and Tiffen 1994). What may be important in the final analysis is not how well an African country reforms or adjusts under the tutelage of IFIs, but rather how a country can position itself to participate more vigorously in the New International Division of Labour (NIDL) (Mittelman 1994).

Indeed, this may be the ultimate question facing both Kenya and South Africa as the two countries position themselves in terms of (a) developing bilateral relations, (b) improving their relative positions in the global economy, and (c) deepening their respective domestic economies. I would argue that (b) and (c) may be more important considerations in the short term (5-10 years) than (a), in spite of the seeming importance of an available market for each other's products. South Africa, for example, long isolated in international trade, has begun an aggressive program to increase trade with the Gulf States, China, South Korea and South America—all areas of rapid economic growth and important players in the NIDL. South Africa has joined China in a licensing agreement to produce the Volkswagen Jetta and has also entered into a similar agreement with the Korea Motor Company (SARDC 1993: 21). If South Africa is able to create a niche for itself in global manufacturing, then there exists a possibility of rapid economic growth similar to that experienced by the Newly Industrialized Countries (NICs) of Southeast Asia and Latin America (Gereffi and Wyman 1990). In contrast Kenya, along with other sub-Saharan countries, stands little chance of achieving NIC or near-NIC status given both the predominance of neo-liberalism in the current global restructuring process, and the relative weakness of the state and essential factors of production in these countries.[2]

Economic trends in Africa may thus suggest that South Africa is poised to overwhelm the rest of the continent in terms of economic prowess. Yet there are signs that after all, South Africa faces challenges that may not be easy to overcome given the structural rigidity of its economy and other regional dynamics. These challenges include the relative high cost of labour within South Africa compared to neighbouring countries such as Zimbabwe. Lower labour costs could make other countries more attractive to Transnational Corporations (TNCs), as indeed has already happened in the case of Mauritius. Furthermore, South Africa has to balance its economic consolidation strategy in Southern Africa, where it is the predominant partner in SADC, and its economic expansion strategy in the rest of the continent, including Kenya. This latter point needs elaboration in light of Kenya's historical role in the East African region.

Kenya in East Africa: Community Revival or Further Disintegration?

Up to 1977, the East African Community (EAC), comprised of Kenya, Uganda and Tanzania, served as a model for regional integration in Africa. Studies have shown that, on balance, the EAC produced positive results in terms of economic growth and the synchronization, rationalization and promotion of a regional market (Hazlewood 1975). The EAC had its origins in the colonial period when the British colonial authorities in East Africa established the East African High Commission (EAHC) to oversee the transport and communication network in the three countries. Upon the attainment of independence by Tanzania Mainland in 1961, the EAHC was renamed the East African Common Services Organization (EACSO), but performed the same functions as its predecessor (Nye 1965).

Between 1962 and 1966, Uganda and Tanzania increasingly became unhappy with the way EACSO operated, especially in the location of key sectoral headquarters: railways, harbours, post and telecommunications, airline and EACSO headquarters itself were all located in Kenya. Both Uganda and Tanzania argued that there was a need to redistribute and relocate the headquarters of the various activities of EACSO. Thus in 1966, the East African Community was established as a successor to EACSO. Tanzania became the headquarters for the Community itself in Arusha and the harbours corporation went to Dar es Salaam instead of Mombasa. Uganda became the headquarters of post and telecommunications, and of the East African Development Bank. Kenya retained headquarters for East African Airways and the railway corporation. Nevertheless, the original maldistribution of the community's resources and the political differences between Kenya on the one hand and Uganda and Tanzania on the other, especially after the overthrow of President Obote in Uganda in 1971, created tensions that led to the breakdown of the community in 1977.

Nabudere (1981) has argued that the breakdown of the community was inevitable given its neo-colonial nature, and its original objective in 1948: to serve the economic interests of Britain, the colonial power, and to ensure the expansion of British capital in East Africa. Thus, from the perspective of British capital, economic integration in East Africa provided a much desired framework for stability and expansion of the market with Kenya as the peripheral headquarters of this process. With the independence of Tanzania and Uganda, and the need to create autonomous and internally generated development, EASCO was absolutely the wrong institution for that purpose. The fine tuning of EASCO by East African governments, reflected in the creation of a revamped EAC, could not overcome its legacy as a colonial institution.

What is of contemporary interest is the recent move to revive the community by the governments of Presidents Daniel Arap Moi in Kenya, Ali Hassan Mwinyi in Tanzania, and Yoweri Museveni in Uganda. All three presidents were not on the scene when the Community broke up in 1977, yet the legacy and the bitterness that resulted from the break-up has continued to haunt regional relationships both at the political and economic levels. It is only since December 1993, for example, that passenger railway service has been restored between Nairobi and Kampala (*Weekly Review*, August and December 1993). In thinking about reviving the community, several issues must be addressed.

In 1980 Tanzania became a member of the Southern African Development Coordination Conference (SADCC). SADCC was established as part of a larger strategy to fight against apartheid in South Africa. SADCC's membership incorporated all countries south of Tanzania, except South Africa itself (Lee 1989). As discussed elsewhere in this volume, South Africa has joined the former SADCC members in the re-constituted Southern African Development Community (SADC). The question for Tanzania now is whether it is willing to cast its lot with its former partners in EAC or continue to be part of a larger, and probably more dynamic regional organization—SADC. To be sure, Tanzania's position in SADC is very tenuous given the fact that geographically it is in the organization's periphery and economically it is one of the least developed states in the region. Its influence in SADC is thus bound to be limited. But rejoining a revamped EAC may not necessarily provide a solution to Tanzania's troubled economy. It will be going back to the old structures that led to the breakdown of the community in the first place.

Kenya, on the other hand, may see its fortunes—at least in the near term—tied to a revamped EAC. Tanzania, being both a member of EAC and SADC, may provide an avenue for Kenya to be an active economic partner of the latter. This could then produce mutual benefits for Kenya and South Africa with South Africa being the predominant economic power in the region. As it stands now, however, the situation is too fluid to allow for a clear determination of the nature of the relationship that is likely to develop between EAC and SADC.

Kenya, South Africa and Beyond

Bilateral relations between Kenya and South Africa demand an analysis which takes into account the relative, and relatively marginal, position of both countries in the NIDL. Yet South Africa is now poised to enter a new era. In spite of deep structural impediments, the South African economy provides an opportunity for transnational capital to penetrate the rest of the continent. South Africa has a comparative advantage over Southeast Asia or Latin America in this regard because of its geographical location, and old/existing capital networks between South African capital and Kenya, and between South Africa and EAC. An example of this is the tourist industry networks in the chain of hotels (e.g., Protea and Sun) in East Africa which have their base in South Africa.

Yet the ultimate question in assessing the relationship between Kenya and South Africa is how effective will South African capital be in playing an intermediary role between global capital and production activities in Kenya and the rest of the region? Two seemingly contradictory trends *cum* scenarios emerge as one ponders this question. The first scenario is that of South African domestic capital seeking outlets and new opportunities for capital investment beyond SADC territory. In this regard, banking capital (e.g., Standard Chartered) is making its presence felt, not only in Kenya, but also in Tanzania. The latter had nationalized all foreign banking institutions in the wake of the Arusha Declaration and has only recently opened its capital markets to foreign banks. Thus, in purely regional calculations, South Africa's domestic capital is poised to move into relatively closed markets north of the Limpopo.

The second scenario which emerges is that of South Africa being the facilitator, the entry point for global capital into the Southern African region, including Kenya. This scenario complicates matters quite a bit if we are to consider that South Africa's domestic capital would prefer to have the region exclusively to itself in order to face less competition and have breathing space to allow for more efficiency in its operations. The latter point is especially important because one of the issues coming to the fore now is that sanctions against South Africa during the apartheid era created tremendous hardships in the operation of South African industry. So, as I have noted, even though South African capital is the most dynamic on the continent, it is still backward by global standards (see Shaw, Chapter 2).

As these two seemingly contradictory scenarios play themselves out, we have to be mindful of other processes at work which will inevitably influence the outcome of future relations between Kenya and South Africa. I have in mind the demands that civil society in both countries is placing on the state. Since the recent multi-party elections in Kenya in 1992, various factions in civil society—labour, students, NGOs—have continued their militancy and have demanded more accountability on the part of the state. Furthermore, there is a growing demand for redistribution of resources in society which the Kenyan regime may not be in a position to effect due to the consolidation of inequitable policies in economic development (Ajulu 1995; Barkan 1994). The pressure on the regime suggests that even though Kenya was an attractive destination for foreign capital in the 1970s and 1980s, it may be less so in the 1990s. Foreign capital has always been wary of political instability and would prefer to operate in an environment which allows for maximization of profit. As it stands now, Kenya is one of the most unstable political economies in the region (Barkan 1994). As the Moi regime continues to resist pressure from civil society and is less responsive to demands for more accountability, foreign capital has shown its impatience by, among other things, balking at large capital projects cherished by the regime. One such project is the Eldoret International Airport (*Herald*, 15 March 1995; *New African*, July / August 1995: 24-6). While the Moi regime has insisted that the building of the airport will open up the Rift Valley Province to economic development, critics argue that another airport is not a priority and that, in any case, it is mistaken. They point to the fact that Nairobi and Mombasa international airports need considerable modernization and that they will remain the most important centres for air traffic. When big projects such as the Eldoret airport continue to be in limbo, the attractiveness of Kenya for foreign capital diminishes.

While the Kenyan regime seems confused on how to handle civil society, the Mandela regime in South Africa, given its origins in the protest movement, fully acknowledges the importance of civil society. Thus, instead of alienating important segments such as labour, the Mandela regime has sought a more corporatist solution, much to the criticism of radical elements in the labour movement who see corporatism as a surrender to big capital (Nzimande and Sikhosana 1995: 47-65; also, Shaw, Chapter 2 and Gelb, Chapter 3). But as Jeremy Baskin (1993) has argued, even though there is a trend towards bargained corporatism in South Africa, this strategy is less likely to succeed in the long run because of the relative weakness of labour, thus making industry the prime mover as opposed to a genuinely bargained compromise which would give labour a say in policy-making. Thus what seems to emerge even in South Africa is the diminished significance of civil society—at least the segment that does not own capital—in shaping industrial and economic policy. One can only surmise that the Mandela regime will continue to be squeezed between the desire to deliver on the revolutionary promise of economic redistribution and the "hard" realities of ownership of the means of production by relatively few members of society (Saul 1991).

In essence then, the political economies of both Kenya and South Africa exhibit uncertainties and deep structural problems which are bound to create obstacles in bilateral economic relations. Furthermore, recent data show an escalating imbalance in South Africa-Kenya trade relations. While South Africa's exports to Kenya have risen dramatically (from R205.4 million in 1993 to R664.8 million in 1994), imports from Kenya fell from already modest totals of R30.7 million to R28.1 million (see Tables 8.1 and 8.2). As with the Uganda-South Africa case, and indeed as was the case in the EAC itself, such alarmingly assymetrical terms of trade are bound to give rise to future inter-state political conflicts.

Conclusion

The picture of bilateral economic relations between Kenya and South Africa presented in this chapter is a pessimistic one. In several ways that is true, but I must hasten to add that the picture is a realistic one. As the euphoria of a new democratically-elected government in South Africa fades, the realities of the structural problems are emerging with a vengeance, as many contributors in this collection have noted (see especially Gelb, Chapter 3). South Africa, first and foremost, has quickly become a leading player in Southern Africa in the context of an enlarged SADC. This reality of course creates immediate problems for Kenya, which is not formally tied into the SADC network. Thus, looking further down the road, the identification of Kenya as part of ever-expanding South African economic interests may only be useful as a long-term strategy as opposed to an immediate or even medium term proposition.

Kenya, on the other hand, may see its immediate economic fortunes as lying within a renewed and reinvigorated East African Community, although this is proving to be a much slower development than previously anticipated (*East African Standard*, 21 April 1995). Even though more trade with South Africa is an officially stated goal, what Kenya seems to be exporting more of to South Africa is its skilled human resources—doctors, lawyers, engineers, teachers, etc. This in turn creates a crisis of development within Kenya itself. But in the final analysis Kenya actually still suffers from the classic symptoms of underdevelopment and dependence on countries of the North. Although the NIDL is creating opportunities for some fractions in some parts of the world, it presents few for Africa, let alone South Africa-Kenya bilateral relations.

Notes

1.   The conventional measure of economic trouble on the African continent has been the ubiquity of Structural Adjustment Programs (SAPs) across sub-Sahara and the continued/increased marginalization of the continent in the global political economy (Swatuk and Shaw 1994).

2.   This becomes very apparent when one compares Africa's dismal position in the late-20th century global political economy with the relatively favourable political and economic conditions which obtained for many Asian states in the 1960s and 1970s and ultimately led to the phenomenon of the NICs (Stein 1994; Swatuk and Shaw 1994).

References

Ajulu, Rok. 1995. "The Left and the Question of Democratic Transition in Kenya: A Reply to Mwakenya," *Review of African Political Economy*, 64: 220-35.

Barkan, Joel D., ed. 1994. *Beyond Capitalism vs. Socialism in Kenya and Tanzania*. Boulder: Lynne Rienner.

Baskin, Jeremy. 1993. *Corporatism: Some Obstacles Facing the South African Labour Movement*. Research Paper No. 30. Johannesburg: Centre for Policy Studies, April.

Brown, Michael Barratt and Pauline Tiffen. 1994. *Short Changed: Africa and World Trade*. Boulder: Pluto Press.

Callaghy, Thomas M. and John Ravenhill, eds. 1993. *Hemmed In: Responses to Africa's Economic Decline*. New York: Columbia University Press.

Chege, Michael. 1994. "Swapping Development Strategies: Kenya and Tanzania after Their Founding Presidents", in David E. Apter and Carl G. Rosberg, eds., *Political Development and the New Realism in Sub-Saharan Africa*. Pp. 247-290. Charlottesville: University Press of Virginia.

East African Standard (Nairobi), 21 April 1995.

Gereffi, Gary and Donald L. Wyman, eds. 1990. *Manufacturing Miracles: Paths of Industrialization in Latin America and East Asia*. Princeton: Princeton University Press.

Hazlewood, A. 1975. *Economic Integration: The East African Experience*. London: Heinemann.

Herald (Harare), various issues.

Into Africa (Johannesburg), January 1994.

Kitching, Gavin. 1980. *Class and Economic Change in Kenya: The Making of an African Petite-Bourgeoisie*. New Haven: Yale University Press.

Lee, Margaret C. 1989. *SADCC: The Political Economy of Development in Southern Africa*. Nashville: Winston-Derek.

Ministry of Finance, South Africa. 1993. *Monthly Statistics*, January-December. Johannesburg.

Mittelman, James H. 1994, "The End of a Millennium: Changing Structures of World Order and the Post-Cold War Division of Labour" in Larry A. Swatuk and Timothy M. Shaw, eds., *The South at the End of the Twentieth Century: Rethinking the Political Economy of Foreign Policy in Africa, Asia, the Caribbean and Latin America*. New York: St. Martin's.

Nabudere, D. Wadada. 1981. *Imperialism in East Africa*. 2 vols. London: Zed.

New African, July/August 1995.

Nye, Joseph. 1965. *Pan-Africanism and East African Integration*. Cambridge: Harvard University Press.

Nzimande, Blade and Mpume Sikhosana. 1995. "'Civil Society', Mass Organizations and the National Liberation Movement in South Africa," in Lloyd Sachikonye, ed., *Democracy, Civil Society and the State: Social Movements in Southern Africa*. Harare: SAPES Books.

Saul, John. 1991. "South Africa—between barbarism and structural reform," *New Left Review* 188: 3-44.

Southern African Research and Documentation Centre (SARDC). 1993. *Unfinished Business: South Africa's March to Democracy*. Harare: SARDC.

Stein, Howard, ed. 1994. *Asian Industrialization and Africa*. New York: St. Martin's.

Swamy, Gurushri. 1994. "Kenya: patay, intermittent commitment," in Ishrat Husain and Rashid Farugee, eds., *Adjustment in Africa: Lessons from Country Case Studies*. Pp. 193-237. Washington, DC: World Bank.

Swatuk, Larry A. and Timothy M. Shaw, eds. 1994. *The South at the End of the Twentieth Century: Rethinking the Political Economy of Foreign Policy in Africa, Asia, the Caribbean and Latin America*. New York: St. Martin's.

Weekly Review (Nairobi), various issues. 1992-1994.

10

South Africa and Francophone African Relations

Cyril K. Daddieh

Introduction

States have developed a habit of paying much closer attention to their relations with neighbours or with states in their immediate geographic region rather than with those actors that are further removed from them, if only because important socioeconomic and political developments in neighbouring states have a much greater propensity to reverberate throughout a delimited geographic area. This assertion has perhaps greater validity for a subordinate state system such as that of Southern Africa and more salience for small and medium-sized states than for states with global interests and a global reach.[1] It is precisely in this context that South Africa's two decades-long efforts to establish close ties with francophone West Africa, a region which is not only a considerable distance away from its shores but with which it had no historical ties and limited, if any, prior economic exchanges present an intriguing anomaly worthy of exploration.

In pursuit of its elusive quest for African allies beyond the Southern African region, a quest designed primarily to achieve political respectability and international diplomatic acceptability, South Africa concentrated its efforts on winning the support of Côte d'Ivoire's political leadership. It did so for one simple reason: the Ivorian state was widely acclaimed to be the undisputed leader of francophone Africa. Much of the credit for the attainment of this "subimperial" status and the influence that Abidjan was able to exert over its region rests with the late Ivorian President, Félix Houphouët-Boigny.[2] Indeed, one seasoned observer of francophone African affairs captured the essence of this influence by evocatively dubbing francophone Africa as "Houphouët's region" (French 1986: 9).

Abidjan's power and influence were cultivated by years of extremely cozy relations with France, coupled with the political leadership's dogged pursuit of a developmentalist ideology predicated on an unabashed courting and nurturing of foreign capital by offering attractive economic incentives including tax holidays, repatriation of profits, provision of required infrastructure such as roads, phone lines, office space, etc., at government expense, as well as exploitation of a relatively cheap and quiescent labour force, much of it coming from poorer francophone states. In short, it was able to provide an overall political climate that was stable and supportive.

These collaborative relations with France, the world economy and especially with multinational corporations (MNCs)—initially French and increasingly American—paid handsome dividends in the form of high levels of manufacturing, economic growth, an excellent network of physical infrastructure and relative affluence during at least the first two decades of independence, enough to make Abidjan the diplomatic and corporate hub of West Africa (Daddieh 1984: 122-44). As a result, South Africa surmised that successful cooperation with Côte d'Ivoire would pave the way for other francophone states to seek accommodations with apartheid. In short, Pretoria was trying to win many friends for the price of one. Moreover, Abidjan had the added attraction of having friends in high places in Western capitals.

In an earlier attempt to assess the foreign policies of francophone African states toward southern Africa, I argued that they had opted not to play a promotional role on behalf of the liberation struggle (see Daddieh 1984). As partial evidence for this claim, I drew upon a highly suggestive study of the degree of commitment of African states to the southern African liberation struggle between 1966 and 1971 which revealed that while for the continent as a whole economic success was strongly correlated with support for the nationalist movements, this was not the case for two of the more affluent African states at the time. These two francophone states, Côte d'Ivoire and Senegal, ranked seventh from the bottom and tenth from the top respectively (Khapoya 1976/77: 469-89; Akindele 1976: 557-76). Among African states with substantial economic capabilities, Abidjan showed the least interest in the liberation struggle. Consistent with this disinterest, both Joshua Nkomo and Sam Nujoma paid a brief visit to Abidjan in March 1979 but this did not signal a shift in the Ivorian orientation of quiet commercial and political dialogue with Rhodesia and South Africa (Hecht 1980: 166-73).

Pragmatism or Mischief: Going the Malawian Way?

Indeed, over the past two decades, South Africa has maintained somewhat disjointed but also incremental relations with key francophone African states, including Senegal, Gabon, Togo and the Central African Republic. These relations were often mediated by the personal involvement of

Houphouët-Boigny. While the rest of the continent sought to make pariahs out of the minority regimes of Southern Africa, to isolate them diplomatically and to extend whatever material and logistical support they could muster to the liberation movements, Houphouët-Boigny was advocating 'dialogue' and using his considerable influence in francophone regional organizations to mobilize support for this position.[3] "For South Africans," as John Barratt had earlier argued, "President Houphouët-Boigny has a particular significance because it is he who launched a movement for dialogue with the South African Government, arguing that the problems of apartheid in South Africa cannot be overcome by means of isolation, force, boycott, etc." (Barratt 1976: 12). Abidjan's position was, needless to say, antithetical to the positions and resolutions of the OAU and was opposed by the ANC as well.

France may have been instrumental in finding black friends for the white bastion in Côte d'Ivoire, Gabon, Senegal, etc., since France itself had been a recognized sanctions-buster from the start and continued to cultivate lucrative commercial and military links with Pretoria (also, Legum 1975). However, the Ivorian president's advocacy and leadership on this issue were not imposed by the dense network of relations between Abidjan and Paris. Rather, Abidjan's flirtation with apartheid South Africa was dictated by personal, political and strategic considerations. More importantly, it reflected Houphouët-Boigny's own choices even if with occasional prodding from France. It is not surprising, then, that the Ivorian leadership not only failed to use its privileged association with France to promote African interests in Southern Africa, but it began to advocate dialogue with South Africa in the early 1970s. As Bernard Charles argued, however, dialogue was "impossible" and doomed to failure partly because of the ideological and racial bases of apartheid, memories of Soweto, French military exchanges with South Africa, the increasing repression of the black population, South African collusion with the United States in their Angolan intervention and partly because it was uneven and lacked reciprocity.

> Meetings between African heads of state and the Rhodesian or South African leaders cannot change the situation unless the former are in a position to pressure the latter by offering them something sufficiently attractive to obtain—or squeeze—appreciable concessions from them (Charles 1976: 13).

Houphouët seemed undaunted by such nay-saying for three reasons. First, he wore his self-professed "realism" like a badge of honour. He claimed that there was no prospect that the West would abandon its ally, South Africa. The West, he argued, would not allow Soviet communist influence to be installed at the Cape. This conviction, coupled with the fact that Africa was too weak to challenge South Africa militarily, suggested to him that it was unrealistic as well as imprudent for Africa to go saber-rattling, advocating the use of force. He argued that Africa had to avoid at all cost the spectre of war with South Africa because it would be catastrophic for the continent. Second, while he condemned apartheid as "an affront to all of us," he also considered it an internal affair (Baulin 1985: 206). His own search for regime maintenance, given his long struggle to fend off the perceived subversive 'onslaught' by Nkrumah's Ghana and Touré's Guinea (Daddieh, forthcoming), guided his defence of the principle of non-interference in the internal affairs of states, including non-interference even in one as illegitimate as apartheid South Africa. Third, he sought to disarm his critics by arguing that there were black minorities all over Africa. How have they been treated?, he asked rhetorically. There are all kinds of discrimination in independent African countries, all kinds of apartheid (Documents du Parti 1985).

However, as was often the case with Houphouët, the real rationale behind the policy was camouflaged by the rhetorical flourish of his arguments. The truth of the matter is that Abidjan and Pretoria shared an ideological affinity. President Houphouët-Boigny detested communism and saw in Pretoria the much needed bulwark against this menace to the continent. It was his obsession with the potential destabilization of the continent through the twin Trojan Horses of eastern communism and Arab-Muslim radicalism that made the two states bedfellows.

Hence, it can be argued that South Africa and francophone Africa needed each other at a critical juncture in their political histories. South Africa was faced with an increasing deterioration in its international situation and had come to realize that it could not get into the good graces of the international community without passing through independent African states, especially those states whose favourable positions on the issue of apartheid could in no way be construed to be driven by their dependence on South Africa. Hence, these tentative contacts with Côte d'Ivoire, Senegal, Gabon, etc., were welcomed because they represented the kind of penetration of African states beyond the more captive Southern African region that could be played up to western audiences looking for justifications to maintain ties with apartheid South Africa.

For his part, as already suggested, Houphouët-Boigny embraced South Africa as a fellow crusader against communism. But the contacts with South Africa also allowed him to play his accustomed role as irritant of the OAU, an organization which he despised for its perceived lack of realism and pragmatism. It was also perhaps to return a favour for the role South Africa had played on his behalf and in support of Biafra in the Nigerian civil war (Baulin 1985). For very different reasons, then, Houphouët-Boigny led his country and some of his francophone colleagues down the Malawian path. On the one hand, the conservatism of the two leaders, Banda of Malawi and Houphouët-Boigny of Côte d'Ivoire, made their links with Pretoria less ideologically or politically anomalous, however geographically incongruous it was for Abidjan. On the other hand, as I suggested earlier, this apparent Malawianization of Ivorian and francophone states' foreign policy toward apartheid South Africa was dictated by political rather than economic necessity. Moreover, in the main, it was more clandestine than overt; it was also characterized by fits and starts and was never put on "fast track." Given the sensitive nature of the relationship, Abidjan was impelled to deny some contacts and to characterize others, including even high level visits, as "unofficial" or "private" rather than "official."

The Genesis and Evolution of Emerging Links

As far back as October 1969, Côte d'Ivoire served notice through its foreign minister, Mr. Usher Assouan, that henceforth it would refrain from voting on United Nations resolutions on apartheid or the decolonization of Rhodesia and the Portuguese colonies. Abidjan was apparently peeved by the uncompromising hostility of African states toward any attempt to raise the Biafran issue for discussion at the United Nations. This was followed a year later by Houphouët's insistence at the 5th Congress of the PDCI that dialogue with the white minority regimes was preferable to the insanity of trying to solve the apartheid problem in South Africa by resorting to the use of force. At the subsequent OAU Summit in Addis Ababa, the dialogue proposal was rebuffed by the African Heads of State. Côte d'Ivoire was told that there was to be no dialogue outside the framework of the Lusaka Manifesto of 16 April 1969.

Undeterred by this apparent setback, Houphouët-Boigny initiated the first official contacts with South Africa in October 1971 by dispatching a delegation led by the Minister of State, Mr. Koffi Ndia, to Pretoria. Although the trip was billed as a "private visit," South African Prime Minister John Vorster received the delegation amidst pomp and ceremony. Following that visit, an optimistic Houphouët-Boigny declared publicly that he would go on an official visit to South Africa if he thought his discussions would bear fruit. Not much else seems to have happened between 1971 and sometime in the middle of 1974 when South Africa's Foreign Minister, Dr. Hilgard Muller, initiated a number of secret diplomatic moves with the Ivorians. These preparatory contacts by the foreign minister resulted in a secret meeting at the end of September between Mr. Vorster and President Houphouët-Boigny at the latter's residence in Yamoussoukro. It was later disclosed that President Senghor of Senegal had participated in that encounter. Following this high level secret meeting between the two francophone leaders and Vorster, Abidjan attempted to relaunch the dialogue initiative.[4]

Still in pursuit of this elusive dialogue, a year later, in September 1975, Mr. Laurent Dona Fologo, Minister of Information, visited South Africa. Although it has been speculated that the choice of Mr. Fologo as opposed to Mr. Simeon Ake, the foreign minister, signalled dissension within the ranks of the Ivorian government over the dialogue policy (Bach 1982: 111),

President Houphouët-Boigny indicated in his famous 14 October 1985 press conference in Abidjan that he had sent Fologo to return the visit the South African Minister of Information had paid him. As if to lay to rest the speculation and to answer his critics, he suggested strongly that the choice was deliberate, even ingenious, because Fologo was accompanied by both his white French wife and his biracial ministerial secretary, "the three races that comprise the South African population," he added (Documents du Parti 1985: 33-34). During that visit, true to form, the Ivorians asked for and received South African support for a stop in Soweto and a conference with township residents which produced a memorable exchange. Fologo also launched an unequivocal attack on apartheid.[5]

Meanwhile, South Africa squeezed every ounce of diplomatic and political mileage it could by announcing rather prematurely on the eve of the visit that Côte d'Ivoire was about to establish diplomatic relations and would be naming an ambassador to Pretoria shortly. Abidjan did not take the diplomatic bait. Rather than usher in "a period of more open diplomacy," so that South Africa would not have to make "contacts under the table," as Vorster had confidently predicted a few months earlier, these visits did not produce diplomatic breakthroughs. Another two years would go by before Houphouët-Boigny would meet secretly with the South African Minister of Foreign Affairs in Geneva in September 1977. The subject of this meeting was the Namibian impasse. It is unclear whether Houphouët initiated this move or was approached to mediate between South Africa and the Namibian nationalists as a way of breathing new life into the dialogue movement. The timing was significant because it coincided with the ending of a UN conference on apartheid (Bach 1982: 112).

However, as in the past, this latest round of secret diplomacy did not produce a foreign policy success for either side. This apparent lack of concrete diplomatic success raises two related questions: Why did the two sides continue this relationship? How equitable were these relations?

The apparent persistence is explained in large part by the mutuality of interests and the potential salience of gains for both sides to which I have already alluded. With respect to the equity issue, there is no question but that for the most part the relationship was unequal. South Africa had the better of these interactions. That inequality also explains the elusiveness of the dialogue policy itself (Charles 1976). In addition to the public relations value of engaging black African states further away from its shores or neighbourhood, it was able to get landing rights for the South African Airways (SAA) as of 1975. Abidjan would later open the door to new ties with the South Africans by allowing them to open a trade mission which was later upgraded to ambassadorial level in September 1992. These initiatives paved the way for Pretoria to open a trade mission in Lomé, Togo, and to make high level contacts with other francophone states, including Cameroon and Gabon (Lowe Morna 1991: 28-30). In return, some commercial links were established with South Africa, although according to Ivorian official statistics, these transactions were extremely modest. In 1979, for instance, they amounted to less than one percent of total external trade, underscoring again the political rather than economic bases of these contacts (Bach 1982: 111).

Again, although we have focused on Côte d'Ivoire because of its centrality to the South African search for black friends outside Southern Africa, it should be noted that other francophone states also entertained relations with apartheid. In February 1975, a delegation of South African officials and businessmen were received in Bangui where they apparently convinced Emperor Bokassa of the Central African Empire that they could provide effective economic and technical aid for his country. According to South African sources cited by Legum, a R4m loan was provided for a tourist hotel complex, a construction company was negotiating a R6m housing project, and further tourist projects were being considered. In the same month, South Africa also strengthened its economic ties with Gabon, even though the latter's government apparently bought space in British newspapers to deny that they had any economic involvement with South Africa. Yet, Legum reports that an official South African source revealed that Gabon negotiated a loan for R170m from an international consortium in which South Africa was the chief partner to finance the trans-Gabon railway line. Talks were also held concerning the possibility of South African firms building low-cost housing in Libreville (Legum 1976: 16).

By contrast, Sekou Toure's Guinea remained a consistently militant foe of apartheid throughout. For instance, when he learned of the February 12 talks between President William Tolbert[6] of Liberia and Vorster in Monrovia, he did not mince his words. He is quoted as saying that "to hold a dialogue with the supporters of apartheid is to add to the racists' injury to Africa, an injury inflicted by Africa itself." He called on all African Governments to "reject all proposals for dialogue with South Africa until the day when the indignity which now soils our continent through apartheid completely disappears" (Legum 1976: 15). His reaction to Fologo's visit, which was supported by Liberia's Ambassador-at-large, Adolphus Tolbert, was equally blunt. He said it was "spectacular and eloquent proof of President Houphouët-Boigny's collusion with the hangmen of Pretoria" (Legum 1976: 27). The Congo was also critical of this independent role of Côte d'Ivoire and Liberia.

Understandably, the African National Congress (ANC) and Nelson Mandela were not happy with these developing relations, however modest, between francophone states and South Africa. Like the rest of Africa, the ANC's foreign policy had as its principal objective the isolation and delegitimization of the white minority regime (Johnston and Shezi 1993: 169-80). Even after the ANC, Pan-Africanist Congress (PAC), and South African Communist Party (SACP) were unbanned on 2 February 1990 and

Nelson Mandela was released from prison nine days later, and virtually up to the time of the multi-party elections, the ANC and Mandela struggled to keep sanctions front and center of the global response to even a crumbling apartheid regime. They hoped by so doing to ensure that the National Party and President De Klerk would negotiate in good faith and that genuinely free and fair elections would take place.

The gulf between the OAU/ANC position and the Ivorian/francophone overtures to apartheid South Africa raises a number of questions for our consideration: how will the ANC and Nelson Mandela react to Côte d'Ivoire in particular and francophone Africa in general? How will the previous history of aiding apartheid to break out of its diplomatic straight-jacket affect the new relationship? Will the rather unconstructive engagement of francophone states with apartheid South Africa have a chilling effect on relations with the new South Africa? The balance of this chapter makes a modest contribution to the search for answers.

Prognoses for Future Relations

What one can say with some certainty is that francophone Africa will lose some of its salience in future South African relations, especially because it was hardly a "strategic region" for either the ANC or the apartheid state.[7] In so far as a new South Africa will be preoccupied with domestic reconstruction in the context of limited financial resources, South Africa's energies and diplomacy will be directed toward securing new markets for its products, new investment funds, strengthening its long-standing relationship with its largest trading and investment partner, the European Community, as well as expanding and strengthening its relationships with North America, Japan, and the Pacific Rim economies (see Mandela 1993: 96). While South Africa may not be able to escape "its African destiny," President Mandela has made it abundantly clear that

> Southern Africa commands a special priority in our foreign policy. We are inextricably part of Southern Africa and our destiny is linked to that of a region, which is much more than a mere geographical concept....Increased trade with southern Africa and the wider continent could be of considerable significance for our manufacturing industries. Neighbouring countries, too, could benefit by expanding their exports to South Africa (Mandela 1993: 90-91).

This reaffirmation of the centrality of Southern Africa to post-apartheid South Africa means that the rest of the continent will play second fiddle, as has always been the case. This suggests that relations with francophone Africa will be modest at best. Meanwhile, for a variety of reasons, it is highly unlikely that under the new South Africa the current state and level of relations between the two sides will deteriorate purely as a result of their previous cooperation during the apartheid era. First, notwithstanding his long years of incarceration, Nelson Mandela has demonstrated a remarkable capacity to forgive former adversaries, and continues to pursue a policy of reconciliation at home and abroad. There is as yet no evidence to suggest that his new government's relations with francophone African states will be guided by anything other than this spirit of reconciliation. Second, the late president of Côte d'Ivoire and leader of francophone Africa also orchestrated a successful rapprochement before he passed away. Ever the astute politician, he bestowed the Houphouët-Boigny Peace Prize on both President De Klerk and future President Mandela as additional insurance. Third, Abidjan has assets that make it an attractive partner in West Africa, as we shall see below.[8]

Even when future South African relations are informed, as they are sure to be, by a redefined 'national interest', they will not preclude continuing improvements in relations with Abidjan and other francophone states (see Vale, Chapter 4). As already suggested, the departure of Houphouët-Boigny from the political scene will actually help this process by removing the complication of ANC resentment over his perfidious cooperation with apartheid. It is equally helpful that the successor regime of Henri Konan Bédié has continued where Houphouët left off in singing the praises of President Mandela. One case in point is President Bédié's remarks to the UN General Assembly on 26 September 1994:

> While the world continues to be torn apart, a few remarkably happy events give us real reason for satisfaction and reason to hope. In this regard, it is with a great deal of joy that I extend, in the name of Côte d'Ivoire, a warm and fraternal welcome to the South African delegation among us. As I had the privilege of doing in Tunis at the 30th Summit of the OAU, I would like on this happy occasion to reiterate to President Nelson Mandela our sincere congratulations for his brilliant and historic election as the head of a democratic and multiracial South Africa.[9]

President Bédié's generous remarks may be his way of continuing the political fence-mending. However, South Africa's present relations with Côte d'Ivoire are not only safe, they are sure to be strengthened in the future as development imperatives and economic actors exert influence on both sides. The quantity and quality of commercial transactions between francophone Africa and South Africa will most certainly increase now that the veil of secrecy that constrained the old relationship has been lifted (see Table 7.2). But they will also be characterized by considerable unevenness. Abidjan will remain a privileged partner because of its comparatively more developed transport and communications infrastructure and its agricultural raw material resource base which will be of interest to South African manufacturing industries because it will complement their resource needs. Moreover, both the South African business community and the foreign policy establishment are likely to want to preserve Abidjan as the center for their exchanges in the francophone region because the existing facilities there make life more pleasant, as seems to have happened already.

In short, whatever misgivings may still linger in some ANC quarters, a significant infrastructure of bilateral facilities, services and communications had already been established under apartheid. This infrastructure consists of the landing rights for SAA that had been secured since 1975, the trade mission opened in Abidjan since the beginning of 1991 and subsequently upgraded to a full diplomatic mission a year later, the recently concluded joint venture between SAA and Air Afrique under which two flights a week between Johannesburg and Abidjan beginning with the inaugural flight on 12 November 1992 now take place, the waiver of entry visa for Ivorians entering South Africa for a period up to two weeks, Côte d'Ivoire-South African Friendship Association, etc. The visa arrangement, which is reserved for Ivorians and not for Ghanaians, is already an astonishing diplomatic coup. While, according to South African Embassy sources in Abidjan, the mission is one of the smallest in the diplomatic field, Abidjan's status and role as springboard have already been anointed by the fact that the Ambassador is simultaneously accredited to Togo and Benin. A special relationship has also been established with Mali which gives it a non-residential diplomatic status.[10] The new South Africa would be hard pressed to walk away from this network of relations.

Trade missions to and from South Africa have begun to multiply, according to embassy sources in Abidjan. A July 1994 trade exposition in Abidjan, dubbed *Contact West Africa*, attracted 80 companies. This is a good indication of interest, although the interest has yet to be translated into substantial economic partnership. There is as yet virtually no South African investment in the Ivorian economy. This is largely because South Africa itself is not now (and may not be for some time to come) a capital-exporting country. Moreover, post-apartheid South Africa is going to end up a net recipient rather than a dispenser of aid.[11]

Côte d'Ivoire is the single most important trading partner South Africa has in francophone Africa. It contributed 48 percent of francophone West Africa's total exports to South Africa for 1992 and 1993, followed by Togo which contributed roughly 24 percent. The remaining trade was shared between Benin (7.6 percent), Mali (7.3 percent), Cameroon (6.7 percent), Gabon (3.9 percent), Burkina Faso (1.5 percent), and Senegal (1.3 percent). No trade figures were reported for Guinea. Abidjan also absorbed roughly 41 percent of total South African exports to the region for the same years, with Cameroon, Gabon and Togo sharing 19.6 percent, 8.1 percent and 5.8 percent respectively. The remaining 26 percent of South African exports went to the rest of the francophone regional member states. Among all African states, Côte d'Ivoire ranked sixth in imports from South Africa, and sixteenth (down from tenth in 1993) in exports to South Africa (see Tables 8.1 and 8.2).

The figures underscore the fact that trade relations remain marginal in terms of the overall direction of South African commerce, although they may understate the extent of commercial links between francophone Africa and South Africa. These initial trade figures might change as they are adjusted to reflect the lifting of the veil of secrecy that once surrounded doing business with apartheid. What will also take time to change is the structure of existing trade relations. These relations are not likely to be transformed in the near future because the 'new' South Africa is apparently interested in conserving the 'old' and familiar division of labour in which South Africa supplies manufactured goods (chemicals, plastics, tin for canning and paper for packaging pineapples and bananas, and steel materials for building) and food products (vegetable products, food, meat, and meat products) and base metals to Côte d'Ivoire and other francophone states in exchange for agricultural raw material inputs for South African industry (vegetable oils, cocoa, coffee, natural rubber, hard woods, and textiles) (see Tables 8.4 and 8.5 above).

For now at least, South Africa seems less interested in manufactured goods produced in Côte d'Ivoire or in any other francophone country. According to one South African government source, South Africa is primarily interested in those goods it does not produce at present, excluding bananas and pineapples. The composition of trade may include marginal off-season food products. Thus, the prospects for substantial improvement in investment activities in francophone Africa are not very good. Industrial investment will continue to be marginal except for "very small niche things where it is economical to manufacture in West Africa."[12]

One area in which South African investors may be poised to take advantage of emerging opportunities is that of mining technology and products. In this area, South African mining companies have little choice but to look beyond their borders because of diminishing opportunities at home. The pitch from the South African Embassy sounded quite rehearsed:

> The minerals in West Africa are similar to those found in South Africa. South African companies are African; they know how to do business in Africa. There are human and environmental factors. South Africa is one of the few countries in the world with geological surveys that are very good on both the government side and private SA companies. South Africa can provide much needed assistance in geological surveying, data collection and analysis (massaging) of the various rock samples.[13]

While the obvious places to look for mining investment may still be Southern Africa, the impression one gets from discussions with embassy officials in Abidjan is that they have already received marching orders to use diplomacy to vigorously pursue the opening of mining investment doors to South African companies in their host countries. They seek a role for South Africa which would not necessarily involve capital investments; they expect South Africa to take part in technical cooperation, using its human capital as equity in manufacturing, transport and service fields where they feel South Africa has a decided comparative advantage over other competitors.

Constraints on Future Relations with Francophone Africa

Finally, quantitative and qualitative increases in South Africa's future relations with francophone Africa face important, though not insurmountable, hurdles. Language is the most obvious one, although generally that problem is overcome in ordinary trade relations. The diplomats concede that it becomes more of a problem in daily living. The second, more serious, hurdle is overcoming the current "second scramble" for control of the region by French business interests. It is true that recent changes have undermined the exalted position these interests once occupied in francophone African trade relations which, as Howard French recently wrote,

> [had] earned this region the reputation of being Paris's *chasse gardee*, or private game reserve. The exchange rate for the Africa, or CFA, franc, fixed at 50 to one French franc from 1948 until early this year, gave Paris another strong commercial advantage over other exporters to this region. But since the currency was devalued to where it now takes 100 CFA francs to buy a French franc, France has grown anxious as West Africans have begun scrambling in search of the best deal, rather than automatically looking to France (French 1994).

Thus, while the task of dislodging the French will not be easy, the climate for future commercial relations has considerably improved over what it might otherwise have been at an earlier period.

Conclusions

With the exception of Guinea, which remained an implacable foe of apartheid throughout, South Africa and francophone Africa have had a long-standing and long-distance courtship for about two decades. Like any courtship that is frowned upon by disapproving parents, this one has been characterized by secret or behind the scenes encounters in the homes of intermediaries in Geneva, Paris and New York. These companions engaged in acts of parental defiance by, as it were, sneaking into their parents' home and bed or by occasionally meeting in public and announcing their intention to go ahead with wedding plans with or without parental consent. This South African-francophone African courtship was tantamount to mischief perpetrated by Africa's prodigal son, Côte d'Ivoire's Houphouët-Boigny, for his own political reasons. However, since 1990 the courtship has blossomed as it has come in from the cold.

The quality of present and future cooperation between South Africa and Côte d'Ivoire will be enhanced by Ivorian efforts to exorcise the ghost of the apartheid past, by new leadership, by the extant infrastructure of relations and, perhaps more importantly, by the positive gains that can accrue to both parties now that they are in a position to explore in a more rational and systematic manner the complementarities between their economies. To some extent, Ivorians and their leaders feel that they deserve cooperation from the new South Africa and any material benefits that may result from the relationship. There are lingering official media illusions about the Ivorian role in the final denouement of apartheid in South Africa. It was for this reason that the Ivorians had the audacity to be disappointed when neither De Klerk nor Mandela turned up to say a fond farewell to their beloved Houphouët.[14] Finally, if what might be called "the betrayal" or "the anger" factor has not and is not likely to bedevil francophone West African relations with an ANC-led South Africa, it is because, unlike Malawi, neither Abidjan nor any other francophone African state carried the courtship all the way to the diplomatic wedding altar by establishing formal relations with apartheid South Africa.

Notes

1. For an earlier attempt to theorize about the subordinate state system of southern Africa, see Shaw 1976, pp. 1-15 and Bowman 1976, pp. 16-43.

2. For a substantive discussion of "subimperialism" and the pronounced tendency to explain African international relations by focusing on the idiosyncrasies and ideologies of 'great' national leaders, see Daddieh, forthcoming.

3. Côte d'Ivoire was not the first state to advocate dialogue or to entertain contacts with the apartheid state. Malawi and Madagascar had already developed relations with South Africa. However, it was the only one whose geography and economic circumstances did not provide justifiable cause for doing so.

4. See Bach 1982, pp. 89-121. Interestingly enough, the Ivorian president denied the meeting, although President Senghor was later to confirm it. See Legum 1975, p. 6.

5. For a personal account of that trip, see Dona-Fologo 1985.

6. President William Tolbert of Liberia was the anglophone variant in West Africa of President Houphouët-Boigny of Francophone Africa. The two conservative regimes and leaders often consulted and supported each other on the dialogue issue. See Legum 1976.

7. For more on the ANC Department of International Affairs conception of four "strategic regions," see Johnston and Shezi 1993, p. 171.

8. This prognosis contrasts with that offered by Peter Vale for Malawi. He argues that Banda, or those close to him, understand that Malawi's future in the region may be complicated by past and present cooperation with South Africa. He suggests that the resolution of South Africa's future relations with Malawi will not be easy. However, we share the view that the exit of these two leaders from the political stage will facilitate the process of rapprochement between their countries and the new South Africa. Vale argues that "Perhaps the most promising course is for a future South African government to resite its relationship with Malawi fully when President Banda is removed from office" (Vale 1993, p. 191).

9. See "Discours de S.E.M. Henri Konan Bedie" 1994, p. 6.
10. Interviews at the South African Embassy in Abidjan on 27 July 1994 with the Third (political) Secretary and the Economic Counsellor.
11. There appears to be no illusions among South African Embassy officials about what the 'new' South Africa will be able to offer its new African friends. On the paucity of South African investments, they argue that South Africa is still a developing country, with islands of development. It is also only 'natural' for South African investors to invest in the Frontline States (Interview in the South African Embassy in Abidjan, July 1994). For more on this, see Evans 1991, pp. 709-21.
12. Interview in the South African Embassy in Abidjan.
13. Interview at the South African Embassy in Abidjan.
14. South Africa was represented by former foreign minister, Pik Botha. President Sam Nujoma of Namibia was the only head of state from southern and east Africa to attend the funeral. See Whiteman 1994, pp. 261-3.

References

Akindele, R.A. 1976. "Reflections on the Preoccupation and Conduct of African Diplomacy," *Journal of Modern African Studies* 14(4) (December): 557-76.
Bach, Daniel. 1982. "L'insertion ivoirienne dans les rapports internationaux," in Y.A. Fuare and J.-F. Medard, eds., *Etat et Bourgeoisie en Côte d'Ivoire*. Pp. 89-121. Paris: Karthala.
Barratt, John. 1976. "The Ivory Coast: a general profile and policy towards South Africa," *SAIAA Newsletter* 8(1) (April).
Baulin, Jacques. 1985. *La Politique Africaine d'Houphouët-Boigny*. Paris: Editions Eurafor-Press.
Bowman, Larry. 1976. "The Subordinate State System of Southern Africa," in Timothy M. Shaw and Kenneth A. Heard, eds., *Cooperation and Conflict in Southern Africa: papers on a regional subsystem*. Washington: University Press of America.
Charles, Bernard. 1976. "The Impossible Dialogue with 'White' Southern Africa: francophone approaches," *International Perspectives* (July-August).
Daddieh, Cyril Kofie. 1984. "Ivory Coast," in Timothy M. Shaw and Olajide Aluko, eds., *The Political Economy of African Foreign Policy: comparative analysis*. Pp. 122-44. New York: St. Martin's Press.
———. Forthcoming. "Côte d'Ivoire and Ghana-Guinea: 'A Hair in each other's soups'?" in Ken Eke and Ibrahim Gibrill, eds., *Conflict and Cooperation in Intra-African Relations*. London: Macmillan.
"Discours de S.E.M. Henri Konan Bedie, Président de la République de Côte d'Ivoire, 49eme Session de l'Assemblée Générale de l'Organisation des Nations-Unies," New York, le 26 Septembre 1994, p. 6.
Documents du Parti. 1985. *La Conférence de Presse du Président de la République Président du PDCI-RDA*. Abidjan: fraternité-hebdo editions.
Dona-Fologo, Laurent. 1985. *Côte d'Ivoire: Le Sursaut National. Recueil des discours et des conférences prononces de septembre 1975 à juillet 1985*. Abidjan: Les Nouvelles Editions Africaines.
Evans, Graham. 1991. "Myths and realities in South Africa's future foreign policy," *International Affairs* 67(4): 709-21.

French, Howard. 1986. "Houphouët's Region," *Africa Report* 31(6) (November-December).

——. 1994. "In African Markets Formerly Its Own, France Finds It Hard to Let Go," *International Herald Tribune*, September 12.

Hecht, Robert. 1980. "Ivory Coast," *New African Yearbook 1980*. London: I.C. Magazines: 166-73.

Johnston, Alexander and Sipho Shezi. 1993. "The ANC's foreign policy," in Alexander Johnston, Sipho Shezi and Gavin Bradshaw, eds., *Constitution-Making in the New South Africa*. Pp. 169-80. London: Leicester University Press.

Khapoya, Vincent B. 1976/77. "Determinants of African Support for African Liberation Movements: a comparative analysis," *Journal of African Studies* 3(4) (Winter): 469-89.

Legum, Colin. 1975. *Southern Africa: The Secret Diplomacy of Detente. South Africa at the Crossroads*. New York: Africana Publishing Company.

——. 1976. *Vorster's Gamble for Africa: How the Search for Peace Failed*. London: Rex Collins.

Lowe Morna, Colleen. 1991. "The Pariah's New Pals," *Africa Report* (May-June): 28-30.

Mandela, Nelson. 1993. "South Africa's Future Foreign Policy," *Foreign Affairs* 72(5) (November/December).

Shaw, Timothy M. 1976. "Introduction to Southern Africa as a Regional Subsystem, in Timothy M. Shaw and Kenneth A. Heard, eds., *Cooperation and Conflict in Southern Africa*, Washington: University Press of America.

Vale, Peter. 1993. "Foreign Policy of a Post-Apartheid South Africa," in Alexander Johnston, Sipho Shezi and Gavin Bradshaw, eds., *Constitution-Making in the New South Africa*. London: Leicester University Press.

Whiteman, Kaye. 1994. "The last farewell," *West Africa* No. 3985 (14-20 February): 261-63.

11

Problems and Prospects for Nigerian-South African Relations and Their Implications for Africa's Economic Renaissance

John Inegbedion

Introduction

Is history about to repeat itself in African economic and political relations? Does the demise of apartheid in South Africa resurrect Cecil Rhodes' dream of taking Africa from the "Cape to Cairo" (cf Leistner 1994; *Economist*, 12 August 1995)? Is the "new" South Africa seeking to dominate its neighbours and the continent as the "old" sought to do under Rhodes and apartheid? Are South African foreign and economic policies approaching Africa as a prize to be won?

If so, is the rest of Africa likely to benefit from such a conquest-like approach to post-apartheid social, political and economic relations on the continent? Or will regional interaction after apartheid simply revive Rhodes' design on Africa? If not, to what extent will the politico-economic exchanges between the new South Africa and the rest of Africa enhance the prospects for development and democracy on the continent in the coming decade?

This chapter addresses the specific case of Nigerian-South African relations. When carefully examined, the political and economic relations between these two countries bear more heavily on the question than those of the other "growth poles" examined in this volume. To be sure, Nigeria was one of the most ardent critics of South Africa after the two countries severed all formal economic and political ties over apartheid in 1962. In fact, they remained bitter enemies until South Africa began to dismantle its racist system in 1990 (Inegbedion 1991).

However, it stands to reason that, given the task of rebuilding Africa's economy, international perceptions, and the two states' own role conception and resources, Abuja and Pretoria will figure prominently in each other's regional socio-economic and foreign policy in the post-apartheid era (Inegbedion 1994a and b; *Economist Intelligence Unit* (EIU) 1995a). Nigeria and South Africa constitute *core states* and stand *primus inter pares* in their respective regions, especially within the sixteen-country Economic Community of West African States (ECOWAS) formed in 1975 and the twelve-member Southern African Development Community (SADC) established in 1980 (cf Myers 1991; Adibe 1994; Inegbedion 1994b). This is not to say that either has all the answers to Africa's external debt crisis and economic marginalization. Rather, their combined resources constitute necessary factors in Africa's economic and political renaissance. Otherwise, it is hard to see how Africa's economic decline will be reversed, regional security tackled, and development and democracy attained, as the two have between them natural, human and financial resources that surpass the rest of Africa combined.

In locating this problematic within a political economy framework, it is suggested that the state of Nigerian-South African relations and their effectiveness in approaching the task of rebuilding Africa's economy are a function of

> [d]omestic conditions, including the internal balance of political groups and the degree of political stability or instability. [These] are particularly important for their impact on foreign policy (Dessouki 1991: 157).

Specifically, it is argued that, more than any factor, Nigeria's political paralysis (if not regression)—especially under the current regime of General Sani Abacha—has prevented the development of strong diplomatic ties between Abuja and Pretoria.

Nigeria and South Africa have much in common in their domestic politics. The two countries are conflict-ridden societies—a conundrum of class, gender, ethnic, civil-military, and pro-democracy struggles (Inegbedion 1994a; Adam and Moodley 1993). While these struggles are still very much in flux in South Africa, the patterns of Nigeria's conflicts and political paralysis are well known (see, for example, Herbst 1996 and Joseph 1996). It is widely accepted, as shown below, that political and economic elites and leaders constitute Nigeria's worst problem (Achebe 1983). This has consequences for formal economic ties with South Africa, as politics and economics are closely intertwined.

Undoubtedly, South Africa has its share of political conflicts and economic problems. The difference is how the political class and economic elites approach these conflicts and problems. In South Africa, policy makers seem determined to devise solutions to their problems; in contrast, their Nigerian counterparts seem paralyzed by theirs.

This chapter is organized in nine sections. It serves as a preliminary step in defining the main factors shaping the issues and problems, as Nigerian-South African relations are barely beginning to unfold. The first section introduces the subject. The second situates the marginalization of Africa in its global context. The third outlines Nigeria's and South Africa's economic resources and political positions in the region. The fourth examines the specific nature of the existing relations between the two states. Section five discusses the internal economic and political factors which condition Nigerian-South African relations. Section six discusses how Nigeria and South Africa may both be forced to contribute to peacekeeping on the continent. Section seven introduces ECOWAS and SADC into the discussion. In section eight the chapter looks at how the question of which state occupies Africa's potential seat on the UN Security Council and the issue of whether the continent should be declared a toxic waste free region may give rise to diplomatic conflicts between Abuja and Pretoria. The conclusion then follows.

Globalization and the Paradox of Africa's Marginalization

Several years beyond the Cold War, Western powers have all but abandoned Africa to its own devices. For example, in the case of the United States (US) one need not be surprised

> if it takes the spectacle of open mass graves and children sobbing over their dead mothers to prick American interest in Africa. Africans are far away. They don't supply American needs or threaten American interests (*New York Times*, 7 August 1994).

Views and policies towards Africa in capital cities like London and Paris differ little from the American position.

Little of the "peace dividend" that was supposed to accrue from the end of the Cold War has trickled-down to Africa, be it in terms of regional conflict resolution or enhanced economic resource flows. While the Cold War is over, deadly conflicts and civil wars still flare in countries like Angola, Burundi, Liberia, Rwanda, Somalia and Sudan with minimal action by leaders in Berlin, London or Washington. In short, Africa has ceased to engage the political interest of the big powers since the fall of communism and the disintegration of the Soviet Union (Inegbedion 1994a).

At the same time, major Western policy makers have concluded that Africa's debt and economic crises

> should be left to the World Bank and the International Monetary Fund (IMF), and if their salvage effort works, fine; if not, so be it, the world economy will hardly notice (Callaghy 1994: 32).

Unfortunately, neither the IMF nor the World Bank has shown any willingness to increase aid and resource flows to the continent (*Africa Confidential*, 21 October 1994: 1-3; *Africa Recovery*, December 1994). Indeed, the World Bank's own data supports this policy position (1993: 65).

In the same vein, the Economic Commission for Africa (ECA) reports that Africa received only $14 billion from all foreign aid and loan sources in 1994, against an aggregate external debt of $301.8 billion (*Africa Recovery*, December 1994). Very few countries under structural adjustment show any signs of the economic recovery anticipated by the IMF and World Bank. It is the widespread view that, contrary to all IMF and World Bank claims, Africa's economic debt and crises have only worsened (cf Callaghy and Ravenhill 1993; Adedeji et al 1994; Mengisteab and Logan 1995). In short, IMF and World Bank "market fundamentalism" (Strange 1994) and structural adjustment orthodoxy have done little to ameliorate Africa's debt burden and economic marginalization.

With few exceptions, African states face a stark choice if they want to become more than peripheral actors in the world economy. As the UN Centre on Transnational Corporations notes in its *World Investment Report 1991* (1992), they either join one of the existing regional trade blocs of Europe, North America, Asia or America-Pacific, or form one of their own. Needless to say, the likelihood of (particularly Sub-Saharan) Africa joining any of these trade blocs is quite remote. Even the existing Lomé Conventions—which have put the raw materials of African, Caribbean and Pacific countries at the disposal of the European Common Market since the early 1960s—have not taken these regions beyond dependency. As many analysts point out, these ties have yielded only very poor development and economic dividends for the majority of African people (Zartman 1992).

Sustained external assistance has become a tenuous option for economic development in post-Cold War Africa. This is the paradox of Africa's economic marginalization: the greater the need the less Africa tends to receive from external state actors and international financial institutions (IFIs). Hence, African states have no choice but to begin to rely on their own domestic and sub/regional resources for economic development and democracy in the years ahead (Shaw and Inegbedion 1994). With public accountability, political will and cooperation, African states can do more for their people, countries and regions with their limited financial resources than any external power has ever willingly done. As suggested above and described below, Nigeria and South Africa have more of such resources—human, natural and financial—than the rest of Africa combined.

Core States in Africa's Economic Development

The resources which Nigeria and South Africa combine between them are widely recognized. Private sector and political leaders in both countries often boast of how critical their size, economic resources and political status are in the economic development of Africa. It is widely believed that

> [c]ommercial links between the two largest economies of sub-Saharan Africa would have enormous implications. Nigeria's more than 100 million citizens are perhaps Africa's most voracious consumers, and a ready market for the agricultural and manufactured goods produced by South Africa. Nigeria has petroleum and natural gas which can be traded with South Africa (Arnold, 1994: 195-6).

Even if South Africa is now displacing Nigeria as the perceived leader in Africa (Okolo and Wright 1994), and the latter is replacing the former as a pariah state, what is important, as already noted, is that the two constitute *core states* and stand *primus inter pares* in their regions.

Despite its vast internal economic and political problems, South Africa has the most diversified and industrialized economy on the continent (see Chapters 2 and 3 above). In 1994 for example, with an estimated population of 40 million, South Africa had a gross domestic product (GDP) well over $120 billion—more than the other SADC member states combined (*Economist Intelligence Unit* (EIU), 1995b). The World Bank classifies South Africa as an "upper middle income" country, with a GNP per capita comparable to Argentina, Brazil, Mexico and Venezuela (Overseas Development Institute, 1994: 3).

Nigeria has even greater economic and political problems than South Africa; but, it also has the largest market in Africa. With a population of about 95 million and a GDP of $30 billion, Nigeria is the predominant state in ECOWAS (*EIU*, 1995a; World Bank 1995; Okolo and Wright 1991). By most conventional economic measures, Nigeria and South Africa have between them human, natural and financial resources that far surpass the rest of the continent.

Former Nigerian dictator, General Ibrahim Babangida, recognized this when he told President F.W. de Klerk and his private sector entourage—led by the South African Chamber of Commerce chieftain, J.H. Viljoen—during their historic state visit to Nigeria in April 1992 that

> cooperation and better understanding between Abuja and Pretoria is the key to ensuring a united, stronger Africa that would solve the continent's legion of external debt, food shortages, unemployment, underdevelopment and disinvestment problems (*West Africa*, 26 April 1992: 664).

In response, South African policy makers underlined the role the two countries must play in rebuilding Africa's economy:

> Abuja and Pretoria will be very good business friends since we constitute the main pillars and economic engine room for the continent. This means that we must take the lead in unleashing the full potential of Africa's economy (*West Africa*, 26 April 1992: 664).

Nelson Mandela, in his initial presidential address to the Organization of African Unity (OAU) in June 1994 stated:

Where South Africa appears on the OAU agenda, let it be because we want
to discuss what its contribution shall be to the making of the new African
renaissance. Let it be because we want to discuss what materials it will supply
for rebuilding African economies.

Indeed, this is what the Lagos Plan of Action, the Abuja Declaration, the
African Alternative Framework to (IMF and World Bank) Structural Adjustment Programs (AAF-SAP), among other schemes proposed by the
OAU and ECA for the economic development and political transformation
of Africa, had called for all along (OAU 1981, 1992; ECA 1989). It is also
what makes cooperation between Abuja and Pretoria crucial in enhancing
the prospects for economic development and democracy in Africa in the
coming decade.

What, if anything, have Nigeria and South Africa done in pursuit of these
goals? The next section examines the diplomatic and economic strategies
in place and/or emerging from Nigerian and South African policy statements to rebuild Africa's economy.

Evolving Nigerian-South African Diplomatic Relations

Nigeria was at the forefront of those easing Pretoria back into continental
and international affairs in the early 1990s. No sooner had de Klerk started
the process of dismantling apartheid, than General Babangida was quick
to admit that a non-racist South Africa had a role to play in African politics
and economic development. The rapprochement between the two states
had hardly begun, however, when political events in Nigeria changed for
the worse, undoing the basis for the strong ties which Babangida had
sought to build between the two states.

Ironically, it was Babangida himself who precipitated the crisis by
annulling Nigeria's 12 June 1993 presidential elections, won by Chief
Moshood Abiola and widely held to be the most free and fair in the
country's history. This action destroyed the perception of Nigeria as the
leader in Africa, and attendant international goodwill towards the country.
The interim government—led by Chief Ernest Shonekan and appointed by
the now discredited Babangida to buy time for the military—itself became
a part of the ensuing power struggles.

Thus, few were surprised when, six months later, General Abacha—
minister of defence in the Babangida regime—toppled Shonekan, termi-
nated the transition to democracy and abolished the structural adjustment
program. This not only brought Nigeria's political image into further
disrepute but deepened the country's economic and debt crises, as the
London and Paris Clubs and the IMF refused to talk to the dictator about
debt rescheduling.

Rather than provide Nigeria with a foreign policy direction, Abacha has
devoted state resources to frustrating the internal struggles for democracy

and to ensuring that Abiola—detained by Abacha since June 1994—does not exercise his popular mandate. This is to say that the sporadic successes seen in Nigerian foreign policy in Southern Africa, ECOWAS and the OAU in the 1970s, 1980s and early 1990s relied on a degree of leadership which Abacha utterly lacks (see, for example, Inegbedion and Shaw 1996).

The course of Nigerian-South African relations under Abacha is a poignant example of this.[1] Within Nigeria, the military interred dozens of the country's most prominent journalists and voices for democracy in the name of "treason." They sentenced several prominent Nigerians, including General Olusegun Obasanjo—former head of the Commonwealth Eminent Persons' Group to South Africa—to long prison terms following kangaroo court proceedings. They arrested and put to death nine Ogoni activists, including the writer Ken Saro-Wiwa, on questionable charges and in defiance of pressures for leniency from the world community.

A United Policy Stance?

Nevertheless, given Nigeria's unflagging support of the liberation struggle, when elections were annulled and full military rule reinstated, the ANC-led GNU found it difficult to openly criticize its historical ally. Whereas the US and EU, among others, suggested that sanctions might be a viable strategy, prominent South Africans—Nelson Mandela, Thabo Mbeki, Bishop Tutu—argued in favour of a "slowly slowly" policy. Mbeki, in particular, was keen to see the rest of the world, the West in particular, allow Africans to set their own agenda and sort out their own problems.

These well-intentioned overtures were met with rebuke, leading Bishop Tutu to comment that meeting with Abacha was akin to confronting intransigent white South Africans during the height of apartheid destabilisation. Nigeria's military rulers seemed on a collision course with other Commonwealth Heads of Government slated to meet at Auckland, New Zealand in November 1995.

Hoping to head off a confrontation, in August 1995, President Mandela invited Nigeria's Foreign Minister, Tom Ikimi, to Pretoria to state the military's case over transition to democracy. Mandela openly expressed his desire to forge a united SADC policy/position toward Nigeria. Inside South Africa, political parties were divided. The PAC, for example, was reluctant to condemn Nigeria. Yet, for some, the government's "go slowly" policy was more conciliatory than necessary: the Abacha regime had little to do with the liberation of South Africa. The ANC, SACP and COSATU met to discuss a common position on Nigeria. While some elements of the ANC wanted a stronger stand against the Abacha regime, others, fearing that too much tough talk might have the opposite effect intended, favoured a more guarded response. Overall, according to one report, alliance members wanted a tougher stand. A compromise position was the establishment, with ANC support, of the South Africa-Nigeria Democratic

Solidarity Group, headed by Morakabe Seakhoa. This civil association seemed to speak to the desires of ordinary Nigerians themselves. Indeed, according to a report in the Nigerian daily, *The Guardian* (5 December 1995), "the human rights and pro-democracy movement in Nigeria had begun to call [Mandela] a turncoat for not coming out openly against a vicious military regime."

At the same time, international pressure was mounting for the unconditional release of Abiola, Obasanjo, and those sentenced to death for purportedly attempting to overthrow the Abacha regime. On 1 October, Abacha commuted the death sentences of the coup plotters to life in prison, and announced a new three-year "transition program." But, just when the government's policy seemed to be bearing fruit, Saro-Wiwa and the Ogoni 9 were hanged.

While a deliberate slap in the face of the global community, for Mandela this was especially embarrassing: it had been the policy of his government to "constructively engage" Nigeria on this and related issues. There emerged the feeling that for whatever reason—diplomatic inexperience, political naiveté—South African policy makers had failed where they should have succeeded: if nothing else, to at least stop the killings.

Mandela's response seemed a personal one. He came out swiftly with a policy about-face. South Africa would push for sanctions against a regime he labelled "an illegitimate, barbaric, arrogant military dictatorship."

Changing Policy

There was much early support for this position. In South Africa, there seemed to emerge what might be termed a "democratic moment" where civil society and the government were united in opposition to the behaviour of both Shell Oil and the Abacha regime. At the level of civil society, candlelight vigils outside the Nigerian High Commission in Pretoria combined with popular demonstrations against and boycotts of Shell and Shell products. The South Africa-Nigeria Democratic Solidarity Group supported sanctions, and planned a pro-democracy meeting in Johannesburg.

At the level of the state, South Africa supported Nigeria's two-year suspension from the Commonwealth, became a member of the Commonwealth Ministerial Action Group (CMAG), and sought to lobby other African, particularly SADC member-states in support of sanctions. At a personal level, Mandela and Abacha engaged in an unstately slanging match during which Mandela accused Abacha of being "irresponsible" and "hard in heart," and prominent Nigerians labelled Mandela "senile."

An International Political Reality

Unfortunately for those who hoped the Nigeria issue would provide impetus for a new, progressive and sustainable South African foreign policy, it became clear very early on that Mandela's was a lonely, substantive voice, lost in a sea of international rhetoric. At an 11 December 1995 meeting of the SADC Summit, the organization decided to leave policy making on Nigeria entirely up to CMAG.

Many observers saw SADC's rejection of an embargo against Nigeria as an implicit African rejection of both Mandela's harsh words and his call for sanctions. From January 1996, the issue had become almost wholly identified with the slow and ponderous machinery of state houses and international organizations. In February, South Africa returned its High Commissioner to Lagos. In April, at its annual meeting in Geneva, the UN Human Rights Commission adopted a resolution expressing its "deep concern" with the violation of human rights in Nigeria. However, all concrete, practical steps were gutted from the resolution.

At the 23 April 1996 meeting of CMAG in London, the group brought itself into line with existing EU sanctions, recommending a ban on all sporting links and an embargo of arms exports. CMAG also took a conditional decision to ban air links and freeze assets pending EU/US discussions. Given the unlikelihood of further, substantive EU sanctions, and given the equally unlikely event that US Senator Nancy Kassebaum's private member's bill, called the "Nigeria Democracy Act," will get through congress unscathed, it is clear that CMAG and South African foreign policy makers have retreated to the safety of symbolic politics. This, no doubt, especially pleased South Africa's own parliamentary foreign affairs committee which has urged "multilateralism," not as a means for instituting effective sanctions on Nigeria but as a way to end South Africa's growing isolation on the issue. In August 1996, South Africa formally accepted the credentials of Nigeria's Ambassador to Pretoria.

Domestic Realities

Beyond the juxtapositioning of civil society and official state protests over Nigeria highlighted above, there was never any real attempt by state makers to formally link the policy making process to actions and organizations in civil society. An official state protest, let alone boycott, regarding the activities of Shell Oil was out of the question. Given South Africa's desperate desire to attract capital for the RDP, any harsh words directed toward a major MNC would send the wrong policy signals to purveyors of international capital.

By mid-1996 the diplomatic row between Nigeria and South Africa had abated. Yet, two key questions remain. First, how are Nigeria and South Africa supposed to strengthen trade and investment relations in the presence of Abacha's whimsical and ruthless form of governance? Second, political squabbles notwithstanding, do existing economic conditions in the two countries encourage the development of such trade relations? The next section examines the obstacles which economic conditions within Nigeria and South Africa pose for future bilateral trade and investment relations.

Political Economy of Trade and Investment Relations

In the economic realm South Africa has an industrial class and base far out-stripping that in Nigeria. Since the demise of apartheid, South African companies have been criss-crossing Africa in search of markets for their goods and services (*Economist*, 12 August 1995: 17-19; Leistner 1994). By contrast, Nigerian entrepreneurs remain mostly retailers and contractors. They shun production to such an extent that one could not agree more with Ihonvbere and Shaw's description of Nigerian entrepreneurs as "hustlers" (1989: 93). Not even the structural adjustment and privatization pro-grammes imposed by Babangida in 1987 and 1989, respectively, have changed this behaviour.

Whether in spite or because of economic and political sanctions in the 1970s and 1980s, South Africa was forced to move "beyond import substi-tution to the production of more sophisticated consumer items and of intermediate capital goods" (Southall 1994: 128). Even before he took office, Mandela was already bidding for direct foreign investment and external markets for South Africa's products. Pretoria wasted no time in beginning bilateral trade and diplomatic negotiations with countries in Asia, the Middle East, North America and Europe, which it believed would provide the best access to lucrative external markets (Durr 1994: 171-2).

Policy makers in Abuja, by contrast, continue to wait for oil rents, much of which now go to service the country's $37 billion external debt. The country has done little to move into production, let alone find a niche for itself in the new international divisions of labour and power nor in the unfolding spatial reorganization of global production encapsulated in the notion of globalization. Clearly, the Nigerian state has failed to create the conditions necessary for industrialization and political transformation. Even dependency analysts like Bade Onimode and Thandika Mkandawire have been forced to agree without reservation that

> state policy, by omission or commission, ... accounted for much of ... why Nigeria, so richly endowed in manpower and natural resources and freed from the usual financial and size constraints, failed to set up the type of capital and intermediate goods industries that have historically proved crucial to accumulation and technological acquisition (quoted in Fadahunsi and Igwe 1989: ix).

Even the motor vehicle assembly plants which the country bought from companies like Peugeot, Volkswagen and Leyland in the 1970s have all but collapsed (Adubifa 1993).[2]

Indeed, whether one is a *dependentista*, realist or liberal analyst, the conclusion is unanimous: Nigeria's political paralysis and lack of economic development are principally of its own making.[3] In other words, little of the country's oil surplus and financial independence from external state actors and IFIs in the 1970s and 1980s was used for economic development and socio-political transformation.

Sophie Pedder laments in a recent survey of Nigeria that "It is hard to believe that only 14 years ago the most taxing question in Nigerian politics was how to spend all the oil money" (*Economist*, 21 August 1993: 4). The Nigerian state alone—as opposed to individuals and cabals—collected well over $100 billion in oil rents between 1973 and 1983, but with little of it accounted for publicly. The World Bank is reported to have "reckoned that capital flight from Nigeria during the 1980s may have reached $50 billion" (*Economist*, 21 August 1993: 4). Carol Lancaster estimates that about $11 billion was taken out of Nigeria in 1985-1987 alone (1991: 30).

The Pius Okigbo Panel, appointed by Abacha to probe his former boss, Babangida, concluded that $12.2 billion of the $12.4 billion oil windfall from the Gulf War, supposedly paid into a so-called "dedicated account," was nowhere to be found (Akin Aina, 1995). There has been so much corruption and lack of public accountability that Babangida himself was awed by the fact that Nigeria's economy had not collapsed from the unprecedented looting and waste to which it has been subject since the Second Republic under the civilian presidency of Alhaji Shehu Shagari, 1979-1984. Without a shred of remorse, Babangida told the *Daily Times* of Nigeria in an interview in March 1993 that

> I have kept on asking my economists why it is that the economy of this country has not collapsed until now. What is it that is keeping it up. I still have not found the answer (quoted in Inegbedion 1994a: 241).

Needless to say this is hardly the kind of climate that promotes investor confidence, be it domestic or foreign.

This problem has only gotten worse under Abacha. The Managing Director of the Chemical Banking Corporation, Thomas Trebat, told the international business community in 1994 not to invest in Nigeria. In his words, "I would not invest in Nigeria or recommend it, absolutely not" (*Reuters Financial Report*, 14 October 1994). Nigeria is now "listed just after Iraq and Russia by the Economist Intelligence Unit and the Control Risks security group as one of the highest risk business locations" in the world (*Africa Confidential*, 20 January 1995: 2).

South African entrepreneurs and government officials cannot be expected to ignore these dire warnings. Granted, South Africa is not yet a capital exporting country. Nevertheless, every investor wants a stable and safe country for his/her investment. In other words, even if South Africa were a capital exporting country, there seems little reason for its citizens to invest in Nigeria when other investors, foreign as well as national, are pulling out because of the deteriorating economic and political climate (*EIU*, 1995a). In consequence, even if Pretoria were willing to support its private sector in the latter's quest for foreign investment opportunities, Abacha's Nigeria does not seem to be a likely candidate.

Happily, the international embrace of South Africa is the flip side of the loss of confidence in Nigeria. South Africa was admitted to the OAU and readmitted to the UN and the Commonwealth organizations in June 1994 with fanfare. As the South Africans themselves note, the "transition from international pariah to new jewel of the south was amazingly quick" (*Rainbow*, August 1994: 11). To its leaders' and its peoples' credit, South Africa embarked upon its democratic experiment in April 1994 without the bloodshed widely predicted by pundits of all political stripes (Karis 1995).

The G-7 governments outdid each other in heaping praise and resources on the new South Africa. For example, France and Japan pledged $1.2 billion and $2.0 billion respectively in economic assistance to Pretoria; Germany, meanwhile, was "eager to aid South Africa" (*Rainbow*, August 1994: 5; *Share*, September 1994: 6). So as not to be left out, the US also pledged some $650 million in aid. On an equally positive note, the magazine, *Plant Location International*, ranked South Africa's Western Cape region second among its top 10 best direct investment locations in the world (*Rainbow*, August 1994: 8). Indeed, Mandela and South Africa are now widely perceived as Africa's role models (cf *Economist*, 12 August 1995: 11-12; *Africa Confidential*, 21 October 1994: 1-3).

This is not to suggest that President Mandela has little to worry about in his domestic politics and foreign policy. To begin with, the internal politics and foreign policy of the new South Africa are in flux (see Peter Vale, Chapter 4). As the Minister of Justice, Dullah Omar, points out, the ANC and the black majority may have "won an election, but they have not gained power" (Olojede 1994: 2). Real power remains within the civil service, security forces and an economy dominated by about seven major MNCs, all firmly under white control (Davis 1994; Howe 1994). What exists in South Africa at present can best be described as a black political superstructure on a white economic substructure. Nonetheless, Mandela and the ANC have been pushing ahead on all fronts. If, as it is now clear, Nigeria and South Africa have no diplomatic and economic relations worthy of the two countries' professed preeminent positions on the continent, how will Pretoria and Abuja live up to their earlier policy statements concerning the rebuilding of Africa? There are four issue areas which bear some elaboration: continental peacekeeping; regional economic integration; the search for an African seat on the UN Security Council; and toxic waste dumping.

Peacekeeping as an Area of Joint Interest

Peacekeeping is one area in which Nigeria and South Africa will most likely have to work together, as they will be compelled to provide resources and coordinate efforts. Nigeria has a good record of active peacekeeping inside and outside Africa. Nigeria's lead role in the ECOWAS peacekeeping operation in Liberia has perhaps become the most prominent example (Vogt 1992; Inegbedion 1996). In the case of South Africa, the US did everything possible to involve it in Rwanda even as Pretoria was hoisting its new rainbow flag in May 1994. Such pressures are unlikely to cease, especially as Western countries seek to avoid entangling themselves in post-Cold War African conflicts. Though Nigeria has now become an international pariah, Abuja and Pretoria are increasingly seen by the global community as having the resources necessary to spearhead peacekeeping and conflict resolution efforts on the continent (Mazrui 1994; Soyinka 1994).

Indeed, as Mandela noted in his first address to the Organization of African Unity (OAU) in June 1994:

> Even as we speak, Rwanda stands out as a stern and severe rebuke to all of us for having failed to address the great issues of our day of peace, stability, democracy, human rights, cooperation and development.

Not only did Pretoria pay its general membership dues on the spot; Mandela made an additional contribution of R1 million to the OAU peace fund. If this was a gesture of Pretoria's willingness to contribute to peacekeeping, it bodes well for Africa, as security is both a prerequisite for, as well as an outcome of, economic development and democracy (Shaw and Inegbedion 1991; Hansen 1987).

One must ask, however, how ECOWAS and SADC fit into this picture? These organizations cannot be ignored, since they remain at the core of Nigeria's and South Africa's capacity to play their continental roles.

ECOWAS and SADC in Nigerian-South African Relations

Much has been written about the mixed results (some say failure) of regional integration and cooperation in Africa.[4] Yet no one has suggested a credible alternative strategy to sub/regional integration as a basis for economic development on the continent (Robson 1990). While former Executive Secretary of ECOWAS, Boubakar Diaby-Ouattara, may claim that regional integration is not a *sine qua non* for national development (*West Africa*, 24 July 1995: 1155), the fact remains that besides Nigeria and South Africa, few African states have the basic resources and size necessary for developing viable, competitive national economies.

This is why, in spite of past failures and lacklustre performances across the continent, the Preferential Trading Area (PTA) of Southern Africa, for instance, now aspires to be the Common Market of Eastern and Southern Africa (COMESA). The Mahgreb states, meeting in Casablanca, Morocco, have also begun the process of forming a North African Common Market (NACM). COMESA and NACM are two of the five sub-regional schemes envisioned by the OAU and ECA in the Abuja treaty of June 1992 as building blocks for an integrated African Economic Community which is to be in place by the year 2025. Whatever their shortcomings, ECOWAS and SADC are ahead of these other groups in this process.

ECOWAS had economic integration and security as its ultimate goal from the beginning. SADC has recently redefined its goals beyond mere coordination of policies. As its Executive Secretary, Kaire Mbuende, stated in a 1994 interview, SADC has reached the limits of sectoral coordination of policies among its members; it must now embark on matters of security and economic integration (*Africa Report*, July-August 1994: 46-47). Despite numerous shortcomings, these two experiments remain the most successful of Africa's regional economic development and security schemes to date. They cannot be ignored.

An African Security Council Seat

Direct competition between Abuja and Pretoria is most likely to come from the question of who occupies Africa's spot in the Security Council, if and when the five proposed new permanent positions are created and Africa is allotted one. South Africa's "desire to be the first African country to take a permanent seat on the UN Security Council" (*Share*, August 1994: 3) runs counter to Nigeria's bid and the view among Nigerians that the African seat properly belongs to them.

Suffice it to say that even though the five permanent members of the Security Council did not voice their support for Nigeria's application when the latter tabled it at the 47th session of the General Assembly in October 1992, it was nonetheless generally believed that Abuja had a strong case (Gambari 1994). The criteria for a permanent seat, as listed by the then Foreign Minister, Baba Gana Kingibe, were seen to favour Nigeria. With a population of about 95 million, the country had the largest concentration of black people anywhere in the world. As noted above, Nigeria has demonstrated its capacity to contribute to the maintenance of international peace and security; its track record in international and regional peacekeeping and peacemaking efforts is highly commendable (Ghia 1994: 23-24). Economically, Nigeria has the largest single market in Africa, is an oil exporter, and has huge economic potential.

As South Africa lacks many of these attributes, the basis of Pretoria's challenge to Nigeria's candidacy for a permanent seat on the Security Council will be concrete achievement. As noted above, Nigeria is fast replacing South Africa as an international pariah. It is a country in chaos whose leaders seem either incapable or unwilling to put things right. By contrast, South Africa has a democratic experiment solidly underway, widely commended and supported world-wide.

If the issue were decided today, not only would international perception be on South Africa's side, but most African states would likely support Pretoria, especially in light of the "any state but Nigeria" fever on the continent. For example, Nigeria failed to win its bid for the African Development Bank presidency because it lacked support on the continent. In another instance, Zimbabwe even resorted to espionage to prevent Nigeria from securing the International Labour Organization spot for which Abuja was bidding.

Toxic Waste Dumping

Another issue likely to come between Abuja and Pretoria is whether Africa should be declared a toxic waste-free region. Since General Babangida was embarrassed by the discovery in 1987 of toxic waste dumped in the country by Italian nationals and businesses, Nigeria has been at the forefront of the campaign to make Africa a toxic waste-free region (Inegbedion 1988). But Pretoria may not share this view, as South Africa has toxic waste technology, and it can make money by accepting toxic and other hazardous wastes from overseas for incineration and/or reclamation and reuse.

Waste contractors receive between $2000 and $3000 a ton to dispose of toxic waste in industrialized countries, while African and other poor countries in the South are paid between $3 and $40 a ton to stockpile them (Atteh 1993: 278-288). But Pretoria is most able to negotiate a better deal. For example, between 1986 and 1988 many countries, including Angola, Benin, Djibouti, Equatorial Guinea, Gabon, Guinea, Mozambique, Morocco, Mauritania, Namibia, Nigeria, Sierra Leone, and Sudan received toxic waste for which they were all paid a pittance (Inegbedion 1988). This was what led ECOWAS and the OAU under Nigerian leadership to pass resolutions against toxic waste dumping on African soil.

However, as has been widely noted, most resolutions passed by the OAU and ECOWAS are hardly ever implemented. Thus individual leadership and diplomatic muscle are needed for action. Had Babangida not detained the Italian ship and crew that dumped toxic waste in Nigeria in 1987, it is doubtful whether Rome would have agreed to clean up the mess (Inegbedion 1988). Moreover, it is difficult to punish these foreign "merchants of death," especially if they have the direct or indirect support of state actors and their agents.

One can imagine, for instance, the kind of support US firms dealing in toxic waste might receive from the current US Under-Secretary of the Treasury, Larry Summers, who, as chief economist at the World Bank, proposed that it made good business sense to dump toxic waste in poor countries. In his view, these countries had empty lands and needed money (Strange 1994: 507).

In terms of Nigeria-South Africa relations, this issue may play itself out in one of two ways. On the one hand, this is an argument Pretoria can use against Nigeria and other African states, in order to import toxic waste: clearly, South Africa has the technology and, like all African states, needs the foreign exchange. On the other hand, should South Africa decide to ratify and uphold the OAU's Bamako Convention banning toxic waste from African soil, it could then assist Nigeria and other African countries (e.g., in the policing of coastal waters) with the desire to ban toxic waste but limited capacity to do so. As an issue of importance to all Africans irrespective of politics, toxic waste management could form the basis for future South Africa-Nigeria cooperation.

Conclusion

It is very clear from the foregoing that economic and political relations between Nigeria and South Africa are at best tenuous. It is equally clear that the nature of relations have nothing to do with the absolute level of human, financial and natural resources. South Africa is the economic powerhouse of and the most industrialized economy on the continent. Nigeria is an oil exporter; it has the single largest market in Africa, is the moving force behind ECOWAS, and the bulwark of ECOMOG.

The core problem confounding bilateral (and, perhaps, inter-regional) ties is Nigeria's internal political paralysis and economic irrationality, particularly as presently manifest under General Abacha. This is what has prevented the development of strong diplomatic relations and economic ties between Abuja and Pretoria—the necessary basis on which the two countries could, in theory, jointly rebuild Africa's economy. As little is likely to change or improve in Nigeria under Abacha, President Mandela and his government will just have to face the continental challenge as best South Africa can, and push and hope for the emergence of an amenable government in Abuja.

Notes

1.   The following review and interpretation of Nigeria-South Africa foreign relations is provided by Larry A. Swatuk who spent the period November 1995 - April 1996 in Nigeria and South Africa.

2.   Volkswagon recently closed its Nigerian vehicle assembly plant and shifted production to existing operations in Brazil and South Africa.

3.   See, for example, Mehta 1991; Adubifa 1993; Scherr 1989; Pinto 1987; Pesaran 1986; Taylor et al, 1986; Forrest 1982; Turner 1980; Falola and Ihonvbere 1985.

4.   See, for example, Shaw and Okolo 1994; Okolo and Wright 1991; Akindele 1988; Onwuka and Sesay 1985.

References

Achebe, Chinua. 1983. *The Trouble with Nigeria*. Enugu: Fourth Dimension.
Adam, Heribert, and Kogila Moodley. 1993. *The Negotiated Revolution: Society and Politics in Post-Apartheid South Africa*. Johannesburg: Jonathan Ball.

Adebayo, Adedeji. 1985. *The African Development Crisis: The Paralysis of Multiple Debilitating Crises.* Addis Ababa: United Nations Economic Commission for Africa.

Adibe, Clement E. 1994. "ECOWAS in Comparative Perspective," in Timothy M. Shaw and Julius E. Okolo, eds., *Political Economy of Foreign Policy in ECOWAS.* Pp. 187-217. London: Macmillan.

Adubifa, Akin O. 1993. "Technology Policy in National Development: A Comparative Survey of the Automobile Industry in Nigeria and Brazil." *Journal of Asian and African Studies* 27/1-2: 42-53.

Africa Confidential, (various issues).

Akin Aina, Wale. 1995. "Nigeria: Pandora's Box," *Africa News* (January).

Akindele, R.A., ed. 1988. "The Organization of African Unity 1963-1988: A Role Analysis and Performance Review." *Nigerian Journal of International Affairs* 14/1.

Arnold, Millard W. 1994. "Southern Africa in the Year 2000: An Optimistic Scenario," in Helen Kitchen and J. Coleman Kitchen, eds., *South Africa: Twelve Perspectives on the Transition.* Pp. 185-96. Westport: Praeger/CSIS.

Asante, S.K.B. 1986. *The Political Economy of Regionalism in Africa: A Decade of ECOWAS.* New York: Praeger.

Atteh, Samuel O. 1993. "Political Economy of Environmental Degradation: The Dumping of Toxic Waste in Africa." *International Studies* 30/3 (September/October): 277-98.

Callaghy, Thomas. 1994. "Falling Off the Map." *Current History* (January): 31-3.

——— and John Ravenhill, eds. 1993. *Hemmed In: Responses to Africa's Economic Decline.* New York: Columbia University Press.

Caporaso, James A., and David P. Levine. 1992. *Theories of Political Economy.* New York: Cambridge University Press.

Cox, Robert. 1987. *Power, Production and World Order.* New York: Columbia University Press.

Carolus, Cheryl. 1994. "The Real Struggles Begin." *Africa Report* (July/August): 34-7.

Davis, Robert. 1994. "Approaches to Regional Integration in the Southern Africa Context." *Africa Insights* 24/1: 11-17.

Diaby-Ouattara, Boubakar. 1994. "Regional Integration: A Critical Appraisal." *West Africa* (24 July): 1155-6.

Diamond, Larry. 1988. *Class Ethnicity, and Democracy in Nigeria: The Failure of the First Republic.* Syracuse: Syracuse University Press.

Durr, Kent. 1994. "South Africa and the Commonwealth." *Round Table* 330 (January): 169-73.

Economic Commission for Africa. 1989. *Africa's Alternative Framework to Structural Adjustment Programmes for Socio-Economic Recovery and Transformation.* Addis Ababa: United Nations Economic Commission for Africa.

Economist Intelligence Unit (EIU). 1995a. *Country Report: Nigeria.* London: EIU.

———. 1995b. *Country Report: South Africa.* London: EIU.

Economist, (various issues).

Fadahunsi, A., and Bun Igwe, eds. 1989. *Capital Goods: Technological Change and Accumulation in Nigeria.* Dakar: Codesria.

Falola, Toyin, and Julius Ihonvbere. 1985. *The Rise and Fall of Nigeria's Second Republic. 1979-1984.* London: Zed.

Forrest, Tom. 1982. "Recent Developments in Nigerian Industrialization," in Martin Fransman, ed., *Industry and Accumulation in Africa*. Pp. 324-44. London: Heinemann.

Gambari, Ibrahim. 1994. *West Africa*, 7 February: 12 and 24 October: 1831-2.

Garba, Joseph N. 1987. *Diplomatic Soldiering: Nigerian Foreign Policy: 1975-1979*. Ibadan: Spectrum.

Ghia, Chukwuemeka. 1994. "Democracy Equals Success." *Nigerian Newswatch* (17 October): 23-4.

Hansen, Emmanuel. 1987. "Introduction," in Emmanuel Hansen, ed., *African Perspectives on Peace and Development*. London: Zed.

Herbst, Jeffrey. 1996. "Is Nigeria a Viable State?" *The Washington Quarterly* 19/2 (Spring): 151-172.

———. 1994. "Creating a New South Africa." *Foreign Policy* 94 (Spring): 120-35.

Howe, Herbert M. 1994. "The South Africa Defence Force and Political Reform." *Journal of Modern African Politics* 32/1 (March): 29-51.

Ihonvbere, Julius O., and Timothy M. Shaw. 1989. "Corporatism in Nigeria," in Julius E. Nyang'oro and Timothy M. Shaw, eds., *Corporatism in Africa: Comparative Analysis and Practice*. Pp. 83-103. Boulder: Westview.

Inegbedion, John. 1996. "Nigeria's Role in the ECOWAS Intervention in Liberia." Forthcoming.

——— and Timothy M. Shaw. 1996. "The Decision and Debate Concerning Nigeria's Recognition of the MPLA in Angola," in Margaret Hermann, et al., eds., *Leaders, Groups, and Coalitions: How Foreign Policy Decision is Made*. Boston: Hyman and Unwin.

———. 1994a. *Inside Nigerian Foreign Policy. 1960-1993: Ethnicity, Class, State and Leadership Contradictions*. Unpublished PhD Dissertation, Dalhousie University, Halifax, N.S., Canada.

———. 1994b. "ECOMOG in Comparative Perspective," in Timothy M. Shaw and Julius E. Okolo, eds., *Political Economy of Foreign Policy in ECOWAS*. Pp. 218-44. London: Macmillan.

———. 1991. "Nigerian Foreign Policy in Southern Africa: Frontline State or Rearguard Actor?," in Larry A. Swatuk and Timothy M. Shaw, eds. *Prospects for Peace and Development in Southern Africa in the 1990s: Canadian and Comparative Perspectives*. Chapter 8. Lanham: University Press of America.

Joseph, Richard. 1996. "Nigeria: Inside the Dismal Tunnel." *Current History* 95(601) (May): 193-200.

Karis, Thomas G. 1995. "A Small Miracle Continues: South Africa 1994-99." *The Round Table* 334: 163-78.

Korany, Bahgat, and Ali E. Dessouki, eds. 1991. *The Foreign Policy of Arab States*, 2nd edition. Boulder: Westview.

Lancaster, Carol. 1991. "The Lagos Three: Economic Regionalism in Sub-Saharan Africa," in John W. Harbeson and Donald Rothchild, eds., *Africa in World Politics*. Boulder: Westview.

Leistner, Eric. 1994. "The Role of South African Engineering in African Development." *Africa Insights* 24/1: 18-25.

Maasdorp, Gavin, and Alan Whiteside, eds. 1992. *Towards a Post-Apartheid Future: Political and Economic Relations in Southern Africa*. London: Macmillan.

Mandaza, Ibbo. 1993. *Southern Africa in the 1990s: Problems and Prospects for Regional Cooperation.* Harare: SAPES.

Mandela, Nelson. 1994. "Statement of President Nelson Mandela at the OAU Meeting of Heads of State and Government." Tunis, 13 June.

Mazrui, Ali. 1994. "Africa in Search of Self-Pacification." *African Affairs* 93/370 (January): 39-42.

Mehta, Satish C. 1990. *Development Planning in an African Economy: The Experience of Nigeria, Vol. 1. 1950-1980.* Delhi: Kalinga.

Mengisteab Kidane, and B Ikubolajeh Logan, eds. 1995. *Beyond Economic Liberalization in Africa.* London: Zed.

Mulaisho, Dominic C. 1990. "SADCC: A New Approach to Integration," in World Bank, *The Long-Term Perspective Study of Sub-Saharan Africa.* Background Papers, Vol. 4. Pp. 40-7.

Myers, David. 1991. *Regional Hegemons: Threat Perception and Strategic Response.* Boulder: Westview.

Neary, J. Peter, and Sweder van Wijnbergen, eds. 1986. *Natural Resources and the Macroeconomy.* Cambridge: MIT Press.

New York Times, (various issues).

Nore, Peter, and Terisa Turner, eds. 1980. *Oil and Class Struggles.* London: Zed.

Ojo, Olatunde. 1980. "Nigeria and the Formation of ECOWAS." *International Organisation* 34/4: 571-604.

Okolo, Julius E., and Stephen Wright. 1994. "Nigeria," in Shaw and Okolo, eds., *Political Economy of ECOWAS.* Pp. 125-46.

—— and Stephen Wright, eds. 1990. *West African Regional Cooperation and Development.* Boulder: Westview.

Olojede, Dele. 1994. "The South African Transition: Freedom in Our Lifetime." *Africa Demos* 3/3 (September): 2-3ff.

Onimode, Bade. 1989. *Imperialism and Underdevelopment in Nigeria: The Dialectics of Mass Poverty.* London: Zed.

Onwuka, Ralph, and Amadu Sesay, eds. 1985. *The Future of Regionalism in Africa.* New York: St. Martin's.

Organization of Africa Unity (OAU). 1992. *Abuja Declaration.* Addis Ababa: OAU.

——. 1981. *Lagos Plan of Action for Economic Development of Africa. 1980-2000.* Addis Ababa: OAU.

Overseas Development Institute. 1994. "Economic Policies in the New South Africa." Briefing Paper 1994(2) (April).

Owoeye, Jide. 1994. "What Can Africa Expect from a Post-Apartheid South Africa." *Africa Insight* 24/1: 44-6.

Payer, Cheryl. 1991. *Lent and Lost: Foreign Credit and Third World Development.* London: Zed.

Pedder, Sophie. 1993. "Let Down Again: A survey of Nigeria." *Economist* (21 August): 1-14.

Pesaran, M.H. 1986. "Comment on Macro Model of an Oil Economy: Nigeria," in Neary and Wijnbergen, eds., *Natural Resources and the Macroeconomy.* pp. 225-28.

Pinto, Brian. 1987. "Nigeria During and After the Oil Boom: A Policy Comparison with Indonesia." *World Bank Economic Review* 1/3: 419-45.

Ravenhill, John. 1990. "Overcoming Constraints to Regional Cooperation in Africa: Coordination Rather than Integration?" in World Bank, *The Long-Term Perspective Study of Sub-Saharan Africa*. Background Papers, Vol. 4. Pp. 81-5.

Reuters News. 1994. *Reuters Financial Report*. 14 October.

Robson, Peter. 1990. "The Conceptual Framework of Regional Integration: Analysis and Appropriate Technology," in World Bank, *The Long-Term Perspective Study of Sub-Saharan Africa*. Background Papers, Vol. 4. Pp. 86-9.

Scherr, Sara. 1989. "Agriculture in an Export Economy: A Comparative Analysis of Policy Performance in Indonesia, Mexico and Nigeria." *World Development* 17: 543-60.

Shaw, Timothy M., and Clement E. Adibe. 1994. "South Africa, Nigeria and the Prospects for Complementary Regionalism after Apartheid." *South African Journal of International Affairs* 1/2: 1-19.

Shaw, Timothy M., and Julius E. Okolo, eds. 1994. *Political Economy of Foreign Policy in ECOWAS*. London: Macmillan.

—— and Julius Okolo. 1994. "Introduction," in Shaw and Okolo, eds., *Political Economy of ECOWAS*.

—— and John Inegbedion. 1994. "The Marginalization of Africa in the New World (Dis)Order," in Richard Stubbs and Geoffrey Underhill, eds., *Political Economy and the Changing Global Order*. Toronto: McClelland and Stewart.

—— and John Inegbedion. 1991. "Alternative Approaches to Peace and Security in Africa," in Jorge R. Beruff, et al., eds., *Conflict, Peace and Development in the Caribbean*. London: Macmillan.

South African Government. 1994. *Rainbow* (August).

——. 1994. *Share* (September).

Soyinka, Wole. 1994. "Hope and Horror in Africa." *New Perspective Quarterly* 11/3 (Summer): 61-2.

Strange, Susan. 1994. *Dissent* 11/3 (Fall): 507.

——. 1986. *Casino Capitalism*. Oxford: Basil Blackwell.

Suberu, Rotimi T. 1994. "The Democratic Recession in Nigeria." *Current History* 93/583 (May): 213-18.

Swatuk, Larry A., and Timothy M. Shaw, eds. 1991. *Prospects for Peace and Development in Southern Africa in the 1990s: Canadian and Comparative Perspectives*. Lanham: University Press of America.

Taylor, Lance, et al. 1986. "A Macro Model of an Oil Economy: Nigeria," in J. Peter Neary and Sweder van Wijnbergen, eds., *Natural Resources and the Macroeconomy*. Pp. 201-21. Cambridge: MIT Press.

The Guardian, (various issues), Lagos.

Turner, Terisa. 1980. "Nigeria: Imperialism, Oil Technology and the Comprador State," in Nore and Turner, eds., *Oil and Class Struggles*. Pp. 199-223.

United Nations. 1994. *Africa Recovery*. (December).

United Nations, Centre on Transnational Corporations. 1992. *World Investment Report 1991*. New York: United Nations.

Vale, Peter. 1991. "Points of Re-Entry—Prospects for a Post-Apartheid Foreign Policy." *South Africa International* 21/4 (April): 214-30.

Viera, Sergio, et al., eds. 1992. *How Fast the Wind? Southern Africa 1975-2000*. Trenton: Africa World Press.

Vogt, Margaret A., ed. 1992. *The Liberian Crisis and ECOMOG: A Bold Attempt at Regional Peacekeeping.* Lagos: Gabumo.

Wangwe, Samuel M. 1990. "A Comparative Analysis of the PTA and SADCC Approaches to Regional Economic Integration," in World Bank, *The Long-Term Perspective Study of Sub-Saharan Africa.* Background Papers, Vol. 4. Pp. 34-9.

West Africa, (various issues). London.

World Bank. 1995. *World Development Report 1995.* Washington, D.C.: World Bank.

———. 1993. *Global Economic Prospects and the Developing Countries.* Washington, D.C.: World Bank.

———. 1990. *The Long-Term Perspective Study of Sub-Saharan Africa.* Background Papers, 4 Vols. Washington, D.C.: World Bank.

Zartman, I. William, ed. 1992. *Europe and Africa: The New Phase.* Boulder: Lynne Rienner.

12

The "New" South Africa in Africa: Some Tentative Conclusions and Prognostications

David R. Black and Larry A. Swatuk

Introduction

South Africa's passage from apartheid to majority rule, currently in its transitional "Government of National Unity" (GNU) phase, has been greeted internationally with enormous enthusiasm. Here, in the midst of the mounting conflict and confusion of purpose of the post-Cold War world, is an undeniably good news story: a triumph of peaceful negotiation (notwithstanding the thousands of lives lost) and democracy over violence and racist authoritarianism. It has produced a government led by a man—Madiba Nelson Mandela—sometimes described as the "last twentieth century hero": a truly inspirational figure with unequalled international stature and moral authority. And it has provided a source of optimism on a continent which for more than a decade has been habitually described as being "in crisis." Indeed, former U.S. Congressman and veteran Africanist Howard Wolpe, for one, has launched a mission "to present South Africa to Americans as the door of hope for the rest of the continent."[1]

It is the implications of this relationship between the "new" South Africa and its continental neighbours, near and far, which this collection has sought to critically analyze. The contributions warrant conclusions which can be characterized as analytically sceptical but prescriptively hopeful. That is, while a close and unblinkered analysis of the challenges confronting South Africa and the rest of sub-Saharan Africa leads to expectations of a future marked by strong continuities, increasing inequalities and mounting insecurity, it also reveals clear bases for hope that a more cooperative and constructive future can be brought into being—however slowly, painstakingly, and perhaps haphazardly.

This concluding chapter, like the collection itself, explores these themes within three expanding concentric circles: the "new" South Africa itself, the Southern African region, and sub-Saharan Africa—particularly East and West Africa—as a whole.

Change and Continuity South of the Limpopo

There is no gainsaying the change in the discourse, and indeed the practice, of South African-African relations which has followed the inauguration of the GNU. The new policy elite, centered around the ANC, has repeatedly professed its intent "to become part of a movement to create a new form of economic interaction in the region based on principles of mutual benefit and interdependence" (Booth and Vale 1995: 286; ANC 1994a). Moreover, through a variety of cooperative initiatives with its neighbours, Mandela's South Africa has created "an important impression..., in contrast to apartheid South Africa,... that the new government operates in concert with other states of the region. The GNU has been at great pains to avoid using its predominant power in regional relations" (Suttner 1995: 15; also Department of Foreign Affairs 1996: 11). The contrast with the attitude and activities of the doomed apartheid state during its last decade—the era of destabilization in the 1980s—is stark.

Yet, at levels of policy making, political economy, and popular opinion, the forces of continuity are also very strong. South Africa remains the regional hegemon; and most South Africans of various classes and identities continue to be preoccupied with their own formidable problems first. Without South African commitment and leadership, rooted in a successful domestic transition at the socio-economic as well as political levels, the prospects for a new era of cooperation and community in the region and continent are grim. These conditions will not be easily attained.

Economic Growth, Development and Continuing Decline

The attempt to re-make South Africa—to promote development as well as growth in a manner which begins to address the historical injustices and grossly inequitable life chances which are the legacies of the past—is handicapped from the outset by the impact of prolonged economic decline. Patrick MacGowan has summarized that, in light of its deteriorating relative circumstances in most significant areas since the mid-1970s, "South Africa will be fortunate to retain a place among the world's semi-peripheral powers over the next twenty years." "Rather more likely," he adds, "is relative descent, so that South Africa will increasingly resemble a big Zimbabwe, at the border between the periphery and the semi-periphery" (MacGowan 1993: 58). This is bad news for Africa. As discussed by Stephen

Gelb and Timothy M. Shaw in this collection, South Africa's increasingly marginal place in a global economy which imposes increasing constraints on even the most powerful countries severely limits its room for maneuver, and any inclinations towards generosity.

Granted, South Africa's economic performance has improved since the historic elections of April 1994, but only slowly. Growth estimates for 1996 of 3.3 percent remain short of the 4 percent required to make any inroads into South Africa's acute unemployment problem. This is so despite Nelson Mandela's remarkably successful—and not uncontroversial—efforts to gain the confidence of the South African and international business communities.[2] In the meantime, the traditional mainstay of the South African economy, gold, is experiencing a "crisis" marked by sharply worsening production figures.[3] With these considerations in mind, the Government launched an ambitious new Macro-economic Strategy for "Growth, Employment and Redistribution" in June 1996 which aims to achieve average annual growth of 4.2% between 1996 and 2000, reaching 6.1% in the final year (Government of South Africa 1996). Even if the GNU, and its post-1999 successor, is able to achieve these targets and engineer a reversal of South Africa's relative economic decline, however, the process will be a long and difficult one. It will make it all the more challenging to generate the resources and the political will required to finance South Africa's ambitious Reconstruction and Development Program (RDP).

Post-Apartheid Reconstruction and Development

The RDP has been the centrepiece of the GNU's policy agenda (ANC 1994b). Among other things, it embodies the government's "justice agenda"—those policies and programs which are designed to reduce historic inequalities and provide a better life for the previously disenfranchized black majority. It provides the political assurance that, along with fiscal responsibility, economic restructuring and growth, the ANC (with its "partners" in government) is committed to real change for the poor majority which is its primary base of electoral support. Yet the RDP and its associated programmes will place an enormous strain on South Africa's limited human and financial capacity. To cite just one important example, Health Minister Nkosazana Zuma's widely praised National Health Insurance Scheme, unveiled in mid-1995 and designed to provide free primary health care to all who need it by the end of the decade, would face a financial shortfall of R3.39 billion over this time frame at present levels of expenditure.[4] More broadly, the RDP process as a whole has come under increasing criticism for its preoccupation with bureaucratic structures and limited progress in meeting concrete targets; this would explain in part its controversial 1996 move into the Ministry of Finance (*Weekly Mail and Guardian*, 4-11 April 1996; Blumenfeld 1996). At the same time, the RDP White Paper, which was designed to set out plans for implementation, has been criticized by progressive academics as "a very significant compromise to the neo-liberal, 'trickle down' economic policy preferences of the old regime" (Adelzadeh and Padayachee 1994: 2).

Obviously, the political stakes around the RDP are very high. Notwithstanding the fact that the RDP itself enjoins the "democratic government" to "negotiate with neighbouring countries to forge an equitable and mutually beneficial program of increasing cooperation, coordination and integration" (ANC 1994: 117), it seems likely to absorb a great deal of time, energy, and resources for essentially domestic purposes, with relatively little left over for the region and continent. While progressive politicians and analysts in the "new" South Africa periodically point out the country's historic culpability for much of the hardship which currently besets the region, and note that a strong case can be made for South African reparations, there will be no large-scale influx of South African public resources to help fuel a regional recovery.

Forces of Continuity

Along with the limitations of relative economic decline globally and pressing priorities domestically, the prospects for fundamental change in South Africa-Africa relations are also inhibited by strong forces of continuity in the South African political economy and society. In the political economy, policy options are constrained and "moderated" by the central role which a small number of highly concentrated corporations continue to play. Powerfully reinforced by the prescriptions of the IMF and World Bank, the influence of corporate South Africa will sharply discourage options entailing substantial planning and intervention, at both national and regional levels. Moreover, these corporations are likely to strongly reinforce the position of South Africa's "growth firsters" who argue that, above all, South Africa must generate growth; that to do so, it must attract investment; and that in light of these priorities, its foreign (economic) policy should continue to emphasize extra-continental linkages with South Africa's largest sources of trade and investment in Europe, North America and Asia. On the other hand, South African corporations and other private interests are themselves playing an increasingly prominent role as architects of trans-societal links between South Africa and the rest of the continent.[5]

At the societal level, too, forces of cultural continuity and (mis)perception constrain the prospects for more cooperative intra-regional relations. As Peter Vale has noted, South Africans have historically "lived up against" their neighbours. These habits of mind are resilient. Obviously, much of the white economic elite has traditionally seen itself as "European" and "Western" in identity and orientation. These perceptions, strongly reinforced by patterns of white emigration over the past several decades, will not be easily re-oriented. But there are strains of chauvinism and parochialism among black South Africans as well, capable of generating a sense of both superiority and hostility towards their African neighbours.

A crucial fulcrum for this quite widely shared South African suspicion of, and sometimes xenophobia towards, neighbouring peoples is the issue of migration. For all South Africans, notably including wealthy whites, "illegal immigration" dovetails neatly with a mounting sense of personal insecurity associated with escalating rates of (often violent) crime. South Africa has become one of the world's most crime-ridden and violent societies.[6] It is a small, and not wholly inaccurate, step to attribute a good deal of the cause of this frightening trend to the presence and activities of foreign migrants (Carim 1995: 2).[7] Among the growing black elite, anti-foreign feeling sometimes takes the form of hostility towards professionals from other African countries "taking South African jobs." And among the poor majority of South Africans—those composing the bulk of the roughly 45 percent of the population who are unemployed—it has manifested itself in frightening and sometimes violent outbursts of xenophobia, leading to, among other things, community members turning on "foreign" neighbours of long-standing (Carim 1995; Confidential interview, DFA, 22 June 1995). The upshot is that, in 1993, 96,600 "illegals" were deported, at a cost of millions of Rands and to dubious long-term effect.[8]

The irony, of course, is that "[t]he story of Southern Africa's economic development has been the story of the migration of its peoples. South Africa's economic success rests in no small part on the migration of workers to its industrial heartland" (Booth and Vale 1995: 286). As Swatuk and Omari point out in Chapter Five, extensive migration has always been a prominent feature of the Southern African political economy. There is therefore a historic artificiality, not to mention lack of realism, about the current shrill and defensive reaction to this "new threat." Only a concerted regional effort aimed at broadly-based development can ultimately stem the flow; yet the danger is that the dominant response will be precisely the opposite of this: a heavy-handed unilateralism fuelled by, and fuelling, intra-regional prejudices (see Vale, Chapter 4; and Swatuk and Omari, Chapter 5).

Finally, and returning to the level of the state, it should be noted that even with the best will in the world, a major stumbling block to the decisive re-orientation of South Africa's policy towards its continental neighbours is the onerous challenge of bureaucratic re-organization and re-orientation. Indeed, much of the slowness of policy change in domestic and foreign policy alike can be attributed to the difficulty of engineering change in the machinery of government, and then establishing and implementing new priorities. In other words, there is a problem of simple bureaucratic over-load. Under these circumstances, the forces of inertia can weigh heavily. For example, notwithstanding the GNU's stated intention to make Africa its top foreign policy priority, budgetary allocations to South Africa's foreign missions reflect a different, pre-transition set of priorities. Of R645 million allocated to foreign missions for the 1995-96 budget year, only R105 million will remain in Africa. Similarly, whereas a total of R51.3 million is allocated to SADC missions *as a group*, R59.5 million is earmarked for the United States alone, R24.8 million for Russia, and R30.5 million for France (Suttner 1995: 7).

In sum, the tremendous domestic and global challenges which the new South Africa confronts allow for only cautious optimism concerning the prospects for a qualitatively new, more cooperative and constructive, level of commitment to the region and continent. Yet, it would also be misleading to underestimate the changes which have already occurred. Thus, the emerging South African-Southern African relationship is characterized by ambiguity.

South Africa in Southern Africa: Partner and/or Hegemon?

What, precisely, has changed in regional relations since the South African elections? What are the benefits, and where are the dangers? Above all, the region as a whole has benefitted from the cessation of inter-state hostilities between South Africa and its neighbours, and the former's destructive campaign of destabilization (Hanlon 1986). While the bonds of regional (inter)dependence ensured that a variety of more or less open economic and even political links were maintained throughout the apartheid era, the dawning of a new era of legitimate communications and cooperation creates opportunities for a range of novel bilateral and multilateral initiatives in the region. To use a medical analogy, by excising the cancer of apartheid, the various parts of the regional body are able, for the first time, to begin to function "normally." What forms will this unprecedented "normality" take?

Regional Security

Some of the most dramatic changes have taken place in the security sphere. In a situation replete with ironies, whereas the old South African security establishment—both military and police—was the major *source* of regional insecurity, the "new" security establishment is engaged in a variety of cooperative exercises to *combat* regional insecurity. For example, under the terms of a bilateral crime-combatting agreement code-named Operation Rachel, "South African police specialists ... have destroyed mortars, rocket-launchers, hand-grenades and landmines since starting an operation against illegal weapons with their Mozambican counterparts."[9] Similar agreements and operations have been initiated with other neighbouring states. More broadly, the "new" South African National Defence Force (SANDF), despite strong continuities at the level of personnel with the old SADF, has played a leading role in the planning for a new regional security arrangement—the Association of Southern African States (ASAS)—substantially modelled after its old nemesis, the Frontline States (see Swatuk and Omari, Chapter 5). It is anticipated that the functions of this new, relatively informal and unbureaucratic, security mechanism will include the provision of "intelligence support for preventive diplomacy initiatives in the case of pending or actual conflicts within the region," planning for combined operations, and the establishment of "security arrangements between states on specific issues such as countering weapons smuggling" (Southall 1995: 5; also Nathan & Honwana 1995). Indeed, given the relatively promising development of regional security links, there are some scholars who argue that, in building regional cooperation, "a focus on security should precede rather than follow economic integration" (Mills 1995b: 238).

Democracy and Human Rights

A second important regional effect of the South African transition is that, through the power of its example, a new regional norm of democracy and human rights has been strongly promoted. Whereas in the past the persistence of apartheid allowed the SADC states to largely escape critical scrutiny of their own democratic shortcomings, and indeed justified certain important derogations from democratic norms in light of the security threat posed by Pretoria, the advent of a freely-elected South African government featuring strong constitutional safeguards for human rights has created strong pressures on neighbouring governments to accelerate their own reform processes. Moreover, whereas groups and individuals in South African civil society which opposed the apartheid state were previously reluctant to criticize the FLS, they are now more likely to be willing, in alliance with activists and NGOs in neighbouring civil societies, to do so.[10] This is not to suggest that the trend towards democratic practices and civil liberties is irreversible in the new South Africa. Nor is it to suggest that the new regional norm of democracy and human rights is irresistible by neighbouring governments determined to retain their political control. However, so long as the South African state and society continue to move in this direction, the pressures on regional governments to do likewise will continue to mount. Indeed, the problem-filled but promising processes of political reform and democratization in such countries as Angola, Lesotho, Malawi, Mozambique, Tanzania, and Zambia need to be understood in relation to the process of change in South Africa. In addition, South African policy makers continue to assert that a "cornerstone" of their new foreign policy will be the promotion of a "culture of human rights" in Southern Africa and beyond, though precisely how this is to be done remains distinctly unclear (Confidential Interview, DFA, 22 June 1995; Department of Foreign Affairs 1996: 23).[11]

Continuity and Change in Regional Political Economy

At the level of the political economy, pockets of the region—in both spatial and class terms—are beginning to benefit from increased South African interest and investment. One slightly breathless journalistic assessment has asserted that whereas South Africa has kept a low *political* profile in relation to its neighbours in the year since its first democratic elections, "The emissaries of South African capitalism ... seem to be everywhere" (*Globe and Mail*, 15 July 1995). As highlighted by several of the contributors to this collection, much of South Africa's renewed economic interest in the region and continent is based on the pursuit of new markets for trade rather than opportunities for longer-term investment; yet, particularly in Southern Africa, some substantial new investment projects are coming on line. For example, the powerful electricity parastatal Eskom is developing and/or rehabilitating power grids in Angola, Lesotho and Mozambique, with plans to integrate them into South Africa's electrical network; mining giant JCI, in conjunction with other South African organizations, has entered into a turnkey supply agreement to rehabilitate Maamba Collieries in Zambia; South African hotel companies are making new investments in Southern Africa and beyond; and various South African mining, transportation and energy firms are either considering or undertaking major projects in the extraordinarily difficult but potentially lucrative context of Zaire.[12]

Perhaps most remarkable is the advent of what has been described as "another Great Trek," a process formalized in mid-1995 by an agreement between the South African government and Angola, Mozambique and Zaire "for the settling of hundreds of mainly Afrikaans-speaking farmers on millions of hectares of prime agricultural land in those countries."[13] It was expected that other countries, including Tanzania, Zambia and Zimbabwe, would also welcome South Africa's "new trekkers." Fears concerning the effects of land redistribution, illegal immigration, and loss of protection for agricultural goods, among other things, have persuaded numerous white South African farmers to seek greener pastures (literally) in the more fertile and less regulated rural areas of their increasingly prostrate neighbours. In some respects, this process builds upon the (re)emergence of large-scale, corporate-owned plantation agriculture, notably in Mozambique.

What do these emerging linkages imply for post-apartheid development prospects in Southern Africa? At one level, South African firms and farmers are providing much-needed investment, technology, and employment. There can be no doubt that *some* individuals, groups, and areas in neighbouring countries will benefit materially—in some cases very significantly—from renewed South African interest.

At another level, however, in the absence of effective institutional frameworks and regulatory safeguards, both nationally and regionally, these various projects will significantly exacerbate disparities and promote private networks of patron-clientelism. They are likely, in other words, to reinforce and accelerate the emergence of regional "growth poles" and "backwaters," in both spatial and class terms. At the risk of sounding anachronistic in this era of marketization and privatization, it can be anticipated that this trend will, unmitigated, exacerbate human insecurity throughout the region. Those inside the charmed circles of growth and development will take steps to protect themselves, their families and their property from the immiseration outside, while those outside will resort to various illicit "modes of accumulation" (theft, drugs, wildlife poaching and trade, guns, etc.). Moreover, should the state structures of the region continue to experience declines in effectiveness and legitimacy, this process will continue to be marked by increasing resort to private "protection rackets"—both "legitimate" and "illegitimate."[14]

At yet another level, however, it may rightly be asked how much of this is really novel, versus simply a restoration of the *status quo ante*. After all, South African corporations such as Anglo American have had long-standing holdings and investments throughout the region (Reichardt, interview, 4 May 1994; Reichardt 1996), while white farmers/settlers have maintained a presence in areas as remote as Botswana's far-western Ghanzi district. South African investments in and promotion of tourism in Malawi, Mozambique and Zimbabwe, for example, in some respects simply resurrect pre-independence patterns. From this perspective, it was the relatively brief period when apartheid and majority rule coincided, from the mid-1960s to the end of the 1980s, which is historically aberrant—and, given the maintenance of South African trade and investment links with the region throughout this period, not so very aberrant at that (see Hanlon 1986; Shaw 1974).

Notwithstanding the acceleration of regional interpenetration and concurrent human insecurity, what is occurring is in some respects simply the "normalization" of historic regional economic patterns and trends which have always been particularly beneficial to South Africa (Libby 1987). It is not surprising, therefore, that South African interests, both private and governmental, have been somewhat lackadaisical in their attitude toward the reform and renegotiation of regional trading and investment arrangements.[15]

Institutional Frameworks for Regional Cooperation

All of this points toward the continuing relevance of the institutional frameworks within which regional economic relations take place. As discussed by Rob Davies in Chapter Six above, there have been no shortage of regional organizations in Southern Africa designed, formally at least, to foster regional economic cooperation and/or integration. To this point in time, however, none have been sufficiently coherent and effective to provide a framework within which regional economic relations can be restructured on a more balanced and complementary basis. Of the organizations extant, SACU has long been the most extensively and effectively integrated; yet this arrangement between South Africa and its four smallest and most dependant neighbours is manifestly based on profound assymetries of power, and is not operating to the satisfaction of either South Africa, or Botswana, Lesotho, Namibia, and Swaziland. It is being renegotiated.[16]

SADC, after a long honeymoon with the international donor community, has had trouble adapting to the post-apartheid context and giving shape to its new status as a development "community." It has come under increasing criticism from donors and scholars alike. For example, Erich Leistner has asserted that:

> Since the signing of the SADC treaty in August 1992, virtually nothing has happened to give concrete shape to the new objectives, nor are there signs that the organization's weaknesses have been addressed. SADCC's patently inefficient system of allocating sectoral responsibilities to particular member countries remains (Leistner 1995: 272).

Leistner's criticisms, based perhaps on unreasonably high expectations, are nevertheless unfair. For SADC members have made significant progress—via, among other things, a number of protocols—toward regional cooperation in several key issue areas: power; water; transportation and communication; labour; and security (Green, 1996). It is to be expected that regional cooperation in these areas will build on the past success of SADC cooperation on food security and drought relief.

Finally, COMESA, despite "impeccable credentials in that it constitutes one of the five sub-regions that the ECA has indicated as building blocs for the proposed African Economic Community," has had limited practical impact. This is most fundamentally because "most governments fail to live up to their treaty obligations" (Leistner 1995: 273), although numerous other problems with this organization could be noted. COMESA and SADC, with substantial overlap in membership and objectives and fearing for their organizational lives in a more hostile donor climate, have engaged in increasingly open conflict over how their efforts and mandates should be harmonized. In this conflict, both have their national champions, based on headquarters location, senior staff nationality, and the like.[17]

An added factor, as Swatuk points out in Chapter Seven above, is that while many of the states of Southern Africa may be suffering through a prolonged decline in authority and effectiveness, they remain sufficiently strong and jealous of their sovereign prerogatives to effectively stymie any regional integration schemes they regard as threatening. As a result, Rob Davies has summarized the situations confronting both SADC and

COMESA as "weak commitments by weak states to weak organizations" (quoted in Leistner 1995: 273).

South Africa and the Status Quo

With the emergence of a legitimate, post-apartheid South African state into the regional political equation, there has been some hope and expectation that South Africa would provide the leadership necessary to sort out this confusion of organizational purpose, and to give new direction to the regional institutional "project." Indeed, the story of Southern Africa's regional institutions since the early 1990s might be sub-titled "Waiting for South Africa." However, indications are that the region will be waiting for a while yet. The GNU did give a fillip to SADC and strike a blow to the prospects of COMESA by choosing to join the former but not the latter. However, it has done little to provide leadership in sorting through the problems of organizational overlap. This is partly attributable to the fact that South African policy makers have not sorted out their own policy towards these two regional institutions, despite South Africa's ostensible foreign policy priority on the SADC region. The fundamental problem is that, despite the many looming challenges and opportunities of regional relations, in economic terms, the *status quo* serves South Africa's immediate interests well. Hence, as noted above, Pretoria simply does not share the urgency of many of its neighbours (notably Zimbabwe) concerning the need to give new purpose and direction to regional economic relations and institutions.

Thus, in light of the continuing dominance of economic links with Europe and both the size and promise of links with Asia, a great deal of the new government's energy has gone into the effort to negotiate a new, Lomé-like arrangement with the EU, and talks concerning the creation of an Indian Ocean Forum in which Australia, India and South Africa would be the principals. South Africa's early negotiating priorities have focused, in other words, beyond the (sub)continent—though in fairness, it should also be noted that it has argued that any Indian Ocean Forum must include the entire SADC region.[18]

The one major exception to this extra-regional focus has been SACU. Here, a major, multi-frontal initiative to renegotiate the agreement was launched in 1994. All parties appear to be firmly committed to what is anticipated to be a multi-year process (see Davies, Chapter 6). Meanwhile, non-SACU states and organizations, such as Zimbabwe and SADC, have been left to wait. However, some South African officials and private sector representatives have reportedly suggested that Zimbabwe should consider joining SACU.[19] The point is that, insofar as the GNU's negotiating priorities are an indicator, the "new" South Africa's foreign economic policy priorities appear to be extra-regional on the one hand, and in that portion of the region where it is most clearly hegemonic on the other. Despite discursive change, South Africa's *actions* in this issue area indicate continuity.

There are, however, other issue areas and relationships which hold out the possibility of fostering a new and more equitable degree of regional cooperation. Some of these are highlighted in Chapters Two through Six above. Several others will be discussed below. In the meantime, we turn to our third concentric circle: South Africa in Africa.

South Africa in Africa

Growth Poles, Backwaters and the Politics of Forgetting

The struggle against apartheid was profoundly Pan-African in character. No issue united African governments and peoples like the struggle against white minority rule, above all in South Africa. While the member-states of the Organization of African Unity (OAU) struggled with internecine conflicts and ineffectiveness, they were powerfully welded together by their common opposition to the apartheid state; and African caucuses and organizations found their firmest common ground in lobbying for sanctions against Pretoria in the UN, the Commonwealth, and elsewhere. While much of this opposition was rhetorical in character, and a significant number of African states maintained more or less open economic and political links with South Africa (see Daddieh, Chapter 10; and Nyang'oro, Chapter 9), many others made real commitments of scarce resources to the struggle. These included, above all, those countries immediately adjacent to South Africa, but also others, such as Uganda and Tanzania,[20] which were further afield. Their contributions included hosting refugees and both political leaderships and armed cadres of the ANC and other liberation movements, often in large numbers, as well as providing material assistance to the struggle.

As a result of this long-standing commitment and the bonds of solidarity forged with the ANC, there was a not-unreasonable expectation among African states as a group that the ANC-dominated GNU could be looked to for both material support and enlightened political leadership in increasingly crisis-ridden Pan-African organizations such as the OAU and African Development Bank (ADB). Moreover, it was also reasonable to expect that those states which had been unswerving in their solidarity and had made the largest sacrifices would be "rewarded" by the "new" South Africa, while those which had cooperated, tacitly or otherwise, with the apartheid state could anticipate a cool and difficult relationship.

As the chapters by Daddieh, Mugyenyi and Swatuk and Nyang'oro suggest, these expectations have proven to be largely misplaced. Notwithstanding sincere expressions of gratitude and goodwill towards Africa, the OAU, and leading allies such as Tanzania, South Africa's political leadership has been distinctly reticent about taking on a significant leadership role in its crisis-ridden continent, and providing tangible political or material "rewards" to the ANC's stronger allies.[21] There are a number of fairly obvious reasons for this. Systemically, the end of apartheid coincided with what has been described as a tectonic shift at the level of the world order which had the effect of shaking the ANC (and others) loose from its traditional normative and solidarist anchors. Economically, South Africa's own intimidating needs and challenges have meant that it lacks surplus resources to devote to the continent's manifold problems, while its top priority has been to develop and exploit trade and investment opportunities which can help it re-establish economic growth and generate employment. On the continent, the better short-term economic opportunities have tended to be located in states, such as Kenya and Côte d'Ivoire, which were at best lukewarm in their support for the anti-apartheid struggle; stalwart supporters such as Tanzania and Uganda have rather less to offer at this point (cf. Mugyenyi and Swatuk, Daddieh and Nyang'oro in this collection). Finally, the process of negotiation and compromise on which the South African transition rests, embodied in the awkward executive structure which is the GNU, has led to a significant watering down of the ANC's core influence and more radical alignments and priorities, notwithstanding the 1996 withdrawal of the National Party.[22]

Preventing Conflict, Building and Keeping Peace

This does not mean that South Africa will entirely eschew a leadership role in the continent's political and security affairs and organizations. To some extent, the cautiousness with which the new leadership, including Mandela, has approached continental fora reflects an admirable degree of modesty concerning the need to understand Africa's problems thoroughly and have a clear policy approach *before* "plunging in." Indeed, South Africa's retreat from forthright activism in response to Abacha's Nigeria was partly indicative of its inexperience in the ways of African diplomacy. Similarly, South Africa's officials have been rightly chary of usurping the leadership of continental mediation processes already underway, and thus appearing to seek a position of dominance which would trigger political alarm bells in the State Houses of Africa.[23] On some issues, however, such as regional peacekeeping and the development of the OAU's Conflict Prevention Mechanism agreed to at its 1993 Summit, South Africa is moving toward a more active leadership role (Shaw 1995b).[24]

Ironically, and perhaps worryingly, the initiative in these areas once again rests primarily with the South African defence establishment, as it has with the emergent ASAS. There is a strange (though not unfamiliar) circularity to South Africa's emergence as a leader in addressing issues of continental insecurity and armed violence which it has itself helped to foment, through its arms trading and the covert activities of its apartheid predecessor. Despite these tensions, however, it makes sense that the "new" South Africa should use its relatively strong military-security technology and capabilities to aid in continental conflict prevention, peacekeeping and peacebuilding efforts.[25] As Nathan and Honwana suggest (1995: 6), a "common security approach" remains vitally important in the post-apartheid era:

> [It] could provide the basis for early warning of potential crises; building military confidence and stability through disarmament and transparency on defence matters; engaging in joint problem-solving and developing collaborative programmes on security issues; negotiating multi-lateral security agreements; and managing conflict through peaceful means... [A common security regime] seeks to minimize risks by creating an environment in which states build their security with rather than against each other.

South Africa as Continental Conscience?

Even more troublesome is the question of whether and how South Africa should contribute to the promotion of a "culture of human rights" and the strengthening of democratic norms and procedures on the continent. It is here that Mandela's vaunted moral authority and the country's own powerful example would seem to give it a distinct comparative advantage.[26] Moreover, notwithstanding the continent's traditionally-firm adherence to the norm of non-intervention in the internal affairs of sovereign states, there has been no greater nor more successful derogation from that norm in the interests of fundamental human rights than the case of South Africa. Hence, once again, the political beneficiaries of that derogation (i.e., the ANC and South Africa's black majority) would appear to be in a strong position to extend and consolidate this process of normative change. Yet the issue is an extraordinarily sensitive one, not least for an organization (the ANC) and a society which has, at long last, finally gained control of *their own* state. Suffice it to say that the GNU will confront a number of telling tests on this issue during its five-year lifetime.

Among the earliest of these has been its struggle to craft an appropriate response to the oppressive military regime of General Sani Abacha in Africa's "other great power," Nigeria (see Inegbedion, Chapter 11). Less dramatic but just as telling will be how it deals with the claims to self-determination of the ANC's erstwhile allies in the Polisario Liberation Front of the Western Sahara. Here lies a potent conflict between material interests and core principles, as the ANC has been the object of blandishments and inducements from the Western Sahara's occupying power, Morocco.[27]

Entrepreneurs of "Security"

While official South Africa moves gingerly towards a more prominent role in Africa's political and security affairs, the most immediate impact of change in South Africa on the continent's security equation has come, once again, from the private sector, specifically profit-seeking ex-SADF mercenaries. According to one source, South African mercenaries in Africa are now thought to number in the thousands. Battle-hardened veterans of guerrilla warfare in Southern Africa employed by the Pretoria-based firm Executive Outcomes successfully helped turn the tide of war in Angola from UNITA to their former enemies in the MPLA, thereby facilitating the latest peace process there. They sought the same reversal of fortunes on behalf of the ruling military junta in Sierra Leone against the rebel Revolutionary United Front.[28] As state capacity declines in many parts of the continent and disorder spreads, the prominence of such "private armies" is likely to continue to increase, and South Africans are likely to be prominent among them.

Traders and Investors, Winners and Losers

Beyond this political economy of violence,[29] more conventional South African traders and investors are also having an increased impact on the continent. Both trade and, more slowly but still significantly, investment between South Africa and the continent are growing (see Chapters Eight through Eleven). In trade, South African exports to Africa were up almost 50 percent in two years to a total of almost US$2.5 billion in 1994, while imports tripled over the same period from US$220 million to US$664 million. This placed Africa as a whole fifth among South Africa's trading partners, behind Germany, the UK, the US, and Japan—though continental markets have always been disproportionately important as purchasers of South African manufactures (*Globe and Mail*, 15 July 1995; Mills 1995a: 11-13). While the main criterion governing increasing interaction appears to have been whether African countries offer viable markets for South African goods, and thus short-term opportunities for trade, there have also been a range of new investments in the continent beyond Southern Africa. Predictably, many of these have been in the mining sector, but others have occurred in tourism, transportation, and even brewing.

It would be a mistake to over-estimate the significance of these developments, however. Spread over a whole continent and several hundreds of millions of people, their impact is significantly dissipated. Moreover, as discussed by several authors in this collection, most African countries have relatively little to trade with South Africa. Thus small, debt-distressed economies like those of Uganda and Tanzania, Guinea and São Tomé are likely to experience increasingly unbalanced trade relations with South Africa, particularly in the context of IMF-mandated liberalization conditionalities—that is, when they attract the attention of South African traders and investors at all. Moreover, where significant investments do occur, they will create and reinforce patterns of winners and losers, in a context where the price of losing may be high indeed. In sum, as with the Southern African region, the effects of South Africa's increasing commercial interchange with the rest of the continent are likely to be highly uneven. They are likely, therefore, to increase tensions and insecurity within and between African countries, though the extent to which they alter current trends on the continent is likely to be limited.

It should be added that the "normalization" of South Africa's relations with the continent has opened the door to an increase in a range of illicit forms of exchange. As the continent's formal sectors decay, various forms of buccaneer capitalism flourish, creating new loci of political as well as economic power.[30]

Given this rather chaotic and unpromising set of prospects, it is hardly surprising that some powerful interests in South Africa advocate focusing the country's attention on extra-continental markets and alliances, and that some scholars argue that "a 'fortress South Africa' policy may not be a politically incorrect option at all, but also something of a socio-economic necessity" (Mills 1995a: 12). Yet should South Africa seek to live up against its neighbours, the continent's myriad problems which transcend state-centric solutions (from environmental decay to disease to arms trading to drought and food insecurity) will only worsen. Inevitably, they will spill over into the South African society, economy and polity. How, then, might a more cooperative and hopeful future be constructed?

Bridges of Hope? Building a More Cooperative Future

The contributions to this collection, and the analysis in this concluding chapter, point toward the irresistible conclusion that movement toward a more cooperative and secure South African, Southern African, and Pan-African future will be slow, erratic, and uneven at best. There is nothing to be gained through panglossian attempts to minimize the scale and diversity of the challenges to be confronted. The transition from apartheid in South Africa has not fundamentally altered some important structural challenges and trends in continental affairs, and in some respects may indeed exacerbate inequalities and insecurities in the Southern African region and beyond.

Nevertheless, the slow process of normalizing South African-African relations and the difficult but thus far successful birth of a (more) democratic and non-racial order in South Africa itself have also created a range of new openings and opportunities for positive-sum cooperation and transnational community-building. Where do these opportunities lie, and how can they be encouraged?

As many of our contributors suggest, there are, in fact, a wide range of issue areas in which cooperation is not only possible but, in many cases, imperative. In certain of them, promising beginnings have been made. Some of these have already been noted: bilateral agreements to deal with small arms trading, for example, and the emergent ASAS/ISDSC. Among other key areas in which cooperation is both possible and strongly desirable are: health, particularly in light of the alarming spread of AIDS throughout the region; the environment, notably with regard to scarce water resources and shared watershed ecosystems; energy resources; tourism; agricultural research and food security; and labour. This list is by no means exhaustive, but gives some indication of the potential scope for cooperative efforts.[31]

Such sectoral cooperative efforts should be encouraged to proceed as far and as fast as possible. More and less extensive schemes of regional coordination should be allowed, indeed encouraged, to co-exist, without being forced to conform to some sort of regional "grand design." The ADB's notion of "variable geometry" could usefully serve as a guiding principle in this regard: dynamic sectors should not be held back or deliberately stunted in the hopes of achieving "balanced development." At the same time, however, political efforts should be made to establish linkages and synergies between these schemes, so that they "spill over" into more extensive forms of regional cooperation.

There is, of course, nothing terribly new in this approach to cooperation building. What is proposed is essentially a latter day and region-specific variant of the old idea of "neo-functionalism." However, unlike the neo-functionalism conceived in relation to the process of European integration, it may be that in Southern Africa, attempts to deepen cooperation in the areas of trade and investment should be downplayed, as compared with some of the issues noted above. The fact is that for the developing countries of (Southern) Africa, trade and investment issues are "high politics," and are likely to generate a high degree of inter-state competition and conflict. Hence, although the longer-term goal of a more fully-fledged economic community should not be neglected, regional efforts should probably be concentrated in the first instance on other areas in which positive-sum outcomes will be more readily achieved.

This leads to the question of agency, i.e., how are such cooperative efforts to be encouraged, and by whom? Here, two related points deserve particular emphasis. The first is that, notwithstanding regional and continental fears of South African dominance, much of the leadership for cooperative efforts—technical, entrepreneurial, and political[32]—will need to come from South Africa. The reality is that in many cases, the greatest concentration of the requisite knowledge and skills rests with South African groups and institutions; while on many issues, other African states and groups will be at best hesitant to move forward without a clear signal of South African support. Hence, it is incumbent on those South Africans who "think region-ally" to articulate their position consistently and forthrightly, and to work actively to forge transnational coalitions of like-minded people to provide what Peter Vale has referred to (with apologies to George Bush) as "the vision thing" (quoted in Swatuk 1995).

The second point which bears emphasis is that this leadership—both national and transnational—cannot be expected to come exclusively, or even primarily, from states. Indeed, given the record of formal inter-state cooperation in Africa, it may be that states will frequently constitute stumbling blocks rather than allies in cooperative efforts. Although cooperative schemes are unlikely to be sustainable in the face of active state antagonism, much of the impetus in their conception and consolidation needs to come from regional and continental civil societies. Without trans-societal cooperation, imagination, and pressure on regional states, cooperative efforts cannot be expected to succeed.[33] How realistic is this fashionable prescription in post-apartheid (Southern) Africa?

The short answer is that, given the historic weakness of civil societies throughout the continent, the odds are long. However, despite difficulties in adjusting to the new era, South Africa's civil society remains more diverse, vibrant, and independent than any other on the continent, and has given some evidence of a desire to work with, learn from, and provide leadership to its counterparts elsewhere. To cite several examples of varying scope and significance,[34] Eskom, under the auspices of the newly created Southern African Power Pool, is spearheading efforts to create an integrated regional power grid (Eleri 1996); the Southern African Trade Union Co-ordination Council (SATUCC) drafted a Social Charter on the Fundamental Rights of Workers in Southern Africa in 1990-91, and South Africa's COSATU has continued to take a resolutely transnational approach to issues of migrant labour and inter-African affairs (Keet 1994; COSATU 1995); coalitions of "reds" and "greens" have emerged in united opposition to "dirty industries"; and five energy policy research institutes from South Africa, Zimbabwe, Tanzania, Zambia, and Norway are undertaking an ambitious joint "Southern African Energy and Environment Project" (van Horen, interview, 1 June 1995).

What these examples suggest is that the promotion of effective regional cooperation and community-building will rest on the efforts of a wide range of interests and actors, developing and promoting a "regional consciousness" rooted in concrete and immediately-relevant achievements. These interests and actors will include corporations, universities and research institutes, trade unions, environmental NGOs, women's organizations, and cultural groups, along with state-based organizations. While this approach may appear idealistic, and will indeed require a long-term vision in the face of uncertainty and setbacks, it would appear to be the only alternative to a future of mounting human insecurity and continued continental marginalization.

Conclusion: The Role of Outsiders

Obviously, the challenges before South Africa and its continental neighbours are daunting. The needs for timely and well-targeted international support are wide-ranging and extensive. This is a disheartening statement, given the current mood of "donor fatigue" and the global decline in real spending on development assistance. Still, there is much that the international community can do to support a successful transition in South Africa and beyond, even within the parameters of reduced resources. Several injunctions apply to these efforts.

First, in South Africa itself, international assistance must embody both short- and long-term dimensions. For the South African transition to succeed, popular support must be consolidated through the success of, for example, housing and school feeding programs associated with the RDP. At the same time, policy within and toward South Africa must support much longer-term and larger-scale projects, in health care, education, energy, and the like.

Second, in focusing on the importance of a successful transition in South Africa, external governments, NGOs, and private sector organizations must not lose sight of the rest of the region and continent. They must support those groups and institutions championing a regional and transnational vision, and provide assistance to concrete regional initiatives. This will pose some problems, particularly for official (national and international) aid agencies. The experience of the Canadian International Development Agency (CIDA) in attempting to promote regional integration in the context of its 1991 strategic policy framework *Africa 21* is illustrative (CIDA 1991). CIDA has had considerable difficulty in attempting to organize programming on an integrated regional basis, primarily because the principle political and juridical units with which it must deal are still *national states*. This makes the task of regional programming a trying one, both administratively and politically. Nevertheless, while the modalities of a regional approach may have to be adjusted, the effort and philosophy behind it should be maintained and reinforced.

Finally, it needs to be recognized that the process of South African, regional, and continental "reconstruction and development" will be a long-term and politically-difficult one. It is not one which can be successfully achieved within a straightjacket of economic and political conditionalities. Hence, without abandoning the need for "policy dialogue," donors would be well-advised to avoid dogmatic adherence to and insistence upon neo-liberal policy prescriptions. Such an approach will generate ill-will and thwart the sense of "ownership" necessary for difficult policy initiatives and reforms to succeed (Mugyenyi 1995). This observation suggests one final way in which the emergence of the "new" South Africa may be beneficial to the development and security prospects of the continent. Given the high stakes and profile of the South African transition, and the country's relatively robust capabilities and resources, South African policy makers will be accorded a degree of flexibility and *space*, in the medium term at least, which most of their African counterparts no longer enjoy. By aligning themselves with South Africa in regional and continental initiatives, other African countries can perhaps regain a degree of autonomy and independence in the establishment of their own priorities and processes.

Notes

1. Quoted in Jean-Jacques Cornish, "Wolpe Sees SA as Africa's 'Door of Hope'," *Cape Times*, 29 June 1995. See, also, Rose Umoren, "From pariah to champion of the continent," *Weekly Mail & Guardian*, 15-22 June 1995; Howard W. French, "A Continent Thanks South Africa's Economy," *Globe and Mail* (Toronto), 15 July 1995; and "The joys of normality," *The Economist*, 20 May 1995.

2. On recent economic performance see, for example, "A giant for Africa," *The Economist*, 20 May 1995; Reg Rumney, "IMF Predicts Slower Growth," *Weekly Mail and Guardian*, 12-18 May 1995; and Peter Galli, "World survey gives SA poor rating," *Business Day*, 6 September 1994. On Mandela's various efforts to woo international capital, see, for example, Clive Menell, "How He Took Care of Business," *Globe and Mail*, 10 May 1995.

3. Shaw discusses this crisis in Chapter Two above. See, also, Karen Harverson, "Gold Mining In Crisis," *Weekly Mail and Guardian*, 21-27 May 1995.

4. See, Edyth Bulbring, "The Long Road Ahead to Make it Come True," *Sunday Times*, 25 June 1995; also, Hilary Southall, "Healthy New World," Weekly Mail & Guardian, 30 June-6 July 1995. For a lucid critique of the ANC Health Plan from a primary health care perspective, see Amanda K. Shaw, *Towards a Healthier South Africa: An Examination of the ANC Health Plan*, unpublished honours thesis, University of Waterloo, Canada, May 1995.

5. As the chapters by Mugyenyi, Nyang'oro, Daddieh and Inegbedion point out, this involvement is, at least to this point in time, admittedly weak and haphazard. We return to a discussion of the role of private capital below.

6. Johnston (1994: 202, footnote 11) cites one remarkable account of township violence. In "The toilets that caused all the trouble," Weekly Mail, 12-18 April 1991, it was reported that "clashes between two squatter camps on the east Rand ... left 15 people dead. The theft of portable toilets by one camp which had no facilities or water, and relied on the other, was central to the outbreak of violence between the two settlements, both of which are aligned to the ANC." (See, also, Shaw 1995a; also "Editorial: Criminals put South Africa's hopes under siege," *Sunday Times*, 14 May 1995; Cas St. Leger, "An 'A' to 'Z' of SA's Crime-Ridden Cities," *Sunday Times*, 28 May 1995; "Explosion of Crime, and the Violence of it, Terrifies White South Africans," *Globe and Mail*, 15 July 1995; and *The Economist*, 15 July 1995.)

7. An ironic "benefit" of the escalation of crime in South Africa is the spectacular growth of the security industry. Among those who have found employment in this field are a small but growing number of ex-freedom fighters. See, "A new force in the security industry," *Weekly Mail and Guardian*, 7-13 July 1995.

8. See, for example, "Costs Continue to Mount as Illegal Aliens Continue Pouring Into SA," *The Argus*, 18 May 1995.

9. See, "Operation Rachel Nets Pile Of Mozambique Weapons," *The Star*, 20 June 1995. On rethinking regional security see, for example, Nathan 1992; 1993; Nathan & Honwana 1995; and van Wyk 1994.

10. An interesting example of this arose during the 1995 Zimbabwe International Book Fair. In the face of a Zimbabwean government directive to exclude Galz— Gays and Lesbians of Zimbabwe—from participating, and an inflammatory attack on homosexuality by President Robert Mugabe, South African author Nadine Gordimer helped frame a resolution "describing the government move as a contra-vention of freedom of expression and urging that Galz be reinstated." Moreover, the Publishers Association of South Africa "immediately suspended discussions with the Zimbabwe book fair authorities on a joint Southern African book fair project." See, "Mugabe cracks down on gay rights," *Weekly Mail and Guardian*, 4-10 August 1995. Unfortunately, one year later at the 1996 Book Fair, Mugabe's gov-ernment once again banned Galz from participating.

11. In speaking of the strengthening of a regional norm of democracy and human rights, we are of course sidestepping the issue of what *kind of* democracy is being promoted. Whether the predominantly *liberal democratic* reforms which are being made will successfully contribute to regional cooperation and stability over the medium term remains controversial. See, in particular, the issue of *Southern Africa REPORT* entitled "Regional Roundup: Elections are not Enough" (vol. 10, no. 4, June/July 1995).

12. See, for example, Howard French, "A Continent Thanks South Africa's Economy," *Globe and Mail*, 15 July 1995; Derek Tommey, "Zambian Collieries Look to JCI for Assistance," *Cape Times*, 4 July 1995; and "Survey: South Africa," *The Economist*, 20 May 1995.

13. See, for example, Patrick McDowell, "White farmers look northward to greener fields"; and Tom Cohen, "Water dwindles in fourth year of poor rains," both in *The Ottawa Citizen*, 15 May 1995; also, Norman Chandler, "SA Farmers Poised to Venture Into Africa," *The Star*, 27 June 1995.

14. Some might argue that this is, in fact, the real meaning of "new thinking on security" in Southern Africa (cf. Swatuk and Omari, Chapter 5; Southall 1995; Nathan and Honwana 1995: 3-7).

15. For example, Zimbabwean business and trade officials have been particu-larly exercised by South Africa's apparent disinterest in negotiating a new bilateral trade agreement to replace the 1964 agreement which expired in 1992. Thereafter, South Africa's traditional trade surplus with Zimbabwe ballooned to R1.5 billion on a total of R3 billion in bilateral trade during 1994. Zimbabwean officials have warned that, without a new agreement ensuring the reopening of the South African market to their country's goods and services, their southern neighbour should prepare itself for a huge influx of illegal immigrants. (See, for example, "Mugabe willing to discuss punitive tariffs with SA," *The Herald*, 9 July 1994; Mike Humphrey, "Guest Column: Zimbabwe, South Africa urged to review 30 year old trade accord," *The Financial Gazette*, 15 September 1994; Iden Wetherell, "Zimbabwean Sanctions Against SA?," *Weekly Mail and Guardian*, 23-29 June 1995; and Teigue Payne, "Trade Kept Waiting," *Sunday Times*, 4 June 1995.)

16. See, for example, Bruce Cameron, "Southern African Customs Union Talks Gain Impetus," *Cape Times*, 4 July 1995; also, interview, Keith Jefferis, Gaborone, 21 September 1994.

17. See, for example, Aziz Pahad, "New Thinking on regional cooperation," *Southern African Economist*, July 1994; "A House Divided," *Southern African Economist*, November 1994; and Leistner 1995: 274-5.

18. See, for example, John Fraser, "SA Fears EU Stalling On Lomé," *Cape Times*, 29 May 1995; Ray Hartley, "Aussies Want SA to Join Trade Pact," *Sunday Times*, 28 May 1995; and "Second Coming," *Financial Times* 19 May 1995; Tim Cohen, "EU, southern African pact to be signed," *Business Day*, 2 September 1994; and David Dickinson, "Chilean experience contains lessons for SA," *Business Day*, 2 September 1994.

19. See, for example, Teigue Payne, "Trade Kept Waiting," *Sunday Times*, 4 June 1995; and Iden Wetherell, "Zimbabwean Sanctions Against SA?," *Weekly Mail and Guardian*, 23-29 June 1995.

20. While Tanzania was a member of both the FLS and SADCC, its status as a southern African state has always been ambiguous, with its historical links and geographic location oriented primarily towards East Africa. Under founding President Julius Nyerere, this poor country was a stalwart of the liberation struggles throughout southern Africa, and was host to the OAU's Liberation Committee and various liberation movements.

21. Just as South Africa's Foreign Minister Alfred Nzo warned SADC members not to expect South Africa to solve their employment problems ("Editorial: Influx Control," *Business Day*, 30 August 1994), he warned OAU member states not to expect South Africa to be the continent's saviour ("Cash-strapped OAU looks to SA," *Sunday Times*, 12 June 1994).

22. See, Anton Harber, "A Lame Duck?," *Weekly Mail and Guardian* 19-25 May 1995.

23. See, for example, Cherilyn Ireton & Edyth Bulbring, "Mandela backs off foreign adventures," *Sunday Times* 19 June 1994.

24. Towards this end, organizations like the Institute for Defence Policy and the South African Institute of International Affairs have hosted a number of meetings, large and small, on international peacekeeping and South Africa's potential role therein.

25. There remains the sticky problem of Armscor and the promotion of regional and continental instability through arms exports. See Vale in Chapter Four above. For a review of the now long-running debate over arms exports, see, for example, "SA-Rwanda arms sales ended," *Daily Dispatch*, 16 May 1994; "SA arms exports 'likely to double'," *Business Day*, 27 May 1994; Jeremy Woods, "Armscor aiming for exports of over R3bn," *Business Day*, 10 July 1994; "SA bans export of landmines," *Daily Dispatch*, 30 July 1994; "Cabinet to review policy on arms exports—Mbeki," *Business Day*, 11 August 1994; Paul Watson, "State-owned arms firm a Mandela dilemma," *The Toronto Star*, 9 October 1994; and "Beyond the Border," *The Economist*, 20 May 1995.

26. See, for example, Allister Sparks, "SA—peacemaker twixt two worlds," *Daily Dispatch* 19 May 1994; and Temba Sono, "Africa opens eyes to Mandela wake-up call," *The Star*, 27 July 1994.

27. On the case of Nigeria, see, for example, Herbst 1996. With regard to Morocco and the Polisario, see, Rehana Rossouw, "What Happened to Sahrawi's Diplomatic

Ties?," *Weekly Mail and Guardian*, 4-10 August 1995. On other "moral" issues in South Africa's "new" foreign policy—e.g., trade with Indonesia; relations with Taiwan and China; arms exports to Rwanda—see, for example, the articles by Roger Southall and Peter Vale in *Southern Africa REPORT*, vol. 10, no. 5 1995; Rehana Roussouw, "Foreign Affairs department under fire," *Weekly Mail & Guardian*, 9-14 June 1995; Rehana Roussouw, "Pahad hits back at f.a. critics," *Weekly Mail & Guardian*, 30 June-6 July 1995; Chris Louw, "Beijing Ready to breathe fire," *Weekly Mail & Guardian*, 30 June-6 July 1995; and Department of Foreign Affairs (1996).

28. See, *International Security Digest*, July 1995; also, Edward O'Loughlin, "SA Mercenaries Conquer Africa," *Weekly Mail and Guardian*, 4-10 August 1995.

29. According to information provided in *International Security Digest* (July 1995: 1), Executive Outcomes is reportedly paid US$20 million a year plus US$20 million for weapons and equipment for its work in Angola. In Sierra Leone, it has settled for a diamond concession.

30. These include not only the influx and activities of migrants, but various commercial "scams," such as one centered in the criminal syndicates of Nigeria in which South Africans are persuaded to part with substantial sums of money in exchange for a non-existent "share" of the mythical proceeds from contracts with the Nigerian National Petroleum Company (See, "Nigerians tell of SA targets," *The Argus*, 18 May 1995),

31. Many of these areas of potential conflict and/or cooperation were discussed at an international symposium entitled *South Africa Within Africa: Emerging Policy Frameworks* held in Johannesburg, 24-27 January 1996: see, for example, de Wit and Vale 1996, Eleri 1996, Green 1996, Johnson 1996, Khosa 1996, and Reichardt 1996. See also the collections edited by Minnie Venter (1994) and Ken Cole (1994). On the growing burden of AIDS, see Swatuk and Omari in Chapter 5; also, William Rees-Mogg, "70 percent of HIV Cases are In Southern Africa, says WHO," *The Star* 19 June 1995.

32. On the various *forms* of leadership which successful policy initiatives require, see Cooper, Higgott, and Nossal, *Relocating Middle Powers* (1993), chapter 1.

33. On the importance of civil societies and trans-societal linkages in promoting regional security in southern Africa, see Booth and Vale 1995, pp. 295-303.

34. See, also, the numerous, albeit somewhat anecdotal, examples in the chapters by Swatuk, Nyang'oro and Daddieh above.

References

Adelzadeh, Asghar and Vishnu Padayachee. 1994. "The RDP White Paper: Reconstruction of a Development Vision?" *Transformation* No. 25.

African National Congress. 1994a. *Foreign Policy in a New Democratic South Africa—a Discussion Paper*. Johannesburg: Department of International Affairs.

———. 1994b. *The Reconstruction and Development Programme*. Johannesburg: African National Congress.

Blumenfeld, Jesmond. 1996. "Pragmatists versus Populists in the 'New' South Africa," *The World Today* (July): 185-9.

Booth, Ken and Peter Vale. 1995. "Security in Southern Africa: After Apartheid, Beyond Realism," *International Affairs* 20(20): 285-304.

Business Day (Johannesburg), various.

Canadian International Development Agency (CIDA). 1991. *Africa 21, A Vision of Africa for the 21st Century.* Hull: CIDA.

Cape Times (Cape Town), various.

Carim, Xavier. 1995. "Migration in Southern Africa: Understanding South Africa's Policy Options," unpublished manuscript.

Cole, Ken, ed. 1994. *Sustainable development for a democratic South Africa.* London: Earthscan.

Congress of South African Trade Unions (COSATU). 1995. "Resolution on Migrant Labour; Resolution on Southern Africa, Africa, South South and North North," *International Policy Conference,* 21-23 April, Johannesburg.

Cooper, Andrew, Richard Higgott and Kim Richard Nossal. 1993. *Relocating Middle Powers.* Vancouver: University of British Columbia Press.

Daily Dispatch (East London), various.

de Wit, Martin J. and Peter Vale. 1996. "Collaboration in African Science: Some Provisional Lessons From the Earth Sciences," paper presented at the International Symposium, *South Africa Within Africa: Emerging Policy Frameworks,* 24-27 January 1996, Johannesburg, South Africa.

Department of Foreign Affairs (South Africa). 1996. *South African Foreign Policy Discussion Document.*

Eleri, Ewah Otu. 1996. "Electricity Cooperation in Southern Africa: The Role of South Africa," paper presented at the International Symposium, *South Africa Within Africa: Emerging Policy Frameworks,* 24-27 January 1996, Johannesburg, South Africa.

Financial Mail (Johannesburg), various.

Globe and Mail (Toronto), various.

Government of South Africa. 1996. *Growth, Employment and Redistribution: A Macroeconomic Strategy.*

Green, Reginald H. 1996. "South Africa, Southern Africa and Beyond: Explorations Toward Regional Integration," paper presented at the International Symposium, *South Africa Within Africa: Emerging Policy Frameworks,* 24-27 January 1996, Johannesburg, South Africa.

Hanlon, Joseph. 1986. *Beggar Your Neighbours: apartheid power in Southern Africa.* Bloomington: Indiana University Press.

Herald (Harare), various.

Herbst, Jeffrey. 1996. "Is Nigeria a Viable State?" *The Washington Quarterly* 19/2 (Spring): 151-72.

International Security Digest. 1995. 2(10): 1.

Interview, 22 June 1995, South African Department of Foreign Affairs (DFA) (Confidential).

Interview, 24 May 1994, Markus Reichardt, Public Affairs Officer, Anglo-American Corporation.

Interview, 1 June 1995, Clive van Horen, Energy and Development Research Centre, Cape Town.

Johnson, Phyllis. "Information Access as a Strategic Resource in Socio-Economic Development and Regional Cooperation," paper presented at the International Symposium, *South Africa Within Africa: Emerging Policy Frameworks,* 24-27 January 1996, Johannesburg, South Africa.

Johnston, Alexander. 1994. "South Africa: the election and the transition process," *Third World Quarterly* (15: 2) (June): 187-204.

Keet, Dot. 1994. "Labour Issues in Southern Africa: Critical Choices for Trade Unions," in Minnie Venter, ed. *Prospects for Progress*. Cape Town: Maskew Miller Longman.

Khosa, Meshack M. 1996. "Towards a Sustainable Transport and Communications Sector in Southern Africa," paper presented at the International Symposium, *South Africa Within Africa: Emerging Policy Frameworks*, 24-27 January 1996, Johannesburg, South Africa.

Leistner, Erich. 1995. "Considering the Methods and Effects of Regional Integration," in Greg Mills, Alan Begg and Anthoni van Nieuwkerk, eds. *South Africa in the Global Economy*. Johannesburg: South African Institute of International Affairs.

Ronald T. Libby. 1987. *The Politics of Economic Power in Southern Africa*. Princeton: Princeton University Press.

McGowan, Patrick J. 1993. "The 'New' South Africa: Ascent or Descent in the World System?," *South African Journal of International Affairs* 1(1): 35-61.

Mills, Greg. 1995a. "Introduction: Waiting for the Fig Leaf to Drop?" in Greg Mills, Alan Begg and Anthoni van Nieuwkerk, eds. *South Africa in the Global Economy*. Johannesburg: South African Institute of International Affairs.

———. 1995b. "The History of Regional Integrative Attempts: The Way Forward?," in Greg Mills, Alan Begg and Anthoni van Nieuwkerk, eds. *South Africa in the Global Economy*. Johannesburg: South African Institute of International Affairs.

Mugyenyi, Joshua. 1995, "Rehabilitation and Reconstruction in Uganda: The Political Economy of Structural Adjustment Programmes," unpublished Ph.D. thesis, Dalhousie University, Canada.

Nathan, Laurie. 1993. "'With Open Arms': Confidence- and Security-Building Measures in Southern Africa," paper prepared for presentation at the *Seminar on Confidence- and Security-Building in Southern Africa*, February, Windhoek.

———. 1992. *A Framework and Strategy for Building Peace and Security in Southern Africa*. Cape Town: Centre for Intergroup Studies, October.

——— and Joao Honwana. 1995. *After the Storm: Common Security and Conflict Resolution in Southern Africa*. The Arusha Papers No. 3, A Working Series on Southern African Security. Bellville: Centre for Southern African Studies, February.

Reichardt, Markus. "Capital Movement and Future Investment in Southern Africa: Anglo American in Perspective," paper presented at the International Symposium, *South Africa Within Africa: Emerging Policy Frameworks*, 24-27 January 1996, Johannesburg, South Africa.

Shaw, Amanda K. 1995. *Towards a Healthier South Africa: An Examination of the ANC Health Plan*, unpublished honours thesis, University of Waterloo, Canada.

Shaw, Mark. 1995a. "Partners in Crime? Crime, Political Transition and Changing Forms of Policing Control," *Centre for Policy Studies Transition Series*, Research Report No. 39.

———. 1995b. "The Future of Peacekeeping in Africa," *African Security Review* 4(1): 28-30.

Shaw, Timothy M. 1974. "Southern Africa: cooperation and conflict in an international subsystem," *Journal of Modern African Studies* 12(4) (December): 633-55.

Southall, Roger. 1995. "Regional Security: The 'New Security' in Southern Africa," *Southern Africa REPORT* 10(5) (July): 3-6.

Southern Africa REPORT (Toronto), various.

Southern African Economist (Harare), various.

Sunday Times (Cape Town), various.

Suttner, Raymond. 1995. "Some Problematic Questions in Developing Foreign Policy After April 27 1994," *Southern African Perspectives* No. 44. Bellville: Centre for Southern African Studies.

Swatuk, Larry A. 1995. *"Of Growth Poles" and "Backwaters": The New South Africa in Africa*. York University: Centre for International and Strategic Studies.

———. 1996. *South Africa Within Africa: Emerging Policy Frameworks, A Conference Report*. Ijebu-Ode, Nigeria: African Center for Development and Strategic Studies (ACDESS).

The Economist (London), various.

The Ottawa Citizen (Ottawa), various.

The Star (Johannesburg), various.

The Toronto Star (Toronto), various.

Vale, Peter. 1995. "Prisoner of the Past? The New South Africa Abroad," *Southern Africa REPORT* 10(5) (July): 7-10.

Weekly Mail and Guardian (Johannesburg), various.

Acronyms

AACC	All African Council of Churches
AAF-SAP	African Alternative Framework to Structural Adjustment Programs
ACDESS	African Centre for Development and Strategic Studies
ADB	African Development Bank
AIDS	Acquired Immune Deficiency Syndrome
ANC	African National Congress
APEC	Asia-Pacific Economic Community
APLA	Azamian People's Liberation Army
ASAS	Association of Southern African States
BCP	Basotho Congress Party
BHN	Basic Human Needs
BLNS	Botswana/Lesotho/Namibia/Swaziland
CAMPFIRE	Communal Areas Management Programme for Indigenous Resources
CBI	Cross Border Initiative
CBO	Community-based Organization
CET	Common External Tariff
CIDA	Canadian International Development Agency
CMA	Common Monetary Area
CMAG	Commonwealth Ministerial Action Group
CODESA	Convention for a Democratic South Africa
COMESA	Common Market of Eastern and Southern Africa
CONSAS	Constellation of Southern African States
COSATU	Congress of South African Trade Unions
CSCE	Conference on Security and Cooperation in Europe
CSO	Central Selling Organization
EAC	East African Community
EACSO	East African Common Services Organization
EAHC	East African High Commission
EC	European Community
ECA	Economic Commission for Africa
ECOMOG	ECOWAS Ceasefire Monitoring Group
ECOWAS	Economic Community of West African States
EIA	Environmental Impact Assessment
EIU	Economist Intelligence Unit
EPZ	Export Processing Zone
EU	European Union
FLS	Frontline States
FSU	Former Soviet Union
FTA	Free Trade Agreement

GATT	General Agreement on Tariffs and Trade
GDP	Gross Domestic Product
GEIS	General Export Incentive System
GEM	Group for Environmental Monitoring
GNP	Gross National Product
GNU	Government of National Unity
HCT	High Commission Territories
HDI	Human Development Index
IBRD	International Bank for Reconstruction and Development (World Bank)
IDRC	International Development and Research Centre
IFAA	Institute for African Alternatives
IFC	International Finance Corporation
IFI	International Financial Institution
ILO	International Labour Organization
IMF	International Monetary Fund
IOC	Indian Ocean Community
ISDSC	Inter-State Defence and Security (Ministerial) Committee
IUCN	World Conservation Union
KANU	Kenya African National Union
LDC	Less Developed Country
MFN	Most Favoured Nation (status)
MK	Umkhonto we Sizwe
MMA	Multilateral Monetary Area (formerly the Rand Monetary Area - RMA)
MNC	Multinational Corporation
MPLA	Movimento Popular de Libertaçao de Angola
MVA	Manufacturing Value Added
NACM	North African Common Market
NAFTA	North American Free Trade Agreement
NATO	North Atlantic Treaty Organization
NEDLAC	National Economic, Development and Labour Council
NGO	Non-governmental Organization
NIC	Newly Industrializing Country
NIDL	New International Division of Labour
NIDP	New International Division of Power
NNEWC	Namibian National Eastern Water Carrier
NP	National Party
OAU	Organization of African Unity
OECD	Organization for Economic Cooperation and Development
PAC	Pan-African Congress
PDCI	Parti Démocratique de Côte d'Ivoire
PTA	Preferential Trade Area for Eastern and Southern Africa
RDP	Reconstruction and Development Program

SABC	South African Broadcasting Corporation
SACP	South African Communist Party
SACU	Southern African Customs Union
SADC	Southern African Development Community
SADCC	Southern African Development Coordination Conference
SADF	South African Defence Force
SANDF	South African National Defence Force
SAIIA	South African Institute of International Affairs
SAIRR	South African Institute of Race Relations
SANDF	South African National Defence Force
SAP	Structural Adjustment Program
SATS	South African Transport System
SATUCC	Southern Africa Trade Union Co-ordination Council
SIAS	Swedish Institute for African Studies
TBVC	Transkei, Bophuthatswana, Venda and Ciskei states
UN	United Nations
UNICEF	United Nations International Children's Emergency Fund
UNITA	União Naçional para a Independência Total de Angola
UNDP	United Nations Development Program
UNEP	United Nations Environment Program
WTO	World Trade Organization
WWF	World Wildlife Fund
ZRA	Zambezi River Authority

Index

Abacha, Sani, 200, 204, 205, 206, 207, 209, 210, 214, 233, 234
Abiola, Moshood, 204, 205, 206
Abuja Declaration, 204
African Alternative Framework to Structural Adjustment Programs (AAF-SAP), 204
African Development Bank (ADB), 2, 13, 115, 130, 131, 135, 138, 158, 213, 232, 237
African Initiative Club, 17, 172
African Life Assurance Company, 28
African National Congress (ANC), 5, 14, 17, 28, 29, 30, 47, 48, 51, 56, 60, 61, 63, 75, 110, 130, 132, 154, 155, 156, 157, 159, 160, 185, 189, 190, 191, 195, 205, 210, 222, 223, 232, 233, 234
African People's Liberation Army (APLA), 10
Afrikaner regime, 28
AIDS, 9, 87, 90, 94-5, 237
Ake, Simeon, 187
Amsden, Alice, 55
Anglo American Corporation, 12, 16, 29, 30, 31, 229
Angola, 27, 33, 78, 86, 87, 91, 92, 138, 158, 185, 201, 213, 227, 228, 235
Argentina, 203
arms, 9, 12, 29, 77, 90, 172, 226, 229
Armscor, 11, 30, 31, 77
Arusha Declaration, 178
Asia-Pacific Economic Community (APEC), 35
Association of Southern African States/Inter-State Defence and Security Committee (ASAS/ISDSC), 9, 101, 102, 227, 233, 237
Assouan, Usher, 187
authoritarianism, 41, 55, 221

Babangida, Ibrahim, 203, 204, 208, 209, 213
Bamako Convention, 214
Banda, Kamuzu, 186
Barclays Bank, 30
Barratt, John, 185

Basic Human Needs (BHN), 33
Bédié, Henri Konan, 191
Benin, 192, 213
Biafra, 186, 187
Bokassa, Emperor, 189
Bonn Declaration, 89
Botha, Pik, 171
Botswana, 11, 33, 73, 88, 91, 93, 118, 124, 138, 139, 143, 161, 229, 230
Botswana/Lesotho/Namibia/Swaziland (BLNS), 118, 119, 120, 123
Brazil, 164, 203
Burkina Faso, 192
Burundi, 92, 161, 164, 201
Bush, George, 237
Buzan, Barry, 74

Cameroon, 188, 192
Camus, Albert, 153
Canadian International Development Agency (CIDA), 239
Central African Empire, 189
Central African Republic, 184
Charles, Bernard, 185
Chege, Michael, 174
China, 30, 159, 175
chrome, 27
civil society, 3, 17, 35, 36, 53, 96, 140, 144, 157, 159, 178-9, 206, 207, 227, 238
Convention for a Democratic South Africa (CODESA), 43
Coke (Corporation), 30
Cold War, (see also post-Cold War) 18, 74, 78, 79, 82, 87
Commission on Global Governance, 89
Common External Tariff (CET), 119, 120
Common Market of Eastern and Southern Africa (COMESA), 115, 131, 134, 155, 158, 211, 230, 231
Commonwealth, 18, 31, 135, 210, 232
Commonwealth Ministerial Action Group (CMAG), 206, 207

About the Book

Despite the lingering effects of more than a decade of sanctions and economic stagnation, South Africa retains the most powerful, industrialized, and diversified economy in sub-Saharan Africa. Today, as a post-apartheid future is constructed and as the old political and economic barriers with the rest of the continent crumble, it is probable that there will be a sustained increase in political and economic interaction between the "hobbled leviathan" of the South and its neighbors. What repercussions will follow from this process? To what extent will it enhance or constrain prospects for political and economic development in the rest of the region? Who will be the main agents and beneficiaries of this expanded interchange? What security consequences, broadly conceived, will result? In this volume, contributors explore these issues by carefully situating their analyses within the twin contexts of a changing world order and the demands for South-Africa-centered reconstruction and development.

About the Editors and Contributors

David R. Black is Assistant Professor of Political Science and a Fellow of the Centre for Foreign Policy Studies, Dalhousie University, Halifax, Canada. His publications include work on "middle powers" and Southern Africa, and the Commonwealth and South Africa. He is Visiting Professor of Political Science at the University of Ottawa, 1996-97.

Cyril K. Daddieh is Associate Professor of Political Science at Salisbury State University in Salisbury, Maryland. He holds a Ph.D. from Dalhousie University in Halifax, Canada. He has authored several articles on Côte d'Ivoire and Ghana, including contributions to Watts and Little, *Peasants Under Contract*, and Mengisteab and Logan, *Beyond Structural Adjustment*.

Robert Davies is an ANC Member of the South African National Assembly and serves on the Standing Committees on Finance, Foreign Affairs, and Trade and Industry. He was previously Co-Director of the Centre for Southern African Studies at University of the Western Cape. He has published extensively on Southern African regional cooperation and integration.

Stephen Gelb studied at the Universities of Cape Town, Toronto and Manitoba. He has taught at the University of the Witwatersrand and Natal, York University (Toronto) and the New School for Social Research. He has also worked as an anti-apartheid activist in Canada, and has been an economic advisor to both COSATU and the ANC. He is the author of many articles on South African political economy, co-author of *The Crisis in South Africa*, and editor of *South Africa's Economic Crisis* (1991).

John Inegbedion is Assistant Professor of Political Science, St. Peter's College, New Jersey and a Fellow of the Centre for Foreign Policy Studies, Dalhousie University, Halifax, Canada.

Joshua B. Mugyenyi is Secretary, Administration, Bank of Uganda, Kampala, Uganda. Dr. Mugyenyi has taught at universities in Canada, Swaziland and Uganda. He has contributed several chapters to books on topics as diverse as democracy and popular participation in Africa, structural adjustment in Africa, Swaziland's foreign policy, and reconstruction and development in Uganda.

Julius E. Nyang'oro is Professor and Director of African and African-American Studies at the University of North Carolina, Chapel Hill. He is author of *The State and Economic Development in Africa* and co-editor of *Corporatism in Africa* and *Beyond Structural Adjustment in Africa*. Dr. Nyang'oro holds doctorates in law and in political science and serves as a consultant to the All Africa Council of Churches.

Abillah H. Omari is a Senior Lecturer and Director of the Mozambique/Tanzania Centre for Foreign Relations in Dar es Salaam, Tanzania. He is co-editor of *The Arusha Papers*, a working papers series on Southern African security co-published by the Centre for Foreign Relations and the Centre for Southern African Studies, University of the Western Cape, South Africa. Dr. Omari is also a consultant to the government of Tanzania on regional security.

Timothy M. Shaw is Professor of Political Science and International Development Studies and Director of the Centre for Foreign Policy Studies, Dalhousie University, Halifax, Canada. He is the author of *Towards a Political Economy of Africa* (1985) and *Reformism and Revisionism in Africa's Political Economy in the 1990s: the dialectics of adjustment* (1993). He serves as General Editor of the Macmillan Press Series on International Political Economy.

Larry A. Swatuk is a lecturer in the Department of Political and Administrative Studies at the University of Botswana, Gaborone, Botswana. He is the author of, among other things, *Between Choice in a Hard Place: Contending Theories of International Relations* (1991).

Peter Vale is Professor of Southern African Studies, University of the Western Cape and Visiting Professor at Stellenbosch University. For the calendar year of 1996, he was UNESCO Professor of African Studies at the University of Utrecht, The Netherlands. With Hans-Joachim Spanger, he has recently edited *Bridges to the Future: Prospects for Peace and Security in Southern Africa*.